CAPTURING THE
SUMMIT

ALSO BY TREVOR MARC HUGHES

Riding the Continent: Hamilton Mack Laing,
(editor) 2019

*Zero Avenue to Peace Park: Confidence and
Collapse on the 49th Parallel,* 2016

*Nearly 40 on the 37: Triumph and Trepidation
on the Stewart-Cassiar Highway,* 2013

CAPTURING THE SUMMIT

HAMILTON MACK LAING AND THE MOUNT LOGAN EXPEDITION OF 1925

TREVOR MARC HUGHES

RONSDALE PRESS

CAPTURING THE SUMMIT
Copyright © 2023 Trevor Marc Hughes

RONSDALE PRESS
125A – 1030 Denman Street, Vancouver, B.C. Canada V6G 2M6
www.ronsdalepress.com

Typesetting: Julie Cochrane, in Caslon 11 pt on 15
Cover Photo: Courtesy Whyte Museum of the Canadian Rockies and Richard Mackie
Cover Design: Julie Cochrane

Ronsdale Press wishes to thank the following for their support of its publishing program: the Canada Council for the Arts, the Government of Canada, the British Columbia Arts Council, and the Province of British Columbia through the British Columbia Book Publishing Tax Credit program.

Library and Archives Canada Cataloguing in Publication

Title: Capturing the summit : Hamilton Mack Laing and the Mount Logan expedition of 1925 / Trevor Marc Hughes.
Names: Hughes, Trevor Marc, 1972– author.
Description: Includes bibliographical references and index.
Identifiers: Canadiana (print) 20230193390 | Canadiana (ebook) 20230193552 | ISBN 9781553806806 (softcover) | ISBN 9781553806813 (EPUB) | ISBN 9781553806820 (PDF)
Subjects: LCSH: Laing, Hamilton M. (Hamilton Mack), 1883-1982. | LCSH: Laing, Hamilton M. (Hamilton Mack), 1883-1982—Travel—Yukon. | LCSH: Laing, Hamilton M. (Hamilton Mack), 1883-1982—Travel—Alaska. | LCSH: Mountaineering—Yukon—Logan, Mount—History—20th century. | LCSH: Mountaineering expeditions—Yukon—Logan, Mount—History—20th century. | LCSH: Logan, Mount (Yukon)—Description and travel. | LCSH: Mountaineers—Canada—Biography. | LCSH: Naturalists—Canada—Biography.
Classification: LCC GV199.44.C22 L644 2023 | DDC 796.52209719/1—dc23

At Ronsdale Press we are committed to protecting the environment. To this end we are working with Canopy and printers to phase out our use of paper produced from ancient forests. This book is one step towards that goal.

Printed in Canada

To Richard Mackie ...
whose advice and work revealed
new landscapes of history to explore ...
and to Ron Hatch, who encouraged
my working on this story.

TERRITORY
ACKNOWLEDGEMENT

The author would like to point out that the area where Mount Logan is located is held within the Traditional Territory of the Kluane First Nation and White River First Nation. Kluane National Park and Reserve is within the Traditional Territory of the Southern Tutchone People, its natural and cultural resources managed by Champagne and Aishihik First Nations and Kluane First Nations of the Southern Tutchone, and Parks Canada.

Some of the story happens in Eyak Traditional Territory. Much of the narrative in the Chitina River valley takes place on the Traditional Territory of the Ahtna, an Alaskan Native Athabaskan People.

CONTENTS

Introduction

I was seeing Hamilton Mack Laing move for the first time. After two years of researching his motorcycle adventures between 1914 and 1919, I was finally catching a glimpse of not only Laing in motion but how he looked in his early forties, during the heyday of his expedition career. I was sitting in a large dark room at the Comox Legion Branch 160 with over 200 people, quietly watching a silent film projected on a drop-down screen.

But I've got to set the scene first and go back about an hour . . .

I had driven from Nanaimo to Comox, having taken the ferry from Tsawwassen, near Vancouver, to Vancouver Island. Hamilton Mack Laing had called Comox home for nearly sixty years, and the Mack Laing Heritage Society was screening *The Conquest of Mount Logan*, a silent film that ran just shy of forty-five minutes. As I walked into the hall, packed with dozens of chairs, I was overwhelmed with the turnout. Clearly this was going to be a popular event.

I was soon shaking Gordon Olsen's hand and speaking to him and other members of the Society. Olsen, a friend of Laing's, has been instrumental in keeping his last standing home, Shakesides, from demolition by decision of the town council. But tonight was reserved for an appreciation of Laing and acknowledgement of his cinematographic achievement.

Hamilton Mack Laing, in a frame from *The Conquest of Mount Logan.*
(COURTESY: LIBRARY AND ARCHIVES CANADA)

In 1925, Hamilton Mack Laing set out from Comox to join a crew
of mountaineers determined to climb Canada's tallest mountain. He
would make his way north, firm in the knowledge of his responsibilities,
specifically as expedition naturalist and cinematographer, a unique job
title to be sure.

My responsibility at the screening was merely to give a short intro-
ductory speech, following Richard Mackie. Richard spoke off the cuff,
which impressed me most as I clutched my notes about sixteen rows
back, the only seat available when it was time to sit down. He told the
audience, as the author of the sole full-length biography of Laing, that
it was about time Laing was fully appreciated, written about, celebrated.
In short, he said, "Laing hasn't been done yet."

Next, Gordon Olsen introduced me, and I diligently made my way to
the front and started off telling how, in studying Mack Laing's motorcycle-naturalist period, I became fascinated with what he packed, or
didn't pack, in his motorcycle's panniers.

For about two years, I had been researching Laing's motorcycle-naturalist years, a period in his life when he believed that his Harley-Davidson made for the ideal form of transportation to get into the natural world, where he could study nature's creatures, specifically its birdlife, to his heart's content. He was in his thirties, full of vim and vigour and looking to make his unique mark on the world as a freelance writer and naturalist who was gaining quite a reputation. He had already published a book, through Outing Publishing Company, *Out with the Birds*, in 1913, which focused on his natural explorations around his home province of Manitoba. I related how Laing would travel by two wheels up to about 1919, when his expedition career as an ornithologist and naturalist for museums and other organizations would take up much of his time. He even ventured across the U.S. in 1915, travelling it by motorcycle in six weeks. But, as I explained to the standing-room-only crowd, during his motorcycle-naturalist years, he was building his reputation as a writer, typing articles about his adventures in the natural world. He would write for *Sunset*, *Outing*, *Tall Timber*, and others. In one article for *Recreation* magazine, titled "A 'Been There' Motorcyclist's Touring Outfit," he wrote specifically about what he packed in his panniers.[1]

I was hoping at this point that a member of the audience wouldn't stand up and ask, "What does this have to do with his going on the Mount Logan Expedition?" So I moved along a little quicker.

I had read the report Laing had co-authored for the National Museum of Canada and told the audience that he'd written how he "was enabled to accompany the Mount Logan Expedition to Alaska as naturalist and cinematographer" and wrote of how "Hubrick's camp [would be] the headquarters for biological work, and through the next three months field work was carried on in the vicinity of the foot of the Chitina moraine" as the mountaineers ascended the tallest mountain in Canada. But I noted that nowhere in this report did Laing mention what he packed.

I continued, clutching the microphone a little tighter, saying that Laing was a man of simplicity. He prided himself on it. His article for *Recreation* about what he packed on his motorcycle, the simplicity that was required for him to provide everything needed for a long-distance journey, showed a man of ingenuity and discipline. I was hoping the

Hamilton Mack Laing during his motorcycle-naturalist period in 1914.
(PHOTO: H.M. LAING, COURTESY: RICHARD MACKIE)

National Museum report would give me more of a glimmer of Laing's views on simplicity, views that no doubt were reinforced by his earlier travelling across the United States on a Harley-Davidson 11-F he named Barking Betsy. I asked the audience to think of a trip they had taken, short or long-distance, and what they chose to pack, what they thought might be useful but could be left behind.

You see, I continued, on a motorcycle there are few places to put things, so Laing needed to be frugal, to say the least. He had this frugality down to a science, so much so that he wrote several thousand words on the subject. Here's how he put it when launching into his story: "You may get along very nicely with that new camper's outfit of forty-seven odd pieces catalogued and sworn to as the complete thing . . . but you will be lucky if you reach your destination with a dozen pieces." Clearly Laing was speaking from experience.

That experience must have been gathered from other times of his life, at Heart's Desire camp in Manitoba or the rural farm life of his up-bringing. But being on the move on two wheels had Laing going farther and faster and being increasingly self-reliant and simple in his approach. In the *Recreation* article, he wrote further: "When one gathers a camping outfit for the first time he soon realizes that it is a clear case of re-verting to primitive conditions. He must have something with which to eat, something in which to sleep and also a shelter.

"My culinary kit is light and more on the luncheon order," he wrote. Also "tinned stuffs" came in handy such as "pork & beans, spaghetti, soups heated on the coals."

For clothing: "One spare shirt, a heavy sweater [which also doubled for Laing as bedding], two changes of under clothing and three or four of socks is ample. . . . I plead guilty to the army shirts and riding trousers and leggings. But of whatever make, both shirt and trousers ought to be of wool. . . . I do not carry a spare pair of trousers; when I tear them, I turn to the mending kit."

Laing had a small kit for seemingly everything. "Thus I have an eating kit (knife, fork, etc.), a shaving kit (razor, tooth-brush)—some probably would omit this—a mending kit, and another of tools seldom used. The trick is to get just what you need in the kit and nothing more."

I was on a roll as I continued. As for shelter, Mack Laing knew the gear in this category was packed but not often used, "but when it is needed it is needed badly. The tarpaulin tent, a flat rectangular sheet about 8 by 12, and equipped with steel pegs, put out by some of the dealers, is about right, providing you get it made of balloon silk . . . [it] has the advantage of being absolutely water-proof; it folds into a smaller roll, and of course takes up less room in the outfit."

Taking up less space with cumbersome belongings is something I think Mack Laing prided himself on. Somehow he also fit in a Kodak camera, film and a folding metal tripod amongst a flashlight, tools, a motorcycle lock and some spare straps. There is no mention as to how he shoehorned all of this into three satchels. However, his concluding bit of advice in this article is clear: "Go light if you would go right."

So why was I mentioning Mack Laing's packing habits in my speech? Well, I found in my research that they had much to do with his later success as a key figure in some major Canadian expeditions. His experience made him a reliable outdoorsman, someone who was prepared with a minimal amount of gear, who was also organized and able to not think too much about how to look after himself in remote locations because it was old hat to him, who could concentrate on his work: note-taking, collecting, photographing or, as the case may be, filming.

As I pointed at the screen behind me, I asked the audience whether, in viewing the film, we might get any hints as to Mack Laing's style from his time as cinematographer. Perhaps simplicity would dictate how he did that as well.

Cale Lacasse was next up at the podium. Lacasse Construction, his family's construction company based in the Comox Valley, had volunteered to restore Shakesides. He spoke eloquently about preserving the heritage buildings of Comox. Tom Dishlevoy, a local architect whose enthusiasm for not only restoring Shakesides but upgrading it to be energy-efficient and environmentally friendly, was nothing short of captivating.

Then, after a further introduction from Gordon Olsen, the lights died down, the buzzing room quietened and the film began. We first saw a black-and-white image of an institutional building, almost castle-like, with the superimposed title, "Distributed by The National Museum of Canada, Ottawa." This was followed by the white title, *The Conquest of Mount Logan*, which looked hand-drawn, to the right of a sketch of a mountain, the "f" in "of" appearing slightly askew, looking like, perhaps, a bit of mountaineering equipment to hook on to the imposing mountain.[2]

With a faint image of a dominating mountain peak shown, a title faded in overtop: "Mount Logan, 19,850 feet above the sea, the highest peak in Canada, and with the exception of the Himalayan Giants the highest mountain in the British Empire, is situated in the southwest corner of the Yukon Territory."

Next, a map of Canada, black ink on a white background appeared. Slowly, as if by stop-motion animation, a dotted line made its way north from Seattle in the bottom left of the screen, by sea, to Cordova, Alaska. A dot to the northeast shows the location of the town of McCarthy, with "Logan" written south of that.

Great Salt Lake, Utah. Laing pauses on his Harley-Davidson 11-F during
his 1915 motorcycle adventure across the continental United States.
(PHOTO: H.M. LAING, COURTESY: RICHARD MACKIE)

The next bit of text, white lettering on a black background, read:
"At the 10,000 foot level Logan is 16 miles long and 4 1/2 miles wide.
It stands upon a base 100 square miles in extent and is the most stupen-
dous mountain mass known."

At the bottom right, behind the text, we see a small image of a moun-
tainous area, an indication of Mount Logan's unique character.

We now see an inset of the earlier map, only showing the Alaska
and Yukon portion. A pen sneaks in, points out a spot just south of
McCarthy, then disappears, leaving a rectangle displaying "Valley of
the Chitina River." Another rectangle appears below it and states "Com-
mencement of the ice, Hubrick's Camp." It disappears and instantly
another appears just east of it displaying "Logan Glacier." The next
rectangle states "Crossing into Canada" noting the border between
Alaska and Yukon Territory. Then another replaces it, reading "Ogilvie
Glacier," and to the east again "Cascade Cache Base of Logan" and
another to the east stating "King Col Camp" and finally "Mt Logan The
Summit." The quiet audience, barring the occasional cough, had been
given a précis of the route to the summit.

If the nature of the Logan massif was being sold as unique, the makeup of the expedition's funding reads as even more so with the next text to appear: "Sponsored by the Alpine Club of Canada and financed by the Dominion, the United States and Great Britain, the expedition reached the summit of June 23, 1925." I thought, this sounds like a battle waged by allied nations keen to see the common foe vanquished.

Next we looked at what is perhaps a photograph or painting of the area traversed to reach the summit, unfortunately dark across the centre and right of the image. What can be made out is the title at the base "The Great Logan Massif from the North." Rectangles, reminding me of comic book speech bubbles, begin appearing, pointing out features of the massif, almost like the labours needed to be conquered by a mythological heroic figure before reaching the treasure that lay ahead. "The Great Stream of the Logan Glacier." "Cliffs along the North Face 7000 feet high." "An Array of Ice Clad Summits." "The Summit of Mount Logan" is finally listed at the very top, an arrow pointing out the exact spot achieved in the harsh landscape.

As we further our understanding of the inhospitable and seemingly dangerous massif of this part of the Yukon, peppered with glaciers and daunting peaks, we are given a play-by-play of the camps achieved along the successful route to the summit. An image of the massif appears, "Seward Glacier" written across a white expanse at the base with several downward arrows, from left to right, denoting the ascending camps met by the expedition. After King Glacier Trench, we see King Col Camp, Windy Camp, several others which are hard to make out, ending in "Summit of Mt. Logan (19,850') Reached 8 p.m. June 23rd." A pen moves across the camps, pointing them out for the viewer.

A slow fade-out, then a fade-in to the previous Great Logan Massif image, returns us to the successful ascent, but an indication that there was more to come afterwards, with rectangles pointing out "bivouac in the open" and "Hurricane Ridge." Perhaps not all went to plan on the way down?

But it is the next bit of text that generates an especially detectable intake of breath and sudden faint sounds of anticipation from the Mack Laing appreciators in the audience, myself included. "A party of nine constituted the expedition. H.M. Laing, Government biologist, remained at the edge of the timber."

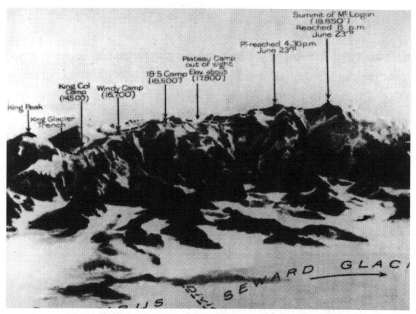

A frame from *The Conquest of Mount Logan* of landmarks and camps
of the expedition. Photograph taken from Mt. Saint Elias, 1897.
(PHOTO: ALLEN CARPE, COURTESY: AMERICAN ALPINE CLUB LIBRARY)

And with a sudden cut to a live-action shot at just under four minutes into the nearly forty-five-minute film, I see Laing in motion for the
first time. He is wearing a cap, a double-pocketed collared shirt, perhaps
army-issue, and belted pants. He appears in a "cowboy frame," we can
see him from the waist up. Are his hands in his pockets? He is casually
talking to somebody to his right, then he seems to address the camera
itself, with what looks like a satisfied look on his face. It's almost as
though he might be telling a joke, or perhaps this was his attitude towards the odd experience of being in front of the camera, having been
the cinematographer already for some time. I couldn't help but think
that here he was, in his early forties, ten years since he had ridden his
Harley-Davidson across the United States. He was bearded and clearly
comfortable in this natural setting, foliage gently swaying in the breeze
behind him.

In that five-second clip, I had seen more of Laing in the prime of his
expedition career than in any photographs viewed in my research the
previous year. Here he was in motion, with a facial expression that told

me he was comfortable in nature, assured of himself, and able to laugh among his company as the camera was turned on him. He was both naturalist and cinematographer in this setting, at a camp along the Chitina River and a vast valley where he would conduct his work, for the most part, on his own. He was self-sufficient, confident and in good health. His work in Alaska would take several months and have him closely associating with the assorted mountaineers, from different countries, who would make up the crew that would ascend the tallest mountain in Canada for the first time. What did he learn? What firsts did he achieve? How did he balance his work as a naturalist and his new role as cinematographer? How did he survive in camp for months at a time and go about conducting his work while the mountaineers struggled against what was clearly a daunting environment?

The five seconds of seeing Laing in motion generated many more questions for me. I sought to answer them by looking into his involvement in possibly the most prolific expedition he would be attached to as naturalist, by consulting his handwritten diaries, preserved at BC Archives in Victoria. There were reports to read, including the various ones written by the mountaineers as well as Laing in the 1925 *Canadian Alpine Journal*, a 1926 *Geographical Journal*, and the report that Hamilton Mack Laing co-authored with P.A. Taverner and R.M. Anderson entitled *Birds and Mammals of the Mount Logan Expedition*, tucked into the National Museum of Canada's Annual Report of 1927.

In the following pages, I've written about Laing in his own historical context, describing what he did as a naturalist of his times. The names of the flora and fauna he noted and studied, as well as their scientific names, come from these reports. I've not sought to update them but present them to the reader in the context of Laing's day, in the 1920s, and the scientific framework with which he was familiar. I've done this as well in describing the work of the mountaineers.

In his own diaries, Hamilton Mack Laing referred to himself as "the tail of the kite," in reference to his following the mountaineers partway in their high-profile quest to climb Mount Logan. He would prove to be successful in his own right, in his own adventure.

CHAPTER 1

Departure

April 11, 1925.

Memorandum re Duties of Mr. Hamilton M. Laing
on Mount Logan Expedition

Mr. Hamilton M. Laing
Comox, Vancouver Island,
British Columbia.

Dear Mr. Laing,

The Victoria Memorial Museum, Department of Mines, Ottawa, has
made arrangements to have you accompany the Canadian Alpine Club
Expedition of 1925 to Mount Logan, Yukon Territory, as naturalist for
this Museum, your period of employment to extend from approximately
April 15th to approximately August 31st, as Junior Zoologist, at the rate
of $105.00 per month, under the same conditions of your employment
by the Museum during previous field seasons. . . . It is desired that you
stop at Sidney, Vancouver Island, British Columbia, to confer with Mr.
A.O. Wheeler, of the Canadian Alpine Club Committee, on your way to
Seattle.

Yours very truly,
L.L. Bolton,
Acting Director, Victoria Memorial Museum
Department of Mines, Ottawa, Canada.

The rain fell in a fine mizzle as Hamilton Mack Laing waited for his train. He stood on the Esquimalt & Nanaimo Railway platform in Courtenay, the one-and-a-half-storey building's Canadian Pacific Railway red dulled on this overcast Thursday morning, April 16, 1925. He noted the rain, but also that it was not cold. He admired how spring was breaking in all loveliness upon Vancouver Island. He was planning to ride the 10:25 a.m. Royal Mail Service train, which would have a mail car in tow, ensuring a timely arrival at its terminus in Victoria. However, his final destination was far beyond that.

His view from the window as the train took him south reminded him in sight and quality of those he had seen in Niagara country of Ontario. He noted alder appeared to be into their green leafage. He took in the maple trees, admiring how they appeared in bloom, showing tiny leaves that crowded after tassels, but the flowers were the highlight. He saw certain trees as having human traits, such as the evergreens, trees he deemed unchanging and uninteresting, like people set in their ways. The madronas he found much more interesting, bark peeling to reveal smooth red nakedness beneath. As he was leaving British Columbia before long, it was notable that he would also spot the bright yellow-cream dogwood blossoms. Fields of yellow buttercups streaked by. Strawberries were also bright sights, white flowers promising summer fruit.

To his disappointment, he noticed that birds were scarce. The ducks had all but gone from the bays passed by. He spotted a few coots, scaups, and horned and Holboell's grebes, what we might refer to today as red-necked grebes. Several mergansers and loons were seen. But to his dismay there were very few gulls. But his disappointment of the showery day was alleviated by the sight of black poplars with firs in the distant landscape accompanying the flow of a river. It seemed to absolve what was a dull first day in advance of an extraordinary adventure.

Victoria seemed to give Mack Laing mixed feelings. He did admire its prettiness, but countered it with its dullness. His train pulled in to the station at 5 p.m. He made his way to Eldon Lane Cottage at Foul Bay.

The next day, he would wake early, listening to the waves murmuring below. But in contrast to the day before, he found himself surrounded by birds in song, and in sight, among the madronas, oaks and shrubbery:

western meadowlarks, towhee, black-winged gull, horned grebe, loon, Seattle wren (or as we might call it today, Bewick's wren), Nuttall's white-crowned sparrow, northern flicker, violet-green swallow.

Laing wanted to get a move on to the nearby town of Sidney this particular afternoon as he had an appointment with something of a mountaineering legend. A.O. Wheeler was one of the founders, and the current director, of the Alpine Club of Canada, and had been its first president after its creation in 1906. He was also, at Laing's visit, the editor of the *Canadian Alpine Journal*, and the spark behind the Mount Logan Expedition of 1925 as its director. He was also the father of E.O. Wheeler, surveyor on the first expedition to Mount Everest in 1921, who was on the advisory board for the Logan expedition. Laing thought that the quickly moving Flying Line jitney he was taking to his meeting was the only thing moving fast in Victoria. He did, however, manage to appreciate the pretty rural scenery of the Saanich Peninsula.

Wheeler welcomed Laing into his Sidney home and, once settled into his office, explained the details of the expedition. Laing would act as naturalist and cinematographer, aiding the expedition by filming the mountaineers on their historic assault on the mountain. The film would be a remarkable visual record and complement Laing's work in the form of specimens, notes and a report, assembled for the Victoria Memorial Museum.

Wheeler familiarized Laing with the climbing party personnel and their history behind the expedition. Not long after the 1922 proposal made by veteran geologist and mountain climber A.P. Coleman, a professor at the University of Toronto, to the Alpine Club of Canada that an attempt to conquer Mount Logan should be made, a special meeting was held in Vancouver to consider it. This took place in the fall of 1923, when they determined to proceed, and an executive committee was created. Considering the international interest in attaining the summit of Mount Logan, representatives were requested from the Alpine Club (England), the American Alpine Club as well as the Alpine Club of Canada.

The American Alpine Club elected Allen Carpe as a representative, an accomplished mountaineer hailing from New York City. Three other

Americans volunteered, and had been accepted, into the expedition: Henry S. Hall Jr. of Boston, Robert M. Morgan of Milwaukee (president of the Dartmouth Snowshoe and Ski Club) and Norman H. Read of New York City, with ties to Manchester, Massachusetts. The executive committee appointed by the Alpine Club of Canada was chaired by William Wasbrough Foster of Vancouver, British Columbia. He would also be part of the climbing party, as would be the team's leader, Albert H. MacCarthy of Wilmer, British Columbia. Andy Taylor, a local prospector and guide from McCarthy, Alaska, would join the climbing party en route. H.F. Lambart, who had worked extensively with the Geodetic Survey of Canada and was the vice-president of the Alpine Club of Canada, would be deputy leader. So it would be MacCarthy, Lambart, Foster, Carpe, Read, Hall, Morgan and Taylor who would make their way to the summit. Laing's role capturing the mountaineers' adventure would end just beyond Hubrick's Camp, where he would make a base of operations to collect his specimens and gather film as his work required. He would most likely not be expected to go beyond what was known as "Turn" where the Ogilvie Glacier began.

After careful consideration of three routes to Mount Logan, the favoured option was one noted as well-known and highly possible from the International Boundary Surveys done in 1912 and 1913. Laing would begin training on the motion picture camera in Seattle, where he also would get outfitted for the expedition. From there a steamship would take him, and much of the personnel of the expedition, to Cordova, Alaska. From there, over the Copper River and North Western Railway, it was 191 miles until McCarthy. Then they would travel by pack train eighty-eight miles to the Chitina Glacier, near where Laing would part with the mountaineering team, and return to his base of operations at Hubrick's Camp to conduct his work as naturalist.

With a warm handshake, Laing parted with the mountaineering pioneer and, in a last glance out his office window, noted several Nuttall's white-crowned sparrows flitting around in the nearby trees.

April 18 dawned cold, raw and windy, a day Laing believed to be thoroughly unpleasant. He would spend much of the day at the Provincial Museum studying bird specimens from British Columbia. The next day, he got into his naturalist role more fully by studying rocks and plants near the cottage where he was staying at Foul Bay. He noted that many plants were in bloom: strawberry, saxifrage, yellow parsnip, camas lily and blackberry bushes.

On April 20, Laing was scheduled to board a steamship for Seattle. He walked in through the impressive entrance of the newly built steamship terminal building designed by Francis Rattenbury (architect of the nearby Parliament Buildings, opened in 1898, and the Empress Hotel, finished in 1908). A fixture of the Canadian Pacific British Columbia Coast Steamships, the building may have been new, but it resembled a Greek temple with its pylons and columns, an impressive entry point to Victoria. This was where Canadian Pacific's *Princess* ships took passengers to Vancouver and Seattle.[1] It was an auspicious day at Victoria's Inner Harbour, as a new steamship, the *Princess Marguerite*, would arrive that evening, having travelled all the way from the John Brown & Company shipyards in Clydebank, Scotland, to start a new era of service for the British Columbia Coast Steamships.[2] But once through the terminal, Laing found himself passing the time waiting for his ship (either the *Princess Victoria* or the *Princess Charlotte*) by studying two birds resting on a float. At first he took them to be loons, but upon a closer look, he discovered they were large cormorants. One red-necked grebe was performing a terrific dance that drew him in for a while, but he soon determined it wasn't a wedding march but an attempt to part with oil on its feathers.

At 4:30 p.m., Laing left Victoria for Seattle. He counted about thirty gulls as the ship entered Juan De Fuca Strait on a journey that would take approximately five hours. There were more red-necked grebes, and he counted a half dozen lesser scaups and up to 100 greater scaups before the ship committed to its southerly course.

The bird prospects were barren as he walked the decks of the ship. Once nearing Port Townsend, however, he met what he described as a congregation. Fifty gulls were excitedly fishing. He also saw an unconfirmed number of marbled murrelets. As the sun sank, he spotted a dozen pigeon guillemots and hundreds of geese in formation, high over the ship, honking in concert. The lights of Seattle grew closer.

The next day, Laing found himself prospecting for something other than wildlife; he was looking for supplies for the months ahead. It would be the only full day he would devote to this hunt. He did his utmost to browse successfully but knew he didn't have to rush into purchasing what he needed. The next day he would begin his cinematographer's training.

Allen Carpe and Mack Laing were named the cinematographers of the Mount Logan Expedition. Carpe wrote of Laing as "representing the Canadian Government, Department of Mines," and that he would take "still and motion pictures of the expedition up to its departure from 'Trail End,'" from which point, Carpe would continue taking motion pictures during the mountaineering phase.[3] He also wrote that in choosing motion picture cameras "spring motor drive was essential," and that the only cameras available for his use at the time of the expedition were the Debrie Sept and the Bell & Howell Filmo.

Carpe considered the Sept to be ideal for work below 9,000 feet. This 35mm camera (using what he referred to as "standard gauge film") began with the Italian company FACT, its design being sold in the early 1920s to a French company called André Debrie that would produce it throughout the decade. It had a magazine capacity of fifteen feet of film. The Filmo, on the other hand, was deemed ideal for the mountaineering phase in that, although it used 16mm film (what Carpe referred to as narrow-gauge film), that film would be "ready spooled in daylight loading containers," allowing for easy changing in the low temperatures the alpine environment was promising.[4] The company Eastman Kodak had soothed the expedition's concern regarding the compatibility of the film sizes by ensuring "enlargements could be made from the narrow-gauge film to standard gauge, and a satisfactory test enlargement was so made." The Filmo also had several lenses, which would have optical filters, such as the Wratten No. 3 (Aero No. 1) filters ("in varnished gelatine") installed, in order to cut through "aerial haze . . . and in rendering distant views and cloud effects." Another filter was the Wratten No. 15 (G) of use in black-and-white photography as it would—as did the No. 3—make the sky look darker, which would show in sharp contrast to the snow and ice.[5]

Carpe would use both cameras interchangeably below 9,000 feet. The Sept required frequent reloading of film as it only had a capacity of fifteen feet of standard gauge film, requiring the changing of a film magazine with the use of a change-bag. The Sept, as the name suggested, could do seven jobs. It could function as a still camera, create sequential images, act as a motion picture camera, project still images, project motion pictures, enlarge pieces of film and be a motion picture transfer machine.

Laing, however, would use a Universal 35mm hand-crank motion picture camera. Various machinations, prior to his involvement in the expedition, facilitated this choice of camera, which had been sent to him directly from the Canadian Government Motion Picture Bureau, overseen by the Department of Trade and Commerce in Ottawa. In January 1925, second-in-command of the expedition H.F. Lambart corresponded, from his Ottawa office at the Geodetic Survey of Canada, Department of the Interior, with George Eastman of the Eastman Kodak Company regarding "a new camera that is still in the development department which we might like to have you take on your trip."[6] Lambart and Carpe had also been corresponding about using motion picture cameras to document the upcoming expedition. At the Mount Logan Committee meeting, held in Vancouver, B.C. on January 11, 1925, at which F.C. Bell, A.H. MacCarthy, W.W. Foster and A.O. Wheeler were present, "it was decided to concentrate as much as possible on still photos, it not being considered that movies would be worth while [sic]."[7] Lambart, on his copy of the minutes, underlined this last phrase in red pencil and wrote next to it, "what rubish [sic] HFL." This would set up a conflict between the Alpine Club of Canada's director and the deputy leader of the expedition regarding whether motion picture photography would document the expedition. In a January 14 letter to JWA Hickson, president of the Alpine Club of Canada, Wheeler further declared "that moving pictures were not a necessity and the obtaining of them would be quite expensive while marketing them was a very doubtful matter." Lambart also highlighted this in red and wrote: "Rubish [sic] HFL"[8] "I am sorry the Committee place such little value in the photographer," Lambart wrote to Wheeler on January 20. "I think the motion pictures would be most valuable and of great future value."[9] Lambart continued unabated, receiving a brief note from Eastman that due to the expedition's earlier-than-expected departure, the camera he had in mind wouldn't be ready in time.[10] R.S. Peck, director of the Canadian Government Motion Picture Bureau, wrote to Lambart on February 26, providing him with "pursuant to our telephone conversation this afternoon" information regarding a new 100-foot standard automatic motion picture camera made by the Bell & Howell Company of Chicago, Illinois.[11] Carpe and Lambart continued to correspond about aerial photography and exploring photographic options. By March 26, Lambart had drafted a letter to Wheeler, informing him he was negotiating with the Deputy Minister of the Department of Mines "regarding the addition of a naturalist to the expedition who would be equipped with a moving picture outfit and film and would be free of expense to the expedition." Although Lambart does address the concern of the weight of the motion picture apparatus he would have to carry at an estimated 125 pounds. "You no doubt know him, Mr. Hamilton M. Laing, as he lives at Comox, and is employed often by the Department of Mines. He is young, writes well and is very well liked. I trust the committee will see their way clear of approving him as an addition."[12] In a memo, written the same day, the head of the Division of Biology at the Victoria Memorial Museum, Rudolph M. Anderson, addressed his concerns with R.S. Peck's recommendation of a Bell & Howell Filmo as it used 16mm film, as well as those worries of Head of Ornithology, Percy A. Taverner, and Supervisor of Migratory Birds Protection for the Canadian National Parks, Hoyes Lloyd, that the narrow gauge of film did not suit the museum's exhibition purposes. "The Eastman Co. can make enlargements of the 16mm film to the standard size of 35mm, but loses detail in the enlargements we would require," Anderson wrote. "Enlargements also mean addition expense." Although Anderson pointed out a solution: "Mr. Peck has a good Universal camera, taking standard size of film, 35mm wide, taking film in 200-foot reels, which he will loan to this Department for the trip," while he emphasized, "Mr. Peck advises that if it is decided to have the Universal camera loaned to Mr. Laing for the expedition, that the apparatus be sent out to Seattle as soon as possible, and that Mr. Laing go down there and get some practice and instruction before the expedition starts."[13] Anderson wrote swiftly to the acting director of the Victoria Memorial Museum, L.L. Bolton, that should Laing be approved for such a unique role and be issued a Universal motion picture camera, Anderson would inform two Seattle-based photographers he'd worked with before with filming experience of Laing's arrival and ask for advice and practice:

Mr. WHE Hudson, 3617 35th Ave. W., Seattle.

Asahel Curtis, Curtis Studios, Seattle.

"If they can not give Mr. Laing a little coaching," Anderson wrote, "they can at least tell him where to go, develop film, etc."[14]

The following day, Laing, who was fully expecting to travel to Alberta to work for the museum, got a telegram from L.L. Bolton:

DEPARTMENT WISHES YOU TO ACCOMPANY MOUNT LOGAN YUKON EXPEDITION AS NATURALIST INSTEAD OF ALBERTA WORK LEAVING SEATTLE MAY SECOND. RETURN AUGUST. CAN YOU REPORT SEATTLE APRIL FIFTEENTH FOR MOTION PICTURE PRACTICE? WIRE ACCEPTANCE AND LETTER INSTRUCTIONS AND ADVANCE MONEY WILL BE SENT COMOX.[15]

It was a week later than planned, but for the week of April 22, his life would be absorbed by experimenting with the Universal camera and studying with Hudson and Curtis. He would also do some shopping and outfitting himself for the months ahead. Wheeler had given him much to ponder at their Sidney encounter, but meeting with S. Rathburn at the Game Commission Office on April 29 would fill him in on his responsibilities, including obtaining a permit to collect specimens on American soil in a rustic and inhospitable part of the north. In his memorandum of duties, drawn up in early April, Bolton informed Laing of the details of his permits:

Mr. Hoyes Lloyd, Supervisor of Migratory Birds Protection, Canadian National Parks, is extending your 1925 bird collecting permit to include Yukon Territory, and is sending you a letter which with your British

Columbia permit will serve until your Yukon permit is countersigned. Mr. O.S. Finnie, Director, Northwest Territories and Yukon Branch, Department of the Interior, has wired to the Acting Gold Commissioner at Dawson asking him to issue you a permit to collect four (4) scientific specimens of each species of game and fur-bearing mammals protected in Yukon Territory with request to send permit to you in care of Alaska Steamship Company, Seattle, or Skagway, Alaska. The Department of Mines has also requested the United States Government authorities at Washington, D.C., to grant you permits to collect mammals and birds in the Territory of Alaska and has asked that they be sent to you at Seattle in care of the Alaska Steamship Company.[16]

Laing took the time to admire the stuffed pheasant mounted in the office.

During the evening of May 1, Hamilton Mack Laing walked into the lobby of the Hotel Seattle. He had been invited by A.O. Wheeler to a "little impromptu dinner" prior to departure on the SS *Alaska* the following morning.[17] H.M. Laing, as the record shows, was in attendance as, "naturalist and motion picture operator, representing the Geological Survey of Canada, Department of Mines."[18] Soon he was shaking hands warmly with H.F. Lambart, the assistant leader of the expedition, who had advocated for Laing's involvement as cinematographer and naturalist. He was aware of a large number of people in a dimly lit room, hazy from pipe smoke. Lambart moved Laing over to meet a commanding figure, W.W. Foster of Vancouver, who was Chairman of the Mount Logan Committee and had been named the "recorder of the Expedition."[19] Foster had attended a farewell dinner the evening before in Vancouver, held at the University Club by the officers and honorary members of the 7th Battalion.[20] Near Foster was Allen Carpe, an American, accomplished mountaineer and fellow cinematographer. Laing shook hands with three other Americans: a youthful, tall Henry S. Hall Jr., a strong and smiling Norman H. Read and Robert M. Morgan. These men were volunteers, paying their own expenses for the experience of accompanying the expedition.[21] Soon Laing and the mountaineers were motioned to their seats at a long table. After their dinner and drink orders had been taken, a spoon struck a water glass at the head of the table. Colonel

F.C. Bell, vice-president of the Logan Committee, acted as chairman for the evening. He welcomed all present, and introductions were made round the table. Laing was learning that he was steeped in a gathering of some of the top figures in mountaineering on the continent. Bell regretted that an L.H. Lindsay, a climber for whom Laing could detect those present had a great affinity, could not attend, nor accompany the expedition, as his eldest boy had fallen critically ill. Bell also pointed out that the day coincided with the birthday of A.O. Wheeler, an announcement that was followed by applause. Wheeler stood up, his grey beard and pipe quite distinctive, now a familiar sight to Laing. Wheeler had been born in Ireland in 1860.[22] His words entertained the guests, the veteran climber offering learned advice to the mountaineers about to sail north. Next to Wheeler was seated Mrs. A.O. Wheeler. Also from the Alpine Club of Canada was a Professor Herschel C. Parker. There was a newspaperman there too, Laing noted, a Major L. Johnston from the *Vancouver Daily Province*.[23] The newspaper was giving the expedition some promotion within its pages and would claim that to "Canadians especially the projected climbing of Mount Logan parallels what the attempt to reach the top of Mount Everest is to the whole British Empire."[24]

Representatives of the Mountaineers of Seattle also attended to wish bon voyage to the expedition, including their president, Professor Meany, and secretary, Ralph S. Dyer.

Bell gave a speech to start off what amounted to much well-wishing for the expedition. One by one, Laing noted the wishes of success and *Godspeed!*, followed by the raising of glasses to the expedition members. He was struck with the camaraderie, the familiarity of the expedition members, a company of mountaineers that, apparently, for the most part, had known each other less than a day. Even those not travelling by sea to Alaska the next day would regale the dinner party with tales of their own experience, advise on the risks of having less than four men roped together in the snow fields and emphasize vigilance and discipline.[25]

Laing heard stories of adventure, of great peaks scaled in Alaska and the Alps and much reminiscence pointing out the tradition they were a part of.[26] A.O. Wheeler had read the messages of well-wishers that had come in from the Alpine Club of Canada, the Alpine Club in England and the American Alpine Club, as well as many old friends.[27] Wheeler later wrote that the "little affair" had been a pleasant "get together" for the members of the expedition.[28] Laing, as he escaped the confines of the soiree after photographs were taken for the newspaper, was looking forward to boarding that steamer the following morning and doing his part. After several days of preparations and learning to use a motion picture camera, he was keen to get on with it. The bonhomie, gentility and politeness of the evening's events would be in sharp contrast to the environment they were all leaving for.

CHAPTER 2

En Route to Alaska

The expedition is planned to sail from Seattle, USA, May 2, 1925, under direction of Capt. A.H. MacCarthy, Wilmer, B.C., with Mr. H.F. Lambart, Geodetic Survey of Canada, Department of the Interior, Ottawa, second in command, and in charge of field arrangements. The expedition hopes to reach Cordova, Alaska, May 12, and go by railway to McCarthy, Alaska, reaching McCarthy about May 14. . . . Please notify me of the date when you leave Comox and before you leave Seattle as to how your work there has progressed; also send me brief reports of progress when opportunity offers.

I trust that you may have a pleasant and profitable season in the field.

Yours very truly,

L.L. Bolton,
Acting Director, Victoria Memorial Museum
Department of Mines, Ottawa, Canada.

There was a westerly wind. The cloud was clearing. There was little bird-life to note on Puget Sound. Laing was on board the SS *Alaska* set for a 9 a.m. departure. Laing witnessed a send-off with cheers from familiar faces from the night before, members of the Alpine Club of Canada and the Mountaineers of Seattle.[1] The *Vancouver Daily Province* reported there were "scores at the gangplank eager for a final handshake, eager to give a last word of encouragement."[2] The anticipation for the expedition was hard to ignore. Laing was among a band of adventurers for whom expectations were high and risks were significant. The *Vancouver Daily Province* summed it up in an article published a few days later:

> If they succeed in reaching the summit of Logan, their achievement will be regarded in the brotherhood of mountaineers the world over as second only to the conquest of Everest. If they do not achieve their objective, the tens of thousands who will wait eagerly for news of them from the land of eternal ice and storm may rest assured that they will have failed only in the face of insurmountable obstacles.[3]

Two hours later, gulls began following the ship, increasing, by Laing's estimate, to 150, all of a large type. Glaucous-winged gulls were in abundance and some herring gulls as well.

Laing met with the personnel of the Logan party. He noted expedition members' names and places of origin in his diary. Leader: Albert MacCarthy (Capt.). Fred Lambart, Ottawa. Col. W.W. Foster, Vancouver. Henry Hall, Cambridge, Mass. Allen Carpe. Norman Read. Andy Taylor, McCarthy, Alaska (guide). The naturalist, H.M. Laing, was the tail of the kite.

Later Laing saw another party of 150 gulls on the water, this time Bonaparte's gulls, their darker head plumage distinguishing them from the earlier glaucous-winged gulls, one of the most common. Two pairs of large cormorants made a low pass over the water. There were two murrelets, perhaps marbled murrelets. In the distance, Laing could just make out two sooty shearwaters.

After dinner, Laing spotted a huge company of Bonaparte's gulls, estimating 2,000 on the water, making the surface appear silver. He tried to pick out one bird from another in a grouping of 100 cormorants, some small, some large, bobbing up and down in the waves and awing, the largest gathering of them seen shortly after passing Port Townsend.

Aware that the ship would be silently steaming its way through the Strait of Georgia, there was one last thing he noted in his diary in his cabin before turning in: Pass Comox in darkness.

Expedition team aboard the SS *Alaska* en route to Cordova.
L to R: (man unknown), Read, Laing, Hall, Foster, Carpe, Lambart, Morgan.
(COURTESY: WHYTE MUSEUM OF THE CANADIAN ROCKIES, V14_AC0P_410)

Next day, the ship was navigating Broughton Strait when Laing emerged on deck soon after his 6 a.m. wake-up. He could see it was overcast north, on the mainland, but Vancouver Island, almost close enough to touch, had clear skies. Further south, snowy peaks emerged. Pulteney Point Lighthouse passed quietly by off the starboard bow as the ship emerged from Cormorant Channel to the open water of Queen Charlotte Strait.

Laing couldn't help noting it was rather a birdless voyage that day. In addition to a dozen glaucous-winged gulls, he spotted one tiny auklet not far off the north end of Vancouver Island as the ship entered Queen Charlotte Sound. What Laing found most exciting about sighting an unknown larger auklet was its visible whitish underparts. He also counted four pairs of bald eagles, one pair at its nest with a juvenile. On another occasion, an adult was seen in pursuit of a juvenile.

The mainland now gathered Laing's attention as Vancouver Island faded aft. He noted the high crests of the inland ranges were all white. He could see new snow drifting in the late morning when the wind rose.

Pacific loons, between a dozen and twenty, drew him in. Laing found one pair especially beautiful with striking white patches on their heads. Indicative of the northern reaches of his destination, Laing had fleeting glimpses of red-throated loons that may have been non-breeding pairs travelling south in search of better fish-hunting waters.

As the ship began negotiating the Inside Passage, Laing saw distant small grebes and a pair of harlequin ducks near Bella Bella. The day's viewings were rounded off with white-winged scoters and a modest raft of surf scoters, the northern-breeding sea ducks, giving him further pause as to his destination.

He was up early again on May 4, 7 a.m., but actually 6 a.m. because he had set his clock to Alaska time. Once on deck, he found the landscape not terribly different from the night before, more hilltops with snowy peaks. Initially there were few birds, but some juvenile gulls were floating in the harbour as the ship slipped into sight of Ketchikan.

Off the ship for the first time, Laing stretched his legs with Foster and Lambart, walking up Water Street and admiring the harbour. There was a sound that Laing relished echoing by the sea: the regular croaking of common ravens, this time from a few on the wing. Some familiar northwestern crows were announcing their weak accusations, with one merely rattling away. Two violet-green swallows twittered while performing acrobatic manoeuvres in their search for insects. There were a dozen fox sparrows and several song sparrows. The two or three golden-crowned sparrows were new sights for Laing on the journey so far. Laing counted a few Savannah sparrows, a smattering of slate-coloured juncos and a rattling belted kingfisher. The telltale buzz led to the sighting of a few rufous hummingbirds, and he counted about six American robins and two chestnut-backed chickadees. And there were guesses on fleeting sightings, perhaps a couple of Pacific wrens, and what may have been an Audubon's warbler rounded off the scan of what Laing considered a 200-yard section of suburbs.

Laing found the temperature dropped fast in the afternoon. The northwest wind was raw and biting as the ship got back underway, heading to Wrangell for 6 p.m., where he spotted two short-billed gulls and a Bonaparte's gull.

May 5 dawned with Laing seeing two small cormorants. A dozen playful gulls followed the ship: one short-billed gull, one herring gull and the rest in the glaucous-winged species. He smiled while watching them on the wing.

It was close to noon when the ship arrived at Juneau for a brief stop. Later, when they reached the mouth of Lynn Canal, close to Icy Strait, a small congregation emerged. Laing saw a Pacific loon and could just make out a pair of marbled murrelets, small grey-and-white figures on the water. The weather was unfortunately not all that pleasant; cold and grey, with more snow falling in the distance at around 5 p.m.

The next day, Laing emerged on deck and couldn't even see land. It may have been because the ship was at last plying the waters of the Gulf of Alaska or because the fog produced a gloom that was hard to shake. It was a little warmer than the day before, with a southerly wind.

Like a warning, a dozen northern fulmars shot across the ship's heading, by Laing's estimation about a quarter mile ahead. He could have easily dismissed them as gulls, but they were more albatross-like in appearance, the stalwart ocean-going birds with hearty bodies. Lambart and Foster, knowing Laing's interest in keeping a running tally, reported a Savannah sparrow sighted on the deck, stating that it appeared to be a female, had a very rumbled look and was soaked with fog. Perhaps it was having a rest?

The gloom lifted by afternoon, with visibility, by Laing's estimation, being three-quarters of a mile. Suddenly, at about 6 p.m., Cape Saint Elias loomed out of the fog in the distance. Laing stood in awe of the sharp crag that endured against the power of the sea, what he thought of as an isolated rock castle of Alaskan giants. Reaching this point southeast of Prince William Sound, vulnerable to the full might of the Pacific Ocean, meant the ship was nearing Cordova, where the expedition party would disembark. For now, Laing was revelling in the view ahead, as this sighting of land, Kayak Island, also seems to have meant an arrival at a haven for birdlife. Laing hurriedly started writing down his sightings, including six tufted puffins, the first he had seen. A flock of 500 sooty shearwaters, calling in their muffled staccato squeak, played in the waves and dove in the breeze. A sighting that truly placed the ship at the mercy of the open ocean was two black-footed albatrosses, clearly identified with wide wingspans. As the ship neared land, Laing could make out a dozen birds grouped together that he could only identify as blackish sandpipers, perhaps rock sandpipers, running quickly, avoiding the swell. As a finale to the show being performed, this particular evening, Laing took pleasure in the sight of black-legged kittiwakes, flying by in sixes, perhaps based at a nearby colony, making their "kittiwake" cries. The gloom had lifted indeed.

CHAPTER 3

To the End of Steel
at McCarthy

From the standpoint of the expedition, it is felt that obtaining a better collection of photographs, and particularly motion pictures of interesting features of the expedition, will enhance the value of the expedition, and that a man of your known field experience will be able to help the expedition in other ways.

—L.L. Bolton

Laing noticed a salmon cannery as the ship pulled into Cordova soon after he emerged on deck. It was a dreary morning, raining heavily. He could see the black face of a mountain beyond the community, and snow was falling there. In fact, he noted how the occasional snowflake was among the cold raindrops, and softly melted as it landed on the water. He watched, spellbound, as a small avalanche began its descent on one of the mountains beyond the town. It slid by his estimation a few hundred feet and then stopped in what appeared to be a sudden collapse.

There were fifty gulls, mainly juveniles, waiting at the wharf.

After breakfast, Laing disembarked and explored Cordova. Rain continued. There was low-lying fog. He could hear a Steller's jay screeching somewhere in the deep evergreen woods. The sweet lilt of a pair of hermit thrushes singing, as well as the ring of a few varied thrushes, kept his eyes scanning the treeline. He spotted a raven and two song sparrows that were long of beak and darker than those he was accustomed to. He wrote down Yakutat song sparrow in his diary. Perhaps it diverged from the brown and grey, with a white streak down the front, of the song sparrows he knew? He found a white-crowned sparrow with what he thought was a gaudy head.

The expedition party was reunited with Albert MacCarthy, their leader, who had been preoccupied on the difficult winter freighting expedition for months. Laing turned in, in preparation for departing by train at 8:30 a.m.

Next morning, Laing and the mountaineers found themselves in a passenger car trundling past the calm waters of Eyak Lake on a Copper River and Northwestern Railway train. Laing peered out at an eagle pair, watching one dive suddenly at the water and extract a fish, but it could not get fully airborne with its heavy catch. The bird had to suffice with dragging it to the shore. Laing had seen a Wilson's snipe, its long bill and plump body giving it away, at the Cordova Naval Radio Station. The area around the rudimentary structure consisted of wide flats, wet mud bars and marsh grass coming up green, about six inches tall. It was an ideal location for a probing snipe.

But in the first ten miles of travel on the rails, the eagles provided the most entertaining viewing; Laing had seen eight. He had also spotted a couple of American wigeons and mallards on the lake. The looming mountain ranges, snowcapped, were starting to fascinate Laing. Their image on the horizon, reflected in the water, the scope and scale of them, was wondrous.

The landscape was changing and becoming more inhospitable. There was wind-driven sand on snow. Marshes, muskeg and snow surface were increasing. He saw alder, willow and the most picturesque poplars he had ever seen that looked like ancient oaks.

Three ptarmigan, almost completely white, ran to a white snowy knoll. Henry S. Hall Jr. told Laing that he may have spotted a mink out the window.

Laing had a chance to, on a brief stop, photograph the vast Allen and Heney Glaciers, noting the moraine supported timber. He saw three black-billed magpies, and more ptarmigan, their heads and necks

Increasingly inhospitable landscape as seen on the train journey to McCarthy,
May 8. The environment changing to marsh, muskeg and snow surface.
(PHOTO: ALLEN CARPE, COURTESY: AMERICAN ALPINE CLUB LIBRARY)

featuring darker plumage than the earlier ones. Later, the train went
through a dry region, devoid of snow, that reminded him of Wyoming
or Montana, glorious, picturesque country. Laing saw reddish-purple
flowers, reminiscent of what he had seen in rock gardens, but the speed
of the train kept him from making any further identification.

At a later stop, Laing was within sight of Heney Glacier while dining, an exceptional view. Afterwards, he began snooping for tracks. He
could detect rabbit and perhaps fox tracks. Two swans rose out of the
water near the train. He was quite excited to see a bumblebee whirling
off over the snow. Butterflies flitted near the train.

Soon, there would be a concerning observation, bordering on the
macabre, as the train got back up to speed. Near Heney Glacier, along
Copper River, among the scrubby alders and willows, Laing saw dead
rabbits. Within what he estimated was a forty-to-fifty-mile stretch,
while bouncing along in the passenger car, he counted fifty dead bun-
nies; most were torn apart, disintegrated, in a state of decomposition.

Some were dead just where they sat, like they had been surprised to death. Laing didn't have an explanation for it but was curious and slightly disturbed by the sight.

Once the train lurched to a stop in Chitina at 3:20 p.m., the passengers moved to a different car for the final leg of the journey into McCarthy, starting at 4:30 p.m. They had travelled 129 miles since departing Cordova that morning. Laing continued to pursue the morbid tallying of dead rabbits. There were, by his calculation, as the train continued, now thirteen or fourteen per mile. Starvation? He noted that the spruce was stripped of bark, and fallen trees were also bare of twigs and leaves. The dead rabbits all were of white pelage. But he'd also seen about a dozen live rabbits along the route that day, all of them brown.

When they stopped at a junction called Strelna at 5:20 p.m., the men all ate a good meal. Laing recalled hearing a junco's quick-tweeting song in the distance. A pigeon hawk, otherwise known as a merlin, did a dramatic sweep and perched on a stub nearby.

The train passed by white poplars, the first Laing had seen in Alaska, then more white birches throughout the evening's journey. There were fewer bald eagle sightings now that the party was further inland. He counted only twenty bald eagles that day, and they were all adults.

After just over twelve hours, the train pulled into McCarthy at 8:45 p.m. Before light got too dim, however, Laing got a good view of the imposing Kennicott Glacier. The expedition members were greeted by the bright and wiry white-haired guide, Andy Taylor.

On the morning of May 9, Laing was peering through his field glasses at a slate-coloured junco singing while perched atop a white poplar. He was revelling in the dry, cool air, much different from the humid sea air he had been taking in for days. It was sunny and delightful. He had already admired a white-crowned sparrow and listened with his eyes closed, the sun on his face, to another junco. But he found this particular junco through his glasses, its rapid-fire song piercing the cool air, noticing its head to be quite black. Laing wandered through the town and caught sight of a few pairs of violet-green swallows, twittering sweetly and swirling to and fro, perhaps hunting for the numerous blue-bottle flies buzzing about.

The mountaineers in front of the Kennicott Glacier. Left to right: Read, Carpe, Foster, MacCarthy, Hall, Taylor, Morgan, Lambart. Dog unknown.
(COURTESY: WHYTE MUSEUM OF THE CANADIAN ROCKIES, V14_AC0P_430)

Laing made his way indoors to load his rifle and arrange his gear, including film purchased in Seattle and the Universal motion picture camera. Jack O'Neill's warehouse and Captain Hubrick's cabin and developing room were the gathering places for the expedition members, where trying out exposures, developing film and printing occupied their time.[1] Their days in McCarthy involved much preparation balanced with rest before making way on foot towards Logan.

Another sunny day dawned in McCarthy on May 10, a perfect day, Laing reckoned. For the first time, he secured the motion picture camera on its tripod and captured a portrait of the group of alpinists, taking still photographs as well. Before noon, he and Lambart walked closer to the moraine deposited by the Kennicott Glacier to create a sweeping scenic shot, depicting as best as he could the vastness of the landscape, marking the end of its forty-three kilometres.

It was a chance for Lambart and Laing to work together, and to begin capturing the expedition on film, a process that Lambart had worked on for months. He had also been aware of the weight of their apparatus—about thirty pounds for the camera, twenty pounds for the tripod and thirty pounds for the 4,000 feet of film—and knew he would require assistance.[2] Later the pack train would help convey this. Lambart and Laing walked up towards the moraine, shouldering their packs loaded with photographic equipment, Lambart also bringing his Ross still camera.

The planned panoramic shot would also set the scene for the expedition, panning from left to right, from west to east, across the long bridge over the Kennicott River. With Lambart's assistance, Laing securely mounted the camera to the tripod and began, diligently turning the crank arm as he panned. The shot showed the direction the expedition would take, in this landscape of massive mountains, dwarfing the man-made bridge. Lambart was satisfied with the beginning of the motion picture photography process and also prepared for his own photographs of the landscape. During this first use of the tripod with the Universal camera, the head seemed to have lost its stability. Laing spent some time that afternoon getting to know the tripod head, and mending it where necessary, so that he could use it on future scenic shots, which, in this land of superlatives, he thought for certain he would capture.

Laing decided on a short adventure to Kennicott, referred to locally as the Kennecott Mines. He knew that the rail route to McCarthy from Cordova was mostly due to the discovery of copper nearby, nearly twenty-five years earlier. The Bonanza and Mother Lode had been some of the Kennecott Company's most famed mines. The Copper River and Northwestern Railway was carved out of the landscape to haul the ore out on the nearly 200-train-mile route to the seaside terminus.

On the way, Laing spotted, along the gravel banks of a stream, a small sandpiper, slate-coloured juncos and white-crowned sparrows. A common companion as he strode to the mine site, following the east side of the moraine, was the sweet song of the myrtle warbler. After quickly glancing at the red-painted mine buildings, he turned back towards McCarthy. He would have only one more day, and he wanted to begin collecting his specimens.

CHAPTER 4

From McCarthy to Hubrick's Camp

From McCarthy the route will be up the Chitina River valley by pack-train to the Mount Logan region east of the Alaska-Yukon International Boundary.

—L.L. Bolton

Hamilton Mack Laing knew he was in Alaska, linked up with the mountaineers attempting the ascent on Mount Logan, through an ar-rangement made between the Victoria Memorial Museum (overseen by the Department of Mines) and the Alpine Club of Canada. He was allowed to accompany the expedition, given the dual roles of naturalist and cinematographer. His field work, done in the Chitina River region, would be partnered with filming the expedition's daily progress, from which a motion picture would be produced. The expedition itself was being sponsored by the Alpine Club of Canada and financed by the Dominion of Canada, the United States and Great Britain, which ex-plained the international makeup of the mountaineers. Laing realized that the mountaineers understood he was there as a government biolo-gist, his salary paid by the Department of Mines. In fact, in his article about the prominent expedition for the *Canadian Alpine Journal* in 1925, Arthur O. Wheeler wouldn't even mention the prolific writer and natur-alist at all. Laing knew he truly was "the tail of the kite."

Laing's duties as naturalist included collecting specimens of the plant and animal life, and that field work began the day before departure for the Logan massif, on May 11, slightly ahead of the schedule described in his memorandum of duties written up by L.L. Bolton, Acting Director of the Victoria Memorial Museum. The field equipment of naturalists of the day included a rifle, and Laing's was a .32 auxiliary. He began shooting, or what he would refer to in his diaries as "securing," birds he had observed in McCarthy. This collection would further the biological science community's understanding of the living world.

As the morning cleared, Laing secured a slate-coloured junco, one golden-crowned sparrow, a male and a female white-crowned sparrow, one Savannah sparrow, one myrtle warbler, a pair of white-winged crossbills already thought to have nested, a violet-green swallow and a solitary sandpiper. He would also collect a rabbit—a Mackenzie varying hare—a very large specimen at over three pounds, in his opinion, and a red squirrel.[1] These he would quickly and efficiently clean for preparation as specimens and leave them stored at McCarthy.

May 12 began with the sky half clear. Laing occupied himself with hefting the Universal movie camera and tripod onto the middle of a McCarthy street and filming the expedition preparing to leave town. As part of his equipment, Laing had received from R.S. Peck, Director of the Canadian Government Motion Picture Bureau in Ottawa, five magazines for the Universal camera, one six-inch lens, one two-inch lens, one tripod, two tripod handles, a camera crank and camera carrying case, all on loan from the Bureau.[2] Laing, wearing a visor cap and double-pocketed army-issue shirt, leaned in to the level of the camera and watched the scene unfold. This was the beginning of the long trail, the 138 miles that would bring the mountaineers to the base of Mount Logan. He watched, rolling film by turning the camera crank as he had learned in Seattle, as crates and bundles were methodically taken out of storage at Jack O'Neill's warehouse to the awaiting pack horses, excited, playful and barking dogs dancing at their feet. The gear was gathered into piles, then loaded onto the horses. Once done, there was time for a request, a gathering of the men for a shot, all together before setting out. The men were cooperative, but the dogs continued to jump and bark, unfazed by the cinematographer's attempts to capture the important moment before setting out on several days of drudgery on foot.

As loaded horses trundled down the streets of McCarthy, they were guided by packers Harry Boyden and Pete Brendwick. Laing managed to find higher ground for a shot, filming the pack train before the expedition left the small bastion of civilization for the wilderness. The men and eleven horses were destined for Martin Harris' Cabin.

By 10 a.m., the expedition was on the trail, and it was very muddy. McCarthy was at the conflux of a complex river system, draining glaciers to the north, including the Kennicott Glacier. Laing knew that they would be crossing the Nizina River ahead, on a newly constructed bridge. This was a large tributary of the Chitina River, which was sourced at the Chitina Glacier in the Saint Elias Mountains, close to where Laing would part with the mountaineers and base himself for his fieldwork.

As W.W. Foster later wrote, the estimated cost of the expedition would be $11,500, which provided for each member's transportation, food, tents, sleeping robes, cooking gear and ropes. This didn't include the three volunteers, Henry S. Hall Jr. from Boston, Robert M. Morgan of Dartmouth College and Norman H. Read of New York, "who would go to McCarthy at their own expense."[3] All expedition members would bring in their own personal equipment, clothing and still cameras, the exception being the motion picture cameras. Laing had expensed his own outfit to the Department of Mines, which oversaw the Victoria Memorial Museum that also was covering costs associated with making the film of the expedition, namely the motion picture training in Seattle and 4,000 feet of film. Personal equipment, including clothing and boots suited for the hike into the Chitina River valley, had been sent in during the winter freighting expedition headed by the slightly built, bespectacled and experienced climber Albert H. MacCarthy.

MacCarthy, when he took on the job of expedition leader at the Mount Logan Executive Committee meeting in Vancouver, November 1923, knew little about Mount Logan, only that it was the second-highest peak in North America and was somewhere in Canada. As he developed a further understanding of the objective's isolation, its summit being located in what appeared to be "the centre of the greatest glaciated alpine area known," he realized the magnitude of what lay ahead.[4] He soon saw the expedition's chances for success greatly increasing if it were done in two sections: one in the winter months early in 1925 that would consist of freighting in food, equipment and supplies and storing it in specific caches, and another that would be "the assault on the Peak in the spring and summer."[5] It was to be, from the very beginning, a "campaign against Mt. Logan."[6] But even before then, Laing knew that MacCarthy, along with Andy Taylor and Miles Atkinson, had taken the route they were on now, starting out in June 1924, to do some reconnaissance of what was considered the most practicable route from the northwest into the Chitina River valley via the town of McCarthy. The reconnaissance trip, planned for about forty-five days, had been plagued by the bad weather the region was notorious for, but the trip had determined that their current route, which would take approximately six days on foot, across eighty-six miles up the glacier-fed stream of the Chitina River, would get them to Trail End, eight miles beyond Hubrick's Camp, where Laing would establish his base for his work. But the eight members of the mountaineering expedition still had fifty miles over difficult moraine to cover before the foot of the Logan massif and, after that, an uncertain period of time to reach "the mightiest hump of Nature in the Western Hemisphere," as MacCarthy would term it, the true summit of Logan itself.[7] Much of the gear packed on the expedition members' backs had been brought in during MacCarthy's winter freighting expedition.[8]

Laing kept his mind sharp by noting the birds en route. White-crowned sparrows were whistling regularly, if not seen, certainly heard. Redpolls were churring away, foraging in a green spot of the woods he passed. Slate-coloured juncos were frequent trail companions. There were two northern flickers, one winnowing at a tree. He heard a woodpecker hammering on a dead spruce somewhere off in the distance. He spotted a whisky-jack, or gray jay. When the expedition halted for lunch by the clearing and massive expanse of the Nizina, he saw a large hawk circling.

It was also a good time to start collecting plant life, and Laing began picking up specimens of a lovely anemone, a whitish species he'd never before seen.[9]

Laing walked behind the expedition members with Taylor and the pack train. Lean, strong and knowledgeable, Taylor wasn't a mountaineer, but his reputation preceded him as an excellent hunting guide.[10] As he strolled along the wooded trail, a black bear emerged. The men halted silently as they waited for it to traverse the trail and lumber into the foliage. After a while, they continued, catching up with the party, more aware that they were in grizzly and black bear territory now.

The landscape changed as the expedition party entered a clearing and then proceeded to follow the valley ahead on gravelly bars, streamlets slowly coursing through the fissures, carrying mud and silt, telling of the glacier being drained ahead.

Laing heard the high-pitched holler of an olive-sided flycatcher, perched on a dead spruce on the crest of a hill. He saw more dead rabbits, recalling his tally from the train journey into McCarthy. Before reaching Martin Harris's cabin, a rustic roof over their heads, the party waded across Young Creek and turned into the woods. Laing took off his pack, while the men settled in for the night. He noted the typical Canadian zone life, featuring white and black poplar, some flowers, few birds to be seen at first, but later, walking solo, he spotted a few juncos and the flash of crimson from a redpoll. He secured a male, the report echoing through the trees.[11]

Along this walk, he also spotted a hairy woodpecker, two white-winged crossbills and a goshawk on the wing, with a red squirrel gripped in its powerful talons. Laing felt raindrops land on his arm, swung his rifle over his shoulder and returned to the log cabin to find his bed for the night.

Laing had battled a few huge mosquitos while he slept in his sleeping bag. He rose early, dressed and emerged from the cabin to see it half clear. He looked at the axe embedded at a forty-five-degree angle in a heavy stump. The handle had indents along the length of it that appeared to be tooth marks. Residents of McCarthy had mentioned, when Laing spoke of the dead rabbits seen along the rail journey, that the past winter had been particularly hard on them.[12] This is when starving rabbits would eat doorstops and nibble axe handles, just as porcupines would.

The expedition cooked breakfast and ate quickly before shouldering their packs and resuming their walk towards Hubrick's Camp, following Young Creek. The ground was wet after a night's rain, and even marshy in the woods. The weather, as Henry S. Hall Jr. later noted in his report on their equipment, was "not unlike the Canadian Rockies in June" with a nighttime temperature around 32° Fahrenheit (0° Celsius) and a day-time high of about 50°F (10°C).[13] Laing strapped on a pair of walking boots, his wool socks pulled up over his pant legs, but he noticed some of the other men wore different boots, twelve-inches high and with regular or rawhide lacing. The rubber soles and leather uppers gave them a military look. These were shoe-pacs, colloquially known as "barker boots," derived from the British shoemaker of the same name, and were the expedition's choice of footwear prior to arriving "above the altitude of day-melting."[14]

The party returned to the gravel beds of the valley, following streams, then crossing them. Laing noticed that the streams didn't run with ice on the surface, they froze from the bottom up, a peculiar trait. The ice wore off from the surface. Also, these streams were running with a fair amount of silt mixed in.

Laing decided to keep pace with Lieutenant-Colonel Foster, who was at the head of the party that morning. William Wasbrough Foster had been the president of the Alpine Club of Canada until 1924 (when JWA Hickson had stepped into the role), and he and MacCarthy were climbing partners and highly experienced alpinists, having, along with Conrad Kain, made the first ascent on Mount Robson, the highest peak in the Canadian Rockies, in 1913. Foster was also the chairman of the expedition's committee and had been sworn in two years previously into the Vancouver Police Department. He had served during the Great War, at the front, achieving the rank of Brigadier and had been seriously wounded twice. He had studied engineering, and prior to his wartime service, he was Deputy Minister of Public Works in British Columbia and had been an MLA.[15] They kept up a good pace with the intent of reaching a log bridge to cross Young Creek, but upon reaching it found it had been washed out. While crossing the creek, Laing saw a spotted sandpiper. Lambart was setting a pace of his own and overtook them. The path now took them closer to a treed ridge, and as Laing got closer, he heard a rough ringing call echoing across the valley, then spotted several varied thrushes perched on branches.[16] As he got even closer, slate-coloured juncos and myrtle warblers appeared.

As the horses found their footing on soil after trudging along gravelly bars and sand, the men assessed the route ahead, a single track much eroded from recent rains that looked quite muddy. It was the way to their wooded camp, and with late evening approaching, they decided to push on. While the party discussed the situation and how best to lead the horses, Laing thought to mount the Universal on the tripod to film what appeared to be a difficult climb. He cranked the handle, getting a shot of the horses gaining ground just before the slope began, then scrambled up the hill to capture the pack train with the valley in the background. The horses were increasingly fearful. A trio of horses, loaded down with heavy canvas bags, hind legs struggling to gain a hold on the muddy terrain, climbed at a forty-five-degree incline, hooves roughly shoving mud aside and down the trail.

As the next group of horses came up the trail, Laing continued to roll film. Just ahead of where the last ones struggled to gain a solid hoof-hold, the lead stumbled, sliding into the horse behind, causing a domino effect. No matter how hard the horses struggled, they couldn't maintain their hold on the hillside, and they careened into alder growth to the right, saving them from free falling into the creek below. Laing stopped filming, detached camera from tripod, settled the Universal back in its case and descended, and the men below ascended, to help get the horses upright and back on the trail. With some additional manpower and a fair amount of adrenaline, Laing, Taylor, Boyden, Brendwick and the mountaineers got the remaining horses up the hill. The climb continued but not at such an angle, and the mud decreased as the party pushed on to their camp for the night at the gravel bars.

Laing noted the recent burn further up the ridge, a spruce-poplar forest, where he spotted an olive-sided flycatcher, two whisky-jacks—or Canada jays—and several white-crowned sparrows in song.

Gratefully, Laing dropped his pack at their campsite, dubbed Undercliff Camp, exhausted. Several of the men looked tired after their eventful day's hike. They started putting up tents as a light rain began to fall. After an evening meal, Laing swatted some more large mosquitos away, which seemed less keen to bite, and looked out uphill into deepening shrub and forest, listening to the echoing, low hooting of a horned owl resounding from somewhere within.[17]

May 14 began with a clear morning. Ravens had started an early morning cacophony of croaks and caws that promised fitful sleep for the men. Laing dressed and emerged from his tent before anyone else into a frosty world filled with the chattering and churring of common redpolls. Looking around the camp, he saw Hudsonian chickadees hopping around.

Laing was curious about the burn walked through earlier; it was a desolate landscape. Stepping over fallen timber in the morning mist, he found what he saw pitiable. He theorized that all burned trees gradually fell as they had no depth of roots. It was evident that summers were dry, moss burned off during the fire and the roots died off. And if the morning chill were any clue, frost near the surface meant little recovery time in the winter. All this in combination, in his opinion, accounted for all the dead spruce in muskegs. Depth of root is necessary for trees to thrive, and after a fire, forest recovery is slow, if not impossible. Looking at those spruce that did survive, he thought that age must be great in proportion to their size, as only the hardiest would be able to endure in this land of extremes.

On the return to camp, Laing tried to lure whisky-jacks by using his squeak and owl call. Surprisingly to him, none came near to investigate but minded their own business.

He was preoccupied with the fact that he had not yet seen any waterfowl. Perhaps, he surmised, they had not yet crossed the route of geese.

A rapid breakfast was prepared, tents disassembled and all packed up, and the expedition was on the move by 8:30 a.m. Before they got started, MacCarthy waved Laing over and requested that, if he planned to use his rifle to collect specimens, he keep well behind the pack train so as not to scare the horses and to fire no shots within a quarter mile of them. Laing agreed, then all men shouldered their packs and MacCarthy waved for them to start.

They continued to travel through the muskeg until they headed downhill. Laing noted that the most numerous bird now was the common redpoll, followed closely by the myrtle warbler.

At 12:45 p.m., they stopped for lunch at what Andy Taylor called Rush Pond. Laing decided to give his rifle a rest in favour of his still camera, taking a few photographs. He could hear juncos, the rising staccato and hammerings of a northern flicker, the energetic see-saw song of a ruby-crowned kinglet and more myrtle warblers. The croaks of frogs emanating from the pond completed the scene.

Not long after resuming the trail at 2:45 p.m., they came back out onto the vast valley of gravel bars, an open expanse four miles wide, where sinking footing in gravel and wet sand made it rough going for Laing. At a spot near a hillside, with snow still clinging to the valley bottom in places, just before a deep river that required fording, the men rested for the day, a place they called Flat Camp. As Laing took a break from reassembling his tent, he wiped sweat from his forehead and surveyed the landscape; it was a study in sand, silt and gravel-flat that went on for miles.

Laing sat in front of his tent in the evening, cleaning a specimen from the day before. He looked up the nearby hillside to admire the sight of sixteen Dall mountain sheep. Smaller than bighorn sheep, they munched on plants clinging to the hill.

May 15 was spent hiking to what was known by the expedition members as Bryson's, a cabin at an old survey camp.[18] Early in the morning, Laing perched up on the hill near where he had observed sheep, in a light rain, with the Universal on a tripod aimed on the camp below. He had already struck his tent before setting out on his morning's climb, in anticipation of capturing what promised to be an action-filled shot: the fording of the river. Laing rolled film on the men packing up the tents and gear, loading up the horses. The wide shot encompassed the remaining snow clinging to the edges of the valley floor on the right, the river on the left, the vast emptiness of the sand, silt and gravel out into the distance and the mountains beyond. Having completed that shot, he

Read rests on open bars of Chitina River en route to
Hubrick's Camp. This day, May 15, they stopped at Bryson's Camp.
(COURTESY: WHYTE MUSEUM OF THE CANADIAN ROCKIES, V14_AC0P_433)

waited patiently, with his pack beside him, for the horses and the men
to begin moving to camera left. He planned to slowly swivel the camera
to follow them as they forded the river. His last similar shot had resulted
in the tripod becoming faulty, but he was more confident in making a
smooth pan with the expedition than in that earlier shot in McCarthy.

Between times of rolling film, Laing stood on the hill admiring an
American hawk owl (fairly common since his rail journey from Cordova) that had responded to his squeak call. It came out nearby, twittering its staccato song for a while. Over the course of an hour, it would
perch three times. Several common redpolls (intensely social, often seen
in flocks, he would note) perched above the unwelcome visitor, giving it
the evil eye and barraging it with staccato bursts of calls.

Finally, after the camp had been struck, the men gathered with the
horses, perhaps to discuss the proper way to cross the water, and in what

order. Then they set out, but first came towards Laing, walking over a snowdrift, the horses lumbering along with one of them mounted by Harry Boyden, before the men stopped on a sandbar. They stayed behind while Boyden led the pack train, as Laing deftly panned the Universal to follow their movements, careful to keep the lead horse in frame. The horses were up to their knees, then gradually the waters were tickling their bellies as a horse mounted by Pete Brendwick followed in the rear to keep them in line. Finally, the train emerged from the river crossing, all eleven safe and sound after the fording. Laing stopped cranking and, happy with his panning effort, removed the camera from the tripod and packed them both away. With the redpolls' verbal attack keeping the hawk owl busy, Laing reached for his rifle, took aim and secured the hawk owl with one shot that reverberated through the landscape. He shouldered his pack and retrieved the body. Laing later noted matted fur in its stomach, which led him to determine the hawk owl's last meal had been a red squirrel.[19] It was 9 a.m.

Laing spent much of the day walking through the gravel and sand with Lambart. It was clear, from the last few days' hiking, that Lambart was the optimist of the group, regularly seen with a smile through his short beard, sometimes sporting round spectacles and setting the pace that the rest of the group would follow for the day.[20] Lambart's reputation preceded him as a member of the Geodetic Survey of Canada, and having taken part in the International Boundary Survey of 1913, which determined that Logan was the highest peak in the Saint Elias Mountains.[21] In fact, Logan exceeded the height of Mount Saint Elias, previously thought as the tallest peak in the group by almost 2,000 feet.[22]

More than twenty years earlier, Lambart had written in his article on topographical and geographic exploration of the region that Mount Logan was first spotted by I.C. Russell, the leader of an 1890 to 1891 expedition jointly run by the National Geographic Society and the United States Geological Survey. That expedition's records added a great deal to the regional knowledge the mountaineers had, seeking to top Mount Logan in 1925. He would have seen it while trudging through knee-deep snow at an altitude of above 14,000 feet on the northeastern ridge of Mount Saint Elias. Russell could make out a few higher peaks, certainly above his position, but almost certainly higher than Saint Elias itself. One peak seemed to rise above all others. Looking at its southern exposure, he decided then and there to name it in honour of the founder and long-time director of the Geological Survey of Canada, Sir William E. Logan.[23] With the information and experience from Russell's expedition in mind, along with his knowledge gained from the International Boundary Survey, Lambart, the modest cartographic and geographic expert of the expedition, was perhaps more aware than anyone else, barring the leader MacCarthy and local guide Taylor, of what they were getting themselves into. One thing of interest, that may have very well been exchanged between Lambart and Laing, is that even though the International Boundary Survey had added not only a defined Alaska/Yukon boundary but also 5,000 square miles of newly explored regions to their expedition maps, including some detail of the Logan massif, it did not add anything to the knowledge of the area east of the massif, all the way to Kluane Lake.[24]

They were heading, save Laing, towards an environment that from about 18,000 feet featured a complicated network of glaciers, snowfields and peaks, the highest up to 19,850 feet at its pinnacle.[25] Behind the smile and the optimistic pace, Lambart was holding back, it seemed to Laing, on what he really knew, on what the mountaineers were in for, the unknown of an unstable, barren and temperamental place devoid of vegetation or life. Lambart had, over the course of the last few weeks' advocating for Laing to accompany the expedition, become familiar with his writing and expedition career, complimenting Laing on his reputation of self-sufficiency and reliance in the field. Lambart spoke positively of Laing's expeditions, after the war had ended, to Athabasca and Great Slave Lake in 1920, his summer stints for the Victoria Memorial Museum in 1921 and 1922 in Manitoba, Saskatchewan and British Columbia, and his recent tour as naturalist on the HMCS *Thiepval* up the Alaska coast to Japan and back to Vancouver Island. Keeping up with Lambart was difficult, but he and Laing managed to overtake Read and Morgan and arrived at Bryson's Cabin Camp—located on a huge flat that Laing could describe only as a half-dry land region and half-inundated—by 6 p.m. Lambart and Laing had broken the ice and developed a kinship as men of the field, dreaming of sunshine.[26]

While at Bryson's, Laing started turning his attention to new plants, including bearberry with its tiny blooms. As he wandered, his thoughts turned to the day's walking and how bear tracks were seen more often, impressions in the sand flats. And where there had been bears, there had been droppings. A quick scatological analysis of one of the piles showed a high concentration of highbush cranberries, the seeds of small berries and some rabbit bones and fur. A fluttering ahead took him out of his reverie as a quick brown-and-grey figure burst out of the woods. Without hesitation, Laing swivelled his rifle, took aim and fired. The report echoed in the cool evening air. At closer inspection, Laing's instinct had proven correct. On the ground was a female spruce grouse, and by the looks of her, laying. Delicately packing his specimen away, Laing realized it was getting late. The sun stayed up much longer here, the daylight almost twenty-four hours with the sun only dipping below the mountains, and he was losing track of time in the evenings.[27] He decided to walk back to camp, taking a route where he saw several frozen waterfalls in a canyon and heard the boom of rock slides in the distance somewhere.

Settled into his tent at 10:30 p.m., Laing slowly fell asleep listening to the song of a robin and thinking of how light it was for such a late hour.

May 16 began with a red-tailed hawk rummaging around in the camp. Laing was tying his boots while listening to the robin's song that lulled him to dreams the night before. On his stroll before breakfast, he listened to myrtle warblers and juncos.

After striking camp, the men set out at a pace that would get them to Short River Camp probably by mid-afternoon if they all kept to it. Light rain fell for the traverse, which the men did without stopping, over the accustomed gravel bars and across several streams. It became much more a land of superlatives. Laing and the mountaineers were now familiar with passing massive rocks, glacial deposits. But Gibraltar Rock, a tower several hundred feet high, was something of an island in the riverbed.[28] Laing watched it, and the men looked it up and down in passing without a sound. To the left, the immense brown moraine of the Hawkins Glacier became part of the day's journey, the sandy path interspersed with glances to the grandeur of the glacier. He saw that the moraine appeared to have a convex back. Today, by his reckoning, was a

Short River Camp, which Laing captured with his Universal motion picture
camera, May 16. The next day they would arrive at Hubrick's Camp.
(COURTESY: WHYTE MUSEUM OF THE CANADIAN ROCKIES, V14_AC0P_438)

study in geology everywhere he looked. He would have preferred to
have seen more birds, but the robin song he had become accustomed to
was only heard in the distant spruce woods.

Once Laing had set up his tent, he spotted a flock of thirty-five or
more sandpipers fluttering over the site, far too quickly for him to identify them. Upon sitting down, weary, he was reminded of the bright
red-purple clumps of mountain saxifrage that added a bit of colour to
the landscape. He also noted many orchids in seed, which testified to
the previous year's blooms.

Once again inspired by the landscape and their camp's raised location, giving the men a splendid view down the river valley they had been
travelling the previous six days, Laing found an aspect where he could
erect the tripod and Universal to capture the tents in camp, smoke from

the cooking fire pluming upwards, and pan to the left to reveal the vast sandbars leading the eye to the mountains beyond, a truly jaw-dropping view. He then zoomed in and filmed two men washing and drying the supper dishes at the firepit, Lambart standing, Taylor emerging from a tent. With some energy now, Laing picked up the camera and folded tripod, shouldered the load and made his way to a different vantage point. Walking into the spruce woods, where a few tents had been set up, he unfolded the tripod, positioning the camera on the reverse axis from his earlier shot. From here, he anticipated getting much more of the camp life in one sweeping shot, a pan that would go from right, at the edge of the camp near a precipice leading to the gravel bars of the river valley and deeper into the sheltered woods where the weary travellers were washing their socks and hanging them to dry on a pole hung over a smoking firepit, to the left to reveal the remaining tents and men at the other edge of the site, nestled into the trees. This would allow the viewers to orient themselves in Short River Camp. Laing stopped cranking, perched his chin lightly on the top of the camera and registered how tired he was. Luckily, perhaps as a reward for the lack of birdlife on his arduous hike, Laing looked around, waited patiently and smiled slightly as he began noticing juncos, his companionable robin, myrtle warblers and redpolls in the surrounding woods.

Looking ahead, he noticed one of the packers making his way to the edge of the camp, in front of the picturesque vantage point of the river valley. Once again, propping the camera and tripod on his shoulder, Laing proceeded to a spot where he could catch the sublimity of the landscape. He settled his camera at the view and tightened the tripod's grip on the Universal. Rolling on the valley floor, he caught the man carrying a pan to scrub out its contents. In doing so, Laing captured not only the packers's actions in the life of the camp but also an assessment of scale: a man's size compared to the unforgiving surrounding landscape. Not wishing to waste the moment, as he would not have many remaining opportunities to capture life amongst the mountaineers before their arduous climb, Laing panned across the camp, much closer now, as one of the packers crossed from left to right with a pot of used dishwater. He panned slowly across one of the alpine tents, about seven feet tall with a funnel-shaped entrance, to stay for a moment on Mac-Carthy, Foster and Lambart looking down the valley. MacCarthy pointed with intent as the men discussed the next day's push to Hubrick's Camp. The pan ended on Morgan chopping firewood and settled on one of the lighter fabrication four-man tents. Andy Taylor entered the frame from the left with an axe, embedded it in a block of wood, moving it over to the front of the tent and proceeded to chop it into pieces. It was a microcosm of life in camp, representative of the last few days. Laing stopped cranking the Universal, realizing he would probably need to change the magazine soon. Packing the camera and tripod away, he ruminated on how tomorrow would bring him to Hubrick's Camp, where he would base himself for his biological work for several months while the mountaineers pursued their conquest of Mount Logan. After bringing his pack into his tent and lying down, he acknowledged his sore feet. There are times, Laing wrote in his diary, when the nearest thing to physical paradise was a good bed.

May 17 started out partly sunny. Laing had emerged early from his tent, feeling well-rested after what he considered a solid night's sleep. After tents had been taken down and packed up, and the firepits were breathing out nothing but smoking embers, the men once again shouldered their loads and descended to the river valley, following the gravel bars towards Hubrick's Camp. Laing kept to the rear and, before turning his back on Short River Camp, took some still photographs of the site with his own Kodak camera. He then quickened the pace to keep up with Lambart, who was once again double-timing it to their destination.

A little while later, Lambart stopped, which caused the men and pack train to slow and halt. The group could see a distant slope of bright white, and realized what it was: their first glimpse of a shoulder of Mount Logan. After a moment, Lambart resumed the challenging pace, and without further delay, the expedition proceeded up the narrowing river valley.

Laing continued to hear the song of the white-crowned sparrow in the valley, which, he observed more and more, could occupy open country just as well as the cover of the wood. Also, as the company trudged

Laing in front of his pup tent at Hubrick's Camp, May 17.
(COURTESY: WHYTE MUSEUM OF THE CANADIAN ROCKIES, V14_AC0P_455)

through the gravelly flat, the tinkling song of a horned lark was heard. He did see one take flight and deliver its flight song, another bird of the wide-open spaces. He followed briefly but lost sight of it.

Arrival at Hubrick's Camp, Laing's base of operations, came without fanfare, save the appearance of a black bear walking over the alpine slope above the camp. It featured a collection of wood poles, standing in a tripod configuration, giving the impression of a massive radio transmission tower, that could act as a hide or cache for food. This made it clear to Laing that he was in bear territory and food was to be properly stored and disposed of. With food in mind, and the appearance of a flock of Dall mountain sheep, perhaps as many as thirty up on the slopes, Norman H. Read took inspiration and, without much hesitation, commandeered Harry Boyden, Pete Brendwick and their horses and headed for the hills, a rifle being brandished seemingly out of nowhere by Read. Laing was surprised by this metropolitan figure from New York City suddenly developing a lust for killing. But perhaps, he surmised, the promise of fresh meat to garnish their cached supplies was enough to bring out the hunter in even civilized man.

While the timbered base camp was prepared, tents set up and fires lit, Laing heard several shots in the hills, then nothing for a while. He had set up his small pup tent by one of the poles of the tall hide, lateral poles making for a good place to hang possessions and the large pole giving something of a lean-to for his tent's structure. He spotted some figures down valley on the gravelly flat, then realized what he was seeing. Reaching for the Universal in its case, he quickly placed it on the tripod, legs planted firmly in the sand, and began rolling as Harry Boyden and Pete Brendwick approached, each guiding a horse with a Dall sheep strapped to its back, followed by a triumphant Norman H. Read, a rifle propped against his right shoulder, marching proudly behind his contribution to that evening's meal.

Later, they feasted on fresh sheep meat set up on a long plank that accommodated most of the men. The smoke from the roasting fire wafted across the table as the men ate heartily of Read's kill. Laing set up and rolled film to capture what would be the last time the group—MacCarthy, Lambart, Foster, Carpe, Read, Hall, Morgan, Taylor, Boyden, Brendwick and, the tail of the kite, Laing—would dine together.

CHAPTER 5

Trail End

An attempt will be made by the leaders of the party to reach the summit of Mount Logan, but as animal and vegetable life is virtually absent from the latter part of the proposed route, you will not be required to go beyond a point where there seems a prospect of doing reasonably fruitful work.

—L.L. Bolton

Laing found himself at Trail End on the afternoon of May 18, 1925, the Universal on tripod, capturing quiet moments as the mountaineers wrote their last letters to loved ones to send back, along with many photographs and feet of film to be returned to Colonel Bell at the ACC, to McCarthy with Harry Boyden, Pete Brendwick and the pack horses. Laing noted in his diary that there were very few birds about. Later that day, the expedition party split up, the mountaineers to spend several weeks camped on ice and snow and Laing to return to Hubrick's Camp.

The party had arrived at Trail End at about 1 p.m. Laing knew he would have to roll a significant amount of film depicting the moment of departure. After this day, Allen Carpe would take over, using the Debrie Sept up to 9,000 feet and the Bell & Howell Filmo for the higher-altitude cinematography. Laing would have the Universal for use at Hubrick's Camp and on his day trips.

At a nearby snowbank, Laing rolled film on H.F. Lambart and A.H.

Chitina Valley, en route from Hubrick's Camp to Trail End, May 18.
(PHOTO: ALLEN CARPE, COURTESY: AMERICAN ALPINE CLUB LIBRARY)

MacCarthy, both men wearing their wool trousers and shirts, holding ice axes aloft and carrying packs. MacCarthy had snowshoes strapped to his. The packs weighed on average about eighty pounds and consisted of a bedroll (about eighteen pounds), their individual expedition equipment (food, cooking utensils, still camera, tentage—about twenty-seven pounds), a pack board (five pounds) and personal equipment (thirty pounds).[1]

Laing had assembled the eight men, in similar full gear, for a final shot, all with ice axes, and rolled film of them on the snow. Then the mountaineers walked away from him and the Universal from camera left, MacCarthy in the lead with a quick goodbye wave from his ice axe. They were finally off.

Laing, Boyden, Brendwick and the pack train, much less burdened, turned back at 4:30 p.m., reaching Hubrick's Camp at 7:30 p.m. On the last mile, Laing tried riding one of the bucks, later writing in his diary that he found riding a horse without stirrups drastic medicine in relieving his tired feet. While hanging on as best he could, he looked above camp and saw the dozens of Dall sheep out and about on the slopes as they were when the expedition party had arrived. Sliding as carefully as he could off the horse, stepping onto the sand, he strode to his tent where he placed his pack and looked up the slope to the high camp, spotting what he could only describe as a blackish hawk. A cool breeze made its way up the valley. The three men dined together before turning in early, the beginnings of a rain shower spattering their tents.

May 19 began in rain. Laing shook hands with Harry Boyden and Pete Brendwick as they prepared to return to McCarthy by the Chitina River valley. They all joked about how the horses seemed reluctant to abandon the relatively good living in camp. Then Laing watched as the men and the horses departed, their steps seeming small in comparison with the vast valley landscape they had to traverse. He was now alone and knew he would be for some time. Looking across the valley, cut by streams that seemed too many to count, he estimated it to be several miles across, later describing it as being almost a desert landscape. The proximity of the glaciers, Hawkins and Barnard to the west, Chitina and Logan to the east, camp being positioned close to the Chitina Glacier moraine, made for crude and raw country. Was the wildlife here going to match those qualities? By Laing's assessment, camp was around 2,000 feet above sea level. To the north were white spruce and poplar with treeless slopes above that.

Laing first reviewed his notes on one of the sheep Read shot two days before, prior to being dispatched. Next to the bears sighted, the sheep were certainly the largest mammals he had seen in the valley. The ram, which he thought was six years old, measured 1,480mm from end to end, the tail itself 100mm. The hind foot measured 410mm from toe to back; its height at the shoulder was 900mm. The circumference of the horn at the base was 349mm.

In the afternoon, the rain had stopped, and Laing busied himself cleaning the skins from earlier days. While working at the larger upper tent, he sensed some motion behind him and turned slowly to see what he identified as an American three-toed woodpecker, perched on a stump, which then transferred to the rails of the camera tripod. Slowly reaching for his rifle at the tent's entrance, Laing swivelled around and fired to secure the woodpecker, a female, he would note, for the collection. This was the most common woodpecker in this environment between the river valley and the start of timber. He could hear the slow drumming of another, a male, in various places as he worked. He also secured an adult male and an adult female white-winged crossbill, whose companions seemed everywhere in the woods, Laing determined by their "Chit-it! Chit-it! Weet-weet-weet!" call.

The fog lifted later in the afternoon, and Laing got another look at the flock of sheep on the lower hills to the north. Two golden eagles circled overhead. A few days earlier, Boyden had told Laing that, on May 4, he had seen a golden eagle flying off with a lamb in its talons.

As for his own food needs, Laing had a cache of stores at Hubrick's Camp that had been brought in during MacCarthy's winter freighting expedition. But he looked on with mild concern when he spotted a large Dawson red-backed mouse snacking on a bacon rind.

Ever since McCarthy, Laing had heard the song of the myrtle warbler, a common bird found among the timber. After listening to its song off and on, he wrote it out as "Weece-weece-weece-weece, wichy-wichy-wichy!"

On May 20, after waking up to rain, Laing heard an unfamiliar song coming from the timber as the cloud gave way to sun mid-morning: "Clee-clee-clee-clee!" A high, shrill new call.

It was a cool day, with a westerly wind and a breeze blowing all morning. Laing spent part of it counting sheep, totalling forty on the slopes above camp. He noted two rams of advantageous size that were mingling closer to the camp, where the flock was seen when the expedition party arrived three days previous.

During the rest of the day, he completed the skins, cleaning the specimens then placing them on drying boards. He worked hard at these tasks but looked up at his surroundings from time to time, the crude and forbidding nature of the landscape which he realized was home, beginning to settle on him. A wandering look towards the Chitina Glacier to the left, the upper end of the valley, would take in a vast grey moraine, which, to Laing's view, choked the access to the glacier.

He had another very important job to do, and that was to prepare, from the existing food cache at Hubrick's Camp, a load to cache at Trail End for the eventual returning mountaineers. While packing the load, he spotted a female red squirrel, quickly dispatched it with his rifle and added it to his collection to clean for the drying board. He returned to his packing, which would occupy him for much of the day, but while working, he thought on various subjects. Why had mice not chewed into the sacks of rice, dried potatoes, oats and other dry goods? He wondered why the red squirrels, even from his early observations clearly one of the most abundant mammals of the woods, did not seem too interested in this obvious source of food.

By evening, Laing had cleaned the creatures secured that day and piled their offal at the edge of camp. It was company of a larger species that he was seeking. He waited patiently until, at 9:15, he spied a grizzly bear coming up the gravel flat. Laing reckoned he had been following the scent of the bait for a half-mile, maybe more. He grew fascinated watching the lumbering bear's interest grow into something more, a kind of certainty that his travels were worth his while. Developing a hurried waddle, the grizzly bore down on the pile. Laing thought it was a beautiful animal. He watched patiently before reaching delicately for his rifle. Just as he did so, Laing saw the bear hesitate. He may have stopped at the bait, but he could now smell the man scent nearby, swung around quickly and bounded into a run. Laing had a method to confuse the bear, a whistle that he could blow sharply and momentarily distract it to stand still. It worked, but the bear stopped only for an instant before returning to his former gait, which turned into an ungainly gallop. Laing managed to get a few shots off, one that seemed to cause the massive creature to tumble, but it got up and disappeared. He reloaded his rifle in frustration, but his countenance turned to a smile in admiration of the lumbering creature with the strong nose that came to dinner.

The next day, the sun came through early, shining at 8:30 a.m., brushing off the freezing temperatures of the night. Laing spent the day stocking the mountaineer's cache, or what he continued to call Mac-Carthy's cache, as he was the man behind the provision planning, at Trail End. Laing had packed twenty-two pounds of food into his

Trapper-Nelson packboard, one that he would perspire profusely under, but still what he considered best for open travelling.

Laing studied the tracks of yesterday's ursine visitor. The grizzly seemed to straighten out considerably when at a full run, landing in pairs. His own tracks to Trail End would take him along a noisy stream, certainly it was louder than the silence enveloping him along the gravel flat.

He arrived at Trail End at noon, stored the food in a bag dangling from a high branch and replaced his packboard on his back without ceremony. A magpie was his only companion; the silence was unspeakable. There seemed to be no living thing on the gravel flat. He had another four hours hard plugging to get back to Hubrick's Camp, the return trail taking him along bumpy moraine, in the end a much longer route. Then, there was a sudden surprise: two northern phalaropes appeared in a tiny pothole in the willows. His shots echoed in the gravel valley; they had been secured. While retrieving them, Laing pondered: Would they have nested here?

He had traversed sixteen miles back, and despite his glowing opinion of his packboard when starting out that morning, he was glad to set it down by his tent. In all, he had walked for eight hours. Once settled in, he spotted three white-winged crossbills and managed to swing his rifle around in time to secure one juvenile with his beak not yet crossed. It was his first. Before he gave up, he managed to secure the adult male. Shaking his head as he retrieved it, he asked himself again: Where do these birds nest?

CHAPTER 6

Boundary Cache
and Beyond

After parting with Laing and the pack train, seeing Laing on his return to Hubrick's Camp and the pack train start back for McCarthy, H.F. Lambart would write later, in his account published in *The Geographical Journal* in July 1926, that the mountaineers "were beginning to realize the enormous task which confronted us." He described a sense among them that strength must be conserved for the climb as "now we were facing the test of our lives."[1]

The weather on May 19 was hardly a good omen for the expedition: a wet and overcast morning. But soon the clouds parted. Packs ranged in weight from 52 to 105 pounds. "A steady grind of some three hours," Lambart recalled, "brought us to Chitina Point."[2] The winter freighting expedition had deposited a cache there.

The next day, the mountaineers were already taking unnecessary items from their packs, which they strung "up among the branches of a friendly spruce."[3] The terrain on their seven-mile march was more forgiving as they travelled the edges of the Walsh Glacier, following game trails and traversing alpine meadow. By the end, they were negotiating through rough moraine. Settling into camp, the tired crew rested surrounded by "the last timber and verdure we were to see until our return."[4] The location at Fraser Baldwin Cache was significant for another reason. They could peer out of their tents at the intimidating sight of Walsh Glacier, "on the broken surface of which we failed to discern a single stretch of smooth ice."[5] Lambart noted how diligent Carpe was capturing this day with his motion picture camera.

Perhaps distracting himself from the next day's daunting task for the mountaineers negotiating the glacier, Lambart recalled that their camp's location was close to a base camp of the 1913 Boundary Survey, where exhausted parties would retire after difficult work on nearby glaciers. The mountaineers would benefit from the survey's topographical knowledge of the glaciers and terrain northwest of Mount Logan.

On May 21, the mountaineers were based out of this camp. Fraser Baldwin Cache was how Lambart described it on the map he later created for the Royal Geographical Society. Much of the day was spent "marking a trail through the chaos and ice and *débris* across the Walsh Glacier."[6] This reconnaissance was done with half the loads on their backs until they were assured a clear path could be made to the junction with the start of the Logan Glacier. The ice of that glacier was smoother, and this assured the group of a quicker and more efficient route.

This route made for an ideal day on May 22, where a great deal of progress was made. Sixteen miles were gained to an advance cache at Boundary Camp (or Boundary Cache as W.W. Foster would later term it). Here the mountaineers accessed much-needed supplies, such as the snowshoes considered very important for the trying surfaces ahead. It would be memorable for another reason: the expedition team spent their first night on open ice at approximately 5,000 feet elevation.[7] The condition of the ice which would either spell good tidings for the next day or poor progress, was the new foundation of their lives. Two Yukon sleds that had been cached for the winter would be used to propel their gear. With winter snow still on the glacier, the early morning hours were the most gainful as the sun would have not yet melted the snow. But as they found on this day, once the heat of the noonday sun beat down on them, drawing a sled became impossible, as the weight of it sunk into a melted surface.[8]

As far as the museum is concerned, your work will consist in making as complete collections as possible of specimens of scientific interest, including mammals, birds, and other animals, as well as plants along the route of the expedition. These are to be supplemented with full and careful field notes and photographs illustrating the life, habitat of animals, and other features of interest observed while with the expedition.

—L.L. Bolton

Laing spent May 22 in camp making skins, preparing seven bird and four mammal specimens. But he did take a break to photograph the grizzly's tracks. The Dall sheep were now a regular feature of the natural landscape, twenty visible before noon, the small flocks distributed amid the first line of cliffs before the timberline. While the sun may have been making progress difficult for the mountaineers, Laing was basking in it as he continued to work, knowing what was coming in the afternoon.

Daily, at noon, wind would pick up considerably and blow a great deal of dust up valley. Dust storms happened every afternoon when its surface was dry, creating a powerful wind gusting down from the glaciers to the east, sometimes reducing visibility to near zero. Laing gradually adapted to this inevitable occurrence, working hard before noon to avoid the dust, then retreating to the safety of the large tent.

His companions were the redpolls, who, like the dusty afternoons, were becoming a regular feature of Laing's days. The common redpoll, he was observing, was a very sociable bird, gathering in flocks once nesting duties were complete, and the old and younger generation chattered away alongside the white-winged crossbills. These early nesters would gather among the redpolls, their collective chatter the most frequent sound coming from the spruce woods. But as the wind picked up, an interloper descended, taking advantage of the increased wind. A black hawk, not identifiable, spun over the woods, casting a shadow over the scene as the dust swirled and the chatter quietened. Eventually, the gusts did as well, and Laing would settle into the tent for the night.

"Grouch!" The odd sound woke Laing at 2 a.m. There was still some light. Alarmed by the grating noise, he quickly felt for his clothes and scrambled to put them on. Exiting his tent stealthily, he investigated the

Pulling a sled along the Logan Glacier, the Logan massif in the background, May 23.
(COURTESY: WHYTE MUSEUM OF THE CANADIAN ROCKIES, V14_AC0P_472)

area and found the source of the noise behind some stove-burned wood. It was a porcupine. A "porky," Laing exclaimed to himself. It saw him, stopped gnawing at the wood and bolted. He seized the opportunity, grabbed his rifle and collected his newest specimen: Alaska porcupine. While settling back into his tent, Laing looked at his watch. It was 2:15 a.m. He fell back to sleep listening to a junco's song.

The mountaineers also had an early waking on May 23: 1 a.m. The smell of bacon cooking filled their nostrils as they sipped coffee. After tucking into porridge, eggs and bacon and loading their packs onto the sleds, they were on the move, relieved to be unburdened of the usual weight on their backs. Lambart took many photographs of the men pulling the sleds with Logan very clear in the background. By 9:30 a.m., they had stopped for lunch; however, shortly after that, the sun softened the snow, and their relief turned to frustration with the labour required to keep the sinking sleds moving sapping their strength. This struggle lasted until 5 p.m., when they took a much-needed rest in a medial moraine, among debris of the Ogilvie Glacier, just two miles above its junction with Logan's massive lateral moraine (the debris gathered in a ridge at the side of a glacier). On Lambart's map that illustrates his paper in *The Geographical Journal*, a distinct turn is made south off the path of Logan Glacier and onto that of Ogilvie Glacier, and indeed Turn Camp would be distinct for more than this change of direction. The mountaineers found another cache of equipment and supplies left by the winter freighting expedition. One item discovered would prove to be indispensable in their new existence on the ice: the air mattress. They were inflated with a bicycle pump and not only kept the men from the ice while resting and sleeping but also proved to be an effective insulator, keeping them warm.[9] The men slept well, warm on their new-found mattresses but also because they knew the next day would be spent resting in camp.

Laing emerged from his tent at 7 a.m. despite his waking in the middle of the night. He wanted to bring in the captured porcupine, and secured another one nearby. Later he captured and examined a white-winged crossbill (a faintly red male whose sex organs suggested to Laing it was a time of breeding) and prepared the skins of four birds and the porcupines.

While cleaning one of the porcupines, Laing marvelled at the assembly of its tail, a conglomeration of yellow and black hairs that was also on the rump. The richness of its brownish-black coat on its head, the ruff formed with long yellow hairs on the top of the head and nape, much of the hair blackish becoming brown near the belly, all created a complex system of matted hair that had him looking it over with a sense of wonder.[10]

In the evening, Laing would think about his day's work, the complexity of the porcupine and keep distant company with a red-tailed hawk too far away to secure but swift enough for him to admire as it turned into the wind past camp and out into the gravel expanse beyond his tent.

A persistent drummer ended Laing's slumber. The slow rattle reminded him of a loud tattoo. Having had enough, he swiftly exited his tent, grabbed his rifle, aimed at the source and fired. He soon realized upon awakening more in the cool and hazy morning that he had inadvertently secured an American three-toed woodpecker. It was the commonest of woodpeckers here, usually seen between the river and timberline and not much higher.[11]

Laing decided that a day's expedition was in order. After breakfast, he made his way up the mountain behind camp, staying near to a ravine, and discovered the remnants of a mine. What occupied him more was realizing that the whole mountainside was a sheep's pasture. He turned his attention to the plant life on one of the highest slopes and began collecting specimens of a tiny red-purple flower. This mountain saxifrage Laing had not seen since a meadow near Bryson's Cabin.

Laing observed various types of country: spruce woods, juniper and bearberry were in profusion. And if he was looking for new evidence of the sheep, the lilies that grew in tufts were closely cropped by their munching while wandering the slopes.

Laing reckoned he had climbed about 1,000 feet above the treeline, where he found a spot out of the cold wind and looked over the environment of Dall sheep. It was a view of superlatives, but he soon became engrossed in the flight of a golden eagle below his perch, noting that these hunters usually hovered hopefully above flocks of sheep. Looking down on the bird of prey, he saw the brown markings on its back. It was a crowning achievement of his walk on high.

On the return to camp, Laing picked up a few ptarmigan feathers in the spruce woods, indicating that in the winter they may descend to the level of the river. He also measured grizzly tracks with interest, his recent encounter in mind. The front tracks were seven inches broad as well as long, the hind tracks longer at eleven inches, but only six and a half inches broad. He placed his pencil as a bookmark, closed his diary, shouldered his pack and returned to camp.

May 25 was another milestone in the mountaineers' journey: they left Logan Glacier and began a new trail up the centre of Ogilvie Glacier, taking them from Turn to Advance Base Camp, also called Advance Base Cache. "Rise and shine, cache and carry!" MacCarthy exclaimed at 12:30 a.m.[12] Three hours later, the party left; MacCarthy, Taylor, Carpe and Foster were on the forward sled, and Lambart, Morgan and Read were on the second, while Hall pulled a small toboggan transporting the cook box and Taylor's dunnage. They were moving at two miles an hour, Lambart estimated. Lambart described the glacier as sweeping "12 miles from the south, where it takes its rise in a huge basin fed by a number of small glaciers entering it like the spokes of a huge wheel."[13] At the head of this formidable mass stood an ice cataract that rose 2,000 feet. The relatively brief five-mile traverse of the glacier brought the men and their sleds, at 7:50 a.m., to their last main cache brought in during the winter freighting expedition. They now had all their equipment for the first time, as well as personal items, which they planned to examine in the afternoon. What Lambart saw was, he thought, an embarrassment of riches, much of it superfluous to their needs. After some snow clearing, they pitched three alpine tents and a ten-foot-by-twelve-foot used government tent in a row on four feet of snow. Henry Hall later excavated and found it was five feet above the ice of the glacier. All took photographs of the camp, with Carpe cranking the 16mm Bell & Howell Filmo. As though to indicate their riches at the cache, their dinner, served by Andy Taylor at 1 p.m., featured butter beans, sausage, plum jam, applesauce, cocoa, tea, pickles, mustard, biscuits, butter, cream and rice. Lambart wrote that MacCarthy's cache was complete but offered too elaborate a choice of goods and would do credit to a top restaurant.[14] Perhaps they would need the calories.

From Advance Base Cache, they would relay the stores and equipment, enough, as Lambart would describe, "for ten men for over sixty days," to a camp referred to as Cascades, from which the ascent of Mount Logan was to begin in earnest. Of course, this relaying was easier said than done. There were 5,000 pounds of equipment and supplies to relay the seven miles up Ogilvie Glacier to Cascades.[15] So their short run on this day was tempered with the fact that a week's worth of lung-busting and monotonous toil lay ahead of them going back and forth across Ogilvie Glacier.

⟨⟨⟨⟨⟩

As mosquitos buzzed relentlessly in the tent, rain slapped gently on its sides. Laing only got snatches of sleep, bitter he couldn't have just shot the "moskeets" and skinned them later. What made it even more difficult to settle into slumber was that the sun never sank now. His only satisfaction was that at 1 a.m. he managed to secure another porky, this one also was nibbling audibly at the charred end of a log.

The eerie whistle of the varied thrush followed Laing all morning and rang throughout the valley. After the dust storms subsided, he prepared skins.

Work had generated an appetite, so he decided to make hotcakes, from white flour, cornmeal and rolled oats, cooked over a small fire. Their scent roused one of the most intrepid birds of the forest, a whisky-jack, which Laing would refer to in his report as Canada jay.[16] This curious little bird flitted around, boldly approached him, then suddenly darted away. He tried to accurately put a time to sunset, thinking the lowest point the sun reached was at 8:45 or 9 p.m., although it was not clear. He descended into a deep sleep in his pup tent, the mosquitos seemingly not as numerous. They were temperamental creatures, "moskeets."

⟨⟨⟨⟨⟩

As the mountaineers were now about to undertake the meticulous relaying of equipment and supplies to Cascades and 1,000 feet above that to Quartz Ridge, they had decisions to make. They were at their "jumping-off trench" onto what Lambart referred to militarily as "the assault on the mountain" and had to determine the amount of supplies needed on the climb, calculated based on the twenty-eight days estimated for "the attack on the mountain."[17] Sacks were packed, each with an amount rationed for eight men for two days, in total weighing 764 pounds; equipment weighed 1,083 pounds. About four relays, possibly more, would be necessary to get all 1,847 pounds moved ahead to Cascades.[18] It would be an enormous undertaking.

At Cascades during the relaying of supplies from Advance Base Cache, May 26.
(COURTESY: WHYTE MUSEUM OF THE CANADIAN ROCKIES, V14_AC0P_497)

In the meantime, Allen Carpe had been capturing nomadic life as best he could, considering he was a vital part of the mountaineering team, stealing away for a moment to set up the light tripod and camera, using the Sept and the Filmo until they got above 9,000 feet, where he would use the Filmo exclusively. He had rolled film as the men left the moraine and walked onto the glacial ice, including the increasingly dramatic alpine scenery as they travelled Logan Glacier and the heavily anticipated first glimpses of the Logan massif. The men lugged the sleds behind them as they snowshoed their way across the shot, their tracks mere scratches in the landscape. Indeed, Carpe seemed to be hungry to capture the vastness, the imposition of their new-found overwhelming surroundings and remote location, quickly scanning the landscape in a desperate and failed attempt to fit it all into the camera's chamber. One shot captured the men struggling as the sun warmed the snow's crust and the heavily laden sleds sank into the deep snow. In the film, it is difficult to distinguish one man from another as the dark figures, faces covered in aluminum-frame snow glasses and mosquito netting to protect them from wind and the powerful reflection of the sun's rays off the snow. It was clearly back-breaking labour, physically testing the mountaineers even before they reached their true launching point for the assault on Logan. But once they reached Advance Base Camp, the filming changed in tone, recording camp life in this remarkable landscape. Little footage captured the equipment relay, but some documented the earlier striking of camp, and conferences between parka-clad, snowshoed men before they set out on an inhospitable landscape where they were diminished by the surrounding mountains, as they lugged their new sled-loads with confidence across the Ogilvie Glacier.

One addition of interest in these brief shots by Carpe was the lead sled, pulled by three men, carrying what appear to be a mass of sticks, three feet long. As Lambart reported, these simple willow wands, 1,000 by his count, were an integral part of their mountaineering kit. Because storm systems were known to attack the Logan massif from the Pacific Ocean without much notice, reducing visibility severely and creating whiteout conditions, these willow wands were intended to be trail markers, placed at 100-foot intervals on the right side of their route. Lambart said they proved to be "veritable beacons upon the snow-clad slope of the mountain, where without them our task would have been utterly hopeless."[19]

However, it was sunny and clear when they completed the first relay to Cascades, where Carpe set up his tripod once again to shoot downhill and capture the immense channel of the Ogilvie Glacier as the men descended to gather another load, made tiny by the magnificence created by the glacial surface surrounded by majestic mountains. It was a phenomenal place, potentially dangerous but, for the moment, awe-inspiring.

The enigmatic King Glacier concerned many of the men. As much of the way ahead was a mystery, one question lingered: Did the glacier allow for a traverse to the upper reaches of Mount Logan? When the decision was made to proceed with the expedition in Vancouver, it was not known whether, even with the reconnaissance and photography from the International Boundary Survey sorties, the glacier, overseen by the 17,130-foot King Peak, led to the upper levels of the massif or to cliffs or, indeed, to oblivion. The earlier photographs demonstrated that the area around Cascades was "guarded by towering portals of rock and ice," the massive bend of ice of King Glacier itself and, in photographs taken from Mount Saint Elias, that the glacier's highest point culminated in the cliffs of King Peak.[20] This was all the information the mountaineers had to go on. They were now pioneers in a forbidding place. Lambart's experience from the boundary surveys was to be called on here; indeed everyone's mettle was to be tested at this point, as the future of the expedition rested on a best guess.

Another three-toed woodpecker had made itself very audible, drumming away while Laing washed his face and growing beard in a basin with soap and water. He had already secured two white-winged crossbills, one a female with fecal matter in her throat. This suggested to him that she had a nest of young somewhere nearby. With the constant "Chit-it! Chit-it! Weet-weet-weet!" everywhere, it was clear he was among a community of them, their food, he reckoned, coming from the spruce seeds, as flocks were regularly seen flying over the spruce woods. On this morning, he was preparing for an expedition towards those woods.

Dall sheep were usually found in the pastures above the timberline. Laing hiked up through the spruce woods to have a closer look at where they called home—the sheep beds, he called them. He noted that when the sheep lay in these structures on the cliff face, their noses would take in scents from the hillside and their eyes would be directed towards the downwind side. Could this have been a survival tactic? Golden eagles were regularly circling above, eyeing the flocks for a potential meal.

Laing's late breakfast once again featured pancakes, which his whisky-jack friend found to be an irresistible draw. He decided to test the bird's tenacity by nailing a pancake to the table. The clever creature, which is referred to in one slide of the film as "a very sociable fellow and a great camp thief," began pecking away at the immobilized pancake, chopping it loose until some became available for gobbling. After consuming it, the whisky-jack bounced around making sure no morsel was left, then flitted off to the spruce woods, which is where Laing was bound.

By 11 a.m., Laing, carrying the Universal camera, tripod and rifle, had a good feeling about capturing, and securing, sheep and bear. Heading for the hills, he spotted a ram out in the open at the bottom of a ravine, and reasoning that the sides of the ravine appeared difficult to ascend, he thought he was in luck. But before he could set up the camera, the ram did the unthinkable. He scrambled up the other side, with such precision that Laing watched in fascination, concerned he would miss a moment of this mountaineering demonstration. He scrambled to where a nearby grouping of the flock of thirty was, on the edge of a cliff about halfway to the timberline, and got the still camera from his pack to capture their position. It was rare to see lambs. They seemed to be protected, cached by their mothers until they grew and strengthened, kept away from the talons of the golden eagles circling nearby.

With the only other appearances made by the juncos, myrtle warblers and redpolls, now quite common in Laing's experience at Hubrick's Camp and in the nearby hills, he planned to go a bit further afield tomorrow. He looked askance towards Logan, cloud obscuring its heights. Once back at his tent to unpack, he felt the normal afternoon dusty winds pick up and remembered how the wind had gusted suddenly early that morning, creating whirlwinds—dust columns sending sand and debris high up. It had been a very pleasant day, despite not seeing any bear.

Laing awoke to a hazy morning, but there was enough visibility to see the thirty sheep move from the cliffs halfway to the timberline to what he described as a bald top—a stone clearing nearby. He watched them while he prepared for his day's hike, but then heard something new, which he described as "O sweet cheet cheet to, sweet sweet sweet in Egypt!"

The American tree sparrow had a powerful song that cut through the morning's hazy air which seemed to render it clearer. He listened again, fixing its location to an area where willows grew at valley level near the riverbank. Gathering his field glasses, he looked towards the trees and thought he caught a fleeting reddish crown and spotted breast. Could he have been mistaken? Was this a fox sparrow? The song rang out a few more times then disappeared. Laing decided to put it out of his mind as he had to shoulder his pack and walk, retracing his steps with the pack train of several days ago. Short River Camp was his destination, where he had last been on May 17. It was now May 27.

Laing couldn't keep this new song out of his mind. Had it actually been the tree sparrow or fox sparrow? "Quick! Three beers!" Two olive-sided flycatchers were visible in the heights of a tall dead spruce at the river shore. With a swiftness that was becoming instinctive, Laing raised the sights of his rifle, but they had already disappeared.

Striding, and sometimes stumbling, through the gravel and sand left behind in the dry riverbeds and the silted stones up higher made for difficult travelling. The dusty valley was desert-like in some places with few signs of life in this barren wasteland. Laing occasionally saw horned larks and heard their tinkling, multi-layered rising flight song, as well as spotted sandpipers lunging in hopes of catching flies. He made it as far as the willow thickets near Hawkins Glacier before turning around.

Heading back to Hubrick's Camp, Laing was reminded of the difficulties of identifying birds without a specimen collection. Three or four Savannah sparrows were resting at the edge of the river flat, near the opening of Barnard Glacier, mostly out in the open, but he could not clearly report their identity while alive. He raised his rifle but could not get a good shot. After lowering it and approaching carefully, the cunning tricks of these nimble birds began as they took to the skies and scattered. A merry chase ensued, with Laing tracking one of them into the woods beyond the river's edge, securing it with some difficulty and considering himself lucky. On this sunny day, at 16°C—the warmest so far in the Chitina River valley—carrying his pack, Laing was sweating in the late afternoon heat. He decided to keep to the quieter and cooler woods away from the trickling streams and set up his camp for the night there, with lupine in bloom at the door of his pup tent.

At 3 a.m. Laing woke to the rising song of an olive-backed thrush, the first he had heard. It was heaven to his ears, and he was keen, shaking away his drowsiness, to transcribe its rendering but couldn't quite do so. He would refer to the lilting tune as a "soulful melody."[21] His later report described his campsite as "a narrower belt toward river-level, where grew the bulk of the white and black poplar and an abundance of flowers, typical Canadian forms were spruce grouse, red-tailed hawk, [and] olive-backed thrush."[22]

He found camping among the trees much preferable to the sand and gravel bars near the noisy streams. Up early on this day, May 28, he planned to return to Hubrick's Camp and start making skins. The sounds of the thrushes continued, as if they had suddenly woken up, and seemed to be pervasive in the woods. He recognized a sharp "Peent!" and a "Wheert!" among the rising song several times. Preparing skins was sometimes tedious, but the day was given an extra lift by the on-going company of the thrushes, their calls becoming more frequent.

A new development, one hinted at by the day before, was the rising temperature. On his walk and looking up at the valley faces, Laing noticed that snow was quickly disappearing. Almost in direct response to this, the Dall sheep regularly visible from camp were working their way up higher on the slopes. But he was curious and a little concerned. He could not yet see any lambs. Where were they?

The usual afternoon winds whipped dust down from the glacier and into the valley. Once evening settled, they died down, and Laing set out on an excursion, intent to find more signs of bear. But in the end, he only saw his companionable sheep.

To supplement the diet provided by his usual stores, and perhaps in the interest of sprucing up the regular menu of pancakes, Laing began sampling porcupine stew, using the meat and offal from the cleaned skins, and found it to be quite tasty.

The spoils of Read's sheep hunt on May 17 also added variety to Laing's menu, and his specimen collection. The adult six-year-old and three-year-old rams had been duly catalogued.[23] He rewarded himself by dining on sheep sirloin, thankful for the air at this altitude that allowed it to dry to a leathery texture. He cut it from the bone, put it into the frying pan and found the meat to be quite delicious.

Laing had followed sheep trails through the woods back to camp that morning. During his ascents into the terrain behind camp, he found these trails offered the easiest path as well as fascinating displays of engineering.[24] These sheep highways were well-worn from many seasons of the flocks following them into the woods to the burns where they could eat the newly emergent camas.[25]

As the days of late May progressed into the summer months, Laing found plants flourishing at an astonishing rate.

The heavens opened up on May 29. The morning did not look promising as Laing quartered in his tent and meandered through camp, loading auxiliary ammunition for later use. By afternoon, the rain lessened to a sprinkle, but it did not rejuvenate the dull and silent world of his surroundings. He heard not the song of the thrush or, indeed, any other bird. The highlight of the day was watching two hawks play fighting, the smaller one a goshawk, the other a falcon, perhaps a gyrfalcon as they demonstrated remarkable manoeuvrability in their shows of force.[26] While working his way along the edge of Hubrick's Canyon, he also heard the plaintive barks of a female coyote.[27] Thinking she was close to her den, he investigated further. He later discovered tracks of a nearby family with young in the sand at the edge of the woods.

Despite the cold night, which Laing registered at 38°F (just over 3°C) at 11 p.m. and closer to freezing in the wee hours, his ambitions for the day ahead were not frozen. By 9 a.m., he was tramping the hills along the sheep trails in a morning that featured cool, cloudy conditions. Although he worked hard, he did not add to his collection. He climbed higher than ever before, 3,000 to 5,000 feet above camp, he guessed, using an avenue he called Read's Slide to get above the timberline. Before proceeding, he spotted many red squirrels, and once a goshawk suddenly swooped above his head. Despite his fast reflex bringing the rifle to bear, he was too late to secure it.

At such a high vantage, Laing would have an ideal observation point for winged predators. He had a fairly good view of a pigeon hawk, noticing how its hovering over a burn much resembled that of a sparrow hawk; then it broke off and chased a golden eagle over the lower hills. Laing observed them for some time with his field glasses.

Returning through the spruce woods, Laing noticed large piles of cone scales from white spruce, some up to twenty feet in diameter and a foot or two high. Turning a scale around in his fingers, he saw how these piles told of a complex cycle and food supply system. He had wondered why red squirrels, being as numerous as they were, weren't much interested in the oats the pack train left behind. It would seem the principal source of food for the red squirrel was the spruce seed. As he continued down through the timberline to camp, he saw families of young squirrels at these heaps of cones. He began to see the seed within the spruce cone as the staff of life for the red squirrel, which then provides sustenance for the goshawk, the red-tailed hawk and hawk owl. He guessed that even more creatures, such as coyote, depended upon red squirrel as a food source. Even the redpoll and white-winged crossbills seemed to subsist on the spruce seed, being frequently seen on the treetops where the cones were clustered. These birds were regularly the prey of pigeon hawks.

Later, Laing had another moment of realization on the way down through the timber. He saw two lambs, the first since he arrived at Hubrick's Camp and began his daily focused observation of the flocks. Watching them feed with their families under the canopy of the timber made him pause. Was this the shelter ewes sought to protect their newborn from the attacks of predators? He was reminded of guide Harry Boyden telling him about witnessing a golden eagle "packing off a lamb" in early May.[28]

Nearby, Laing came across torn, white fleece where he guessed a bear had feasted on Dall sheep, which refocused him on searching for the elusive bruin. He had seen footprints lately but no recent sightings. Was sheep regularly on the menu for a grizzly? How had this one met its fate?

From there, Laing headed straight for camp. It was starting to get quite cold. The evening would be marked by extremes. The mercury dipped to 45°F (just over 7°C) by 10 p.m., and the magnificent olive-backed thrush continued to serenade him to sleep.

With renewed purpose, Laing ventured into the woods by 8:30 a.m. the next day, May 31, once again following Read's Slide. He took note of the numerous and increasingly noisy redpolls, as well as about six white-winged crossbills. Nesting was over for the redpolls, and the first young were leaving the nest; the social activity between redpoll and crossbill was becoming increasingly intense.[29]

Laing mimicked the regularly spaced toot of a pygmy owl call to bring out the golden-crowned kinglets that he could hear, but to no avail. This disappointment was tempered by securing a male magpie. The presence of this solitary bird whose flocks weren't meant to appear in the Chitina River valley until late July baffled Laing. But it reminded him that he still a great deal to observe in the months ahead.

Laing had decided it had been too long since he had written to his sweetheart, Ethel May Hart. Describing his tent camp to his future wife, he asked her to "imagine a valley 1 1/2 miles wide—the floor a desert of level gravel with a dozen small rivulets coming across it—muddy, soupy glacial stuff." He guessed in his letter that the mountains up either side of the valley were about 8,000 or 9,000 feet high and that he was positioned "on N. side. S. side is very steep and colder." Reiterating this for her refreshed his confidence that he was on the best side for his work. Further detailing his location at the beginning of timber leading to the lower slopes, he mentioned "black poplars on all the sides and here and there on the hills" and that "deep ravines cut into the mountain—precipitous." His immediate surroundings, he added, featured "the sudden little hills and benches" and that beyond "there is a variety of burns, cliffs, green timber in clumps, bushy slopes until finally you get beyond the line of timber and have only alpine vegetation up to the yellow cliffs and the eternal snows."[30] With that letter sealed in an envelope, he filed it with his diary and settled into his usual daylight slumber, nestled in his valley, many miles from the struggles of the mountaineers among the forbidding glacier landscapes to the southeast.

CHAPTER 7

King Glacier

In "The Story of the Expedition" in the *Canadian Alpine Journal*, W.W. Foster wrote that, in order to finish stocking Cascades, "relaying of supplies was a continuous operation until May 31."[1] From a point approximately halfway between Turn Camp and Cascades Camp where the main winter cache was located at 6,050 feet, the men focused all their efforts, barring part of a day devoted to reconnaissance of the King Trench, to travelling the eight miles from the main cache to Cascades across the Ogilvie Glacier. Luckily, they had good weather as the sun was out. To avoid the strained effort of hauling the Yukon sleds through the melted surface of ice and snow, they started relaying "as soon as possible after 1 a.m. [as] each morning a good crust was obtainable on the snow lying upon the glacier."[2]

Up to May 31, "4,000 lbs. of equipment, provisions, and supplies had been relayed 308 miles by the party itself, each member making an average carry of 70 lbs. forty miles and relaying two tons eight miles."[3] This formidable feat was accomplished in an equally stunning landscape. Foster saw the sublimity of the world around them as a kind of reward for the labour required to make the relay to Cascades over several days. On the first trip up the Ogilvie Glacier to Cascades, May 27, "the party was saluted by a tremendous avalanche falling thousands of feet from the towering heights above" creating icy clouds from its impact onto the glacier for ten minutes afterwards.[4] This was the provenance of its name, Cascades. Describing Cascades Camp, Foster remarked at the design of cliffs and glaciers "and the highly mineralized and consequently multi-coloured rock adds to the beauty of the scene."[5]

However, the stunning scenery was countered by the declining morale in the camp. Lambart wrote, in his expedition diary entry on May 27, "Mac is a man of iron."[6] Getting up at 12:30 a.m. to start relaying at 1 a.m. was beginning to take its toll. On May 29, Lambart listed the weight of each pack being carried to the top of Quartz Ridge, 1,000 feet above Cascades: Read 61 pounds, Morgan 50 pounds, Lambart 48 pounds, Foster 40 pounds, MacCarthy 38 pounds. On that day, Lambart described Henry Hall as "practically a casualty today," having come up with Read and Morgan and not pulling very much, collapsing into a tent, exhausted. He then added, "the present state of affairs is not good and something will have to be done to straighten out matters." Cracks were starting to appear in the chain of command, with MacCarthy keeping his plans to himself. "On active words," Lambart wrote further, "Mac at present is failing to be open with his immediate plans and fails to divulge anything." What's more, it seemed that Read and Morgan were feeling somewhat underappreciated. "There is a general feeling that some are being used to further the interests of the special '4'," Lambart scrawled in pencil. It seems that Lambart, deputy leader, and not the expedition leader MacCarthy, was the one who spoke with Read and Morgan on the subject. In his diary, Lambart reported, "have had a long open confession from Read & Morgan how they are feeling with regards to the present status and promised them that my interest was by our every one having an equal show & that I would always remain on second rope & would not be a party to any 4 getting to the top on their backs."[7] Lambart's reassurance may have sealed a potential rift in the expedition during this period of heavy lifting in consolidating the new camp.

MacCarthy wrote rather jubilantly of their accomplishment: "On the afternoon of May 31st we were consolidated in a camp at the base of Cascades (altitude 7,800 feet) in two ten by twelve by three wall tents and four alpine tents."[8] By his estimate, they were ready for a four-week expedition. Lambart was less assured, writing that MacCarthy "is failing to measure out what will be actually needed … the number of days rations to provide for and also to stick by the plan of consolidating our camps step by step." Apparently, the deputy leader was not pleased with the expedition leader's abundant provisions being moved to Cascades: "He has an awful pile of stuff that he is pushing up to Cascades without any definite plan as to how much he is taking up & how much he is leaving behind."[9] Prepared or not, it was from this scenic and well-stocked camp that the mystery of King Glacier had to be solved if the expedition was to proceed.

The unknown lay ahead of them, with only a few photographs taken from quite a distance away as their guides. What lay ahead up the King Glacier? It was with a fair mix of excitement and trepidation that a reconnaissance party, consisting of MacCarthy, Lambart, Carpe and Foster, left Cascades and pushed on. They had walked around the ice-fall, which gave their new camp its name, and had a clear view of the King Glacier via its slender channel that would be named King Trench. "Imagine with what elation," Lambart wrote, "they saw that the way was clear—that by the narrow trench of the glacier they could reach the heights."[10] The big guess had gone in their favour, and the men returned with the good news, bringing up the spirits for the next leg of transporting supplies: from Cascades up to the place called Quartz Ridge. Then they planned to transport supplies up to a place they named "The Dome" and then to camp on King Glacier: Observation Camp.

During this relaying period at the end of May, Carpe was busy with the motion picture camera, as well as with his role with the front sled. On May 30, Lambart wrote that "Carpe taking short movy [sic] with [Debrie] Sept of sled work & took one of him in black moustache, white teeth and bare arms."[11] It was clear these two mountaineers were united in their love of photography.

There, however, would be no love lost after the relaying of supplies at Cascades had ended. On May 30, Lambart scribbled in his diary, in bed at 4 p.m., "All anxious to get at the 'frill' & cutting down on this wearing relay."[12] But next morning, he reported "feeling splendid," having had the best sleep so far on the expedition.[13]

Expedition leader A.H. MacCarthy's "preliminary schedule" had them all at the top of Quartz Ridge by June 1.[14] But they would need more time to get "twenty-eight packs and one Yukon sled, about 1500 pounds, to the top of Quartz Ridge over an all-snow route of varying gradients."[15] One part of their ascent was at a forty-five-degree angle. They found the snow to be firm, making it possible to get a solid footing. But with the growing risk of deep crevasses swallowing them up, it was deemed that attempting to glissade—sliding down a slope using an ice axe to maintain balance—was not recommended. For two days, they laboured to make this relay. Once established, they were ready to leave Cascades and proceed on foot for the "assault."[16]

On June 1, Lambart scribbled: "Packing to quartz ridge commences. All hand 7. Andy being on the sick list with a bad leg." Despite his good sleep, Lambart, still in a bad disposition about MacCarthy's relentless pursuit of their task, complained: "Mac is making a mistake in the quantity of stuff he is taking and being too constantly on the job, it would do us all good to forget there was a Logan for a whole day & leave people to their own thoughts." MacCarthy was also getting Foster to assist. Lambart reported: "Mack and Billy have been all afternoon on a most foolish undertaking. Packing 4 weeks' supplies into 14 packs of 2 days provisions for 8 men. The result will be that everything must be broken up and from now on we will be pouring out of the bags a mush of paper, biscuits, bags and everything mixed up."[17]

Next day, they packed more to the top of Quartz Ridge, an hour up with loads of 38 to 65 pounds and a half hour back, three to seven loads per man. Lambart, however, was done in after two loads, writing that he felt "thoroughly done up and sleeping a good deal after lunch . . . with a headache and perhaps eating too much of the rich food."[18] The superfluous food stores were seemingly having their effects.

On June 3, a clear and sunny morning, the men set out, at 6:30 a.m., carrying weighty packs with "a month's outfit already above us on Quartz Ridge."[19] By this time, the daylight was constant, which was an omen of success to MacCarthy. By the time they arrived at Observation Camp, they were weary, buoyed by their advance but "suffering considerably from blistering sunburn caused by the reflected glare of light from the snow." Lips were cracked and bleeding, faces were peeling. Even with the liberal application of lanolin, the suffering was not eased completely.[20]

≈

> While these instructions set forth the general desires of the Department and the leaders of the expedition, it is quite impossible to give instructions covering the details of your work. Your long field experience gives us confidence that you will meet emergencies with resourcefulness, and your general knowledge of natural history and of Museum needs assures us that you will make a wise allocation of the time and resources at your disposal for the best interests of the Museum.
>
> —L.L. Bolton

June 1 began with the singing of the olive-backed thrush, its "Peet!" and "Peent!" and soulful rising song a regular feature coming from the spruce woods. Laing first noticed it at 2:15 a.m., waking later to hear it coming from near his tent. He noted how the thrush didn't extinguish its song until near midnight, then, out of the absolute silence, its song and piercing "Peent!" would return. He was beginning to think that the thrush held off its singing until that moment, at dusk and at dawn, when not a sound was coming from anywhere, when all of the world was still and listening. It's almost as though the bird was a pious monk that retreated into a spiritual shelter and whose daily chores included providing music for a sleeping world.

However beautiful the song of the thrush was, when he arose at 6 a.m., drops of rain were landing on his tent, creating a gloom and calm at the same time.

Laing had placed thirteen mouse traps at timber level around the camp. Perhaps he hoped a Dawson red-backed mouse, common at river level, would get lodged in the snare but more likely a Drummond meadow-mouse, frequently seen around camp. The day before, using some raw meat as bait, he had managed to catch one, a juvenile, of a deeper grey than the more mature mice he had observed. Earlier in May, he had secured two red-backed specimens on the river bed, with their winter pelage still on them, quite a distinctive red area on the back, yellow sides and white underneath.[21] Perhaps future specimens would vary in colour and size as summer approached?

The sun was out for a while but regularly ducked behind the clouds. Despite the cover, it was quite warm: 60°F (about 16°C) in the evening. Laing spent the day making skins, some for his most recently captured specimens. He was perplexed by the male and female rabbits with their long white hairs still showing, signs that the winter molt was not completed. The Mackenzie varying hare was not in a good state. He thought back to his rail travels in early May and the dead rabbits that appeared in the woods about fifty miles from Chitina station, then further north in greater numbers. He recalled seeing more around McCarthy and on his walk to Kennicott, then later on the Nizina and lower Chitina. He roughly calculated that this over 100-mile stretch of land (its breadth was unknown) was afflicted with what he called a "dying-off year" for rabbits.[22]

Laing remembered counting from the train car window up to fourteen dead rabbits per mile. There was, he reckoned, twenty yards visible from the car window. Doing some arithmetic, he thought this could mean over 1,200 per square mile. But he did see a dozen living rabbits, in their brown pelage, so not all were afflicted. The dead animals were all in their white winter coats. After asking locals about this phenomenon at McCarthy, whose theories ranged from possible tumours to large-scale starvation, Laing was leaning towards the latter. He had seen shrubbery approaching McCarthy and along the forested route up the Chitina to be eaten clean away, even fallen spruce trees had been picked clean of their bark, leaves and stems, and this lack of food could point to a starvation event.[23]

The rabbits, though, seemed to be in good health from Bryson's Cabin up the Chitina to Hubrick's Camp.[24] He'd made hare sightings at the level of the river's gravel beds on up to the start of timber. These animals were thriving. Perhaps their food source was more dependable in this valley?

While Laing pondered this, he heard an unnatural whistle. As he looked out into the cloudy landscape, there it was again: a distant steam whistle. Closing his eyes, he could also hear a faint humming and the growl of heavy factory machinery. These sounds of civilization, of industrialization, did not add value, nor did they belong in this landscape. He sensed the oncoming daily dust storm and decided to leave the drying board and shelter in the tent. He found that immersing himself in his work, whether it was another sortie or preparing skins, alleviated his loneliness. But if it were left to him, he'd prefer not to be reminded of civilization. He had not even made note of curiosity in his diary as to the progress of the mountaineers. To his surprise, he did not require any soothing when it came to his solitary state, only activity towards achieving his goal.

The next morning, Laing arose unusually late. Perhaps his vigorous specimen preparations the day before had exhausted him far more than he had thought. The day was warmer, the clouds darkening. Expecting rain, he switched from his initial plan of heading back into the hills, to exploring the valley so as to avoid climbing in wet weather. The American tree sparrow he had heard on his jaunt on May 27 was still in memory.[25] He now called this place, where he had had a fleeting possible glimpse of one, Tree Sparrow Point, and he longed to return and try his luck to secure one.

Laing kept close to the riverbank, near the willow trees. Along the way, he heard the repetitive "Peet!" and "Teet!" of the olive-backed thrush, a regular background tone to these past days. After exploring where he thought he had heard the thrush on May 27, but after a brief morning vigil during which the sky cleared, he heard none of the "O sweet cheet cheet to, sweet sweet sweet in Egypt!" of the tree sparrow's song. Disappointed, he proceeded into the woods, buoyed by the song of the thrushes. He returned to camp at noon with ten birds secured, including a juvenile redpoll and another olive-backed thrush.

Laing encountered more hares on his return to camp, further convincing him that famine or disease wasn't present in this part of the valley. What he witnessed on his rail journey and near McCarthy must have been an isolated event. With no dead rabbits seen, or evidence they had been picked off by predators, he decided it would not be amiss for him to add to his menu, having long since run out of mutton. So it was rabbit stew for dinner, which he found to be quite a delicacy.

June 3 began with a disappointment: there were no mice in the traps. But on the bright side, the morning was a clear one. If there was one thing Laing was certain of, it was the uncertainty of Alaskan weather. But it was holding for now. With that cue, he decided to try his luck with the alpine country behind camp. Finding the Universal heavy, he opted to bring the still camera, planning to do some stalking.

Not long into the spruce forest, he spotted what he described at the time as a golden sprite, Wilson's warbler.[26] Could it have been hiding throughout the nesting season? Why was he just seeing one now? With its bright yellow plumage, it did not blend into these surroundings. He brought up his rifle and fired. Laing later examined the specimen, an adult female.

Another first was ahead: Laing was certain he saw a hermit thrush on the top of a spruce tree, its brown body unmistakably giving it away. Although his shot had hit his mark, he cringed. The specimen fell into the canyon and was lost into its depths.[27]

Keen to add to his collection, Laing searched for birds that he hadn't secured yet. He soon came across one, the northern raven, a common creature he'd seen here. Near the canyon, he spotted a healthy-looking adult, raised his rifle and fired. One shot was all it took. After noting it was a female,[28] he stowed it away in his pack.

Once at the canyon, he quickly determined where the female had come from. Just below, on the other side, he saw a nest containing an adult and what appeared to be young ones. He stayed for a while, crouched down, eventually reaching for his field glasses. He counted five young, looking mature enough to leave the nest by his reckoning.[29] He turned back and set out to the west along the slope, the spruce thinning to only those few that could find a hold on the rock face.

There, about a dozen strong, was a flock of sheep. Laing saw ewes and young and one old ram. After so much wondering about where lambs were kept, it was odd to see them out here in the open. He reached into his pack and quietly brought out the camera. But he needed to close the distance. Scrambling up a rocky outcropping, he believed he was within 100 yards to the point over a precipice where the flock had congregated. After he managed to dislodge a rock, which tumbled down the slope, several ewes turned their heads towards Laing and stood still. He got several exposures from this vantage point before the lambs quickly rounded a turn to put a tall spruce between them and Laing; the ewes soon followed, and the old ram, its immense spread of horns on display, turned away last and bounded proudly yet stiffly up the rocky cliff in pursuit of the ewes. Laing was satisfied he got his photographs before they turned away. But he also questioned his assumption that the newborns had been hidden in the cover of willow thickets. Perhaps they were kept up here, concealed among the cliffs. Upon further thought, forest cover would not deter a golden eagle in its search for a meal.[30] Perhaps up here they would have strength in numbers, or maybe the well-trodden trails gave them solace, knowing that many generations had travelled these ways. Thinking more on this, he put the camera away and, looking up, saw the clear skies were darkening. Estimating the time at somewhere around 3 p.m., he decided to play it safe with the uncertain weather and head downhill.

Back near the canyon, Laing spotted something new. This was a thrill! Could it be? Way up the canyon wall, in a place he was now calling Raven Canyon, he heard the echoing flight song of a wheatear and soon spotted him flitting in the inaccessible heights where he thought its nest may be embedded. As he recalled, this bird had a connection to the Old World, mostly common in Eurasia, but this could be the furthest south it might penetrate on its summer route.[31] As it flew excitedly from point to point, it eventually stopped someplace, and Laing did not hear him anymore. This sighting was the cap on an extraordinary day. With another look in the direction of the raven's nest, he turned downwards to camp.

Nearing the tent, Laing caught sight of an olive-sided flycatcher before it too flitted away.[32] His smile was soon turned into a sombre look as, glancing west towards the moraine, he saw a wild sight indeed. It was a squall, far from the regular dust storm that made its way across the river valley. As the wind picked up, it took Laing's hat, and a wall of dust and rain moved quickly towards him. He retreated to the tent above the riverbed, taking shelter as the winds buffeted the canvas. He peered out as the valley went dark, the precipitation taking on an ominous quality. The winds continued for what seemed like several hours. Then, as soon as it swept across Laing's landscape, it dissipated, and the sky opened up to allow the sun to stretch its beams across the vast expanse ahead of him.

CHAPTER 8

Ravens in the Family

Albert H. MacCarthy, moving beyond what he had seen during the winter freighting expedition, was exploring new ground with his fellow climbers. With the necessary equipment and provisions at hand "to ensure a sustained effort" and completely consolidated at 10,200-feet elevation at Observation Camp by June 4, he now estimated, and hoped for, a successful climb to the summit of Logan on June 21 and a return to Advance Base Camp two days later.[1] It was an ambitious plan, but with sunny skies, the route clear from their reconnaissance of King Glacier and the team well-provisioned for a month (in fact, MacCarthy thought they were stocked up for two weeks beyond the estimated twenty-one days needed to accomplish their goal and return back to the Advance Base Camp), the expedition was as ready as it was going to be.[2]

Sleet and heavy gusts of freezing wind in the remaining hours of the day did not bode well for their departure next day. The three alpine tents where the men huddled from the elements were buffeted harshly all night.[3] In his diary, Lambart described dreaming about a butler building a "gorgeous mansion in the country."[4]

Wind and thick fog greeted them as they rose on the morning of June 5. This no doubt was a break for the men suffering from sunburn. By 9 a.m., the fog was starting to dissipate, and putting on packs weighing about thirty-five pounds, some carrying bundles of willow markers,

Observation Camp, preparing to bring sleds up King Glacier to the
icefall, June 5, when the clearing fog gave them the opportunity.
(COURTESY: WHYTE MUSEUM OF THE CANADIAN ROCKIES, V14_AC0P_519)

snowshoed and on two ropes, the eight men set out hopefully in the
direction of the col ahead—a saddle or depression in a ridge—which
they would name King Col, at the head of the glacier, where they hoped
to make their next camp.[5] MacCarthy, Read, Morgan and Foster were
on the first rope; Lambart, Taylor, Hall and Carpe were on the other.[6]
The first part of the day involved ascending King Glacier for about four
miles, pulling their loaded sled. This traverse was where they began placing willow wand markers, approximately every 100 feet of their trail. At
1 p.m., they reached the base of a 1,000-foot icefall, where they had to
abandon the sled. MacCarthy noted that the gradient was relatively easy
and "its hundreds of crevasses all securely filled and bridged by hard
snow so that the footing on snow shoes was safe and good." They snowshoed to the top of the icefalls. At 3 p.m., at an elevation of 13,200 feet
and a mile beyond the top of the falls, as crevasses started to block their

path, and so close to the col at the head of King Glacier, "a sudden change in the weather brought down on us a slashing and penetrating blizzard."[7] They hurriedly cached their packs and retraced their steps to Observation Camp, searching for the willow wands as they went. They arrived in warm sun and could see King Trench and Col in the distance illuminated by sunshine. This was indeed frustrating for the men, and although their route for the next day was plotted out with the willow wands, experience was suggesting several things to the climbers. It was clear that the area was subject to erratic weather, so delaying departure due to poor conditions might be perhaps the wrong approach. Heading out prepared for the weather, with the right clothing in their packs, would be the best policy. And, clearly, consistent use of the willow wands would be advantageous as good visibility was not always available.

Although not completely understood at the time of the expedition, today we know the Saint Elias Range's remoteness and its nature as the highest coastal range in the world made it uniquely dangerous and subject to erratic weather patterns.[8] These mountains, concentrated in an area on a swift rise from the Pacific Ocean, were located in an environment of meteorological extremes. Microclimates existed because of the varying topography and altitude. The area in and around the Logan massif was subject to moist air rising from the ocean and cooling rapidly, resulting in dense fog, fierce blizzard or anything in between, which lead to incredible sudden temperature drops. Laing at Hubrick's Camp was experiencing these Pacific-driven weather extremes with afternoon dust storms created from the dry surface of the river valley inviting high winds down from the glaciers. Whereas, the mountaineers were getting their first taste of high-altitude storm systems attacking them from the Pacific, meeting the barrier of the Logan massif and playing havoc with visibility, then suddenly lifting. Whiteout conditions could descend unexpectedly and create severe problems with navigation. Thus the willow wand method was already proving to be beneficial to the mountaineers for finding their way, like the trail of bread crumbs in *Hansel and Gretel.*[9]

On June 6, assisted by the willow stakes every 100 feet, the mountaineers snowshoed with renewed confidence under clear skies with fresh

Looking nearly due west, down the King Glacier, June 6.
(COURTESY: WHYTE MUSEUM OF THE CANADIAN ROCKIES, V14_AC0P_522)

supplies on a sled to the base of the icefalls in four hours. At this point, 13,200 feet in elevation, they cached the sled and 100 pounds of their freight, slinging packs on their backs with the rest of the supplies to climb the icefalls. About a mile beyond the cache and close to a mile shy of King Col itself, the mountaineers decided to set up their King Col Camp, at 13,875 feet. They extracted shovels from packs and dug out of the deep snow a flat expanse for the alpine tents. Allen Carpe was rolling film while the men set up camp. He had filmed them several times along the route, shrunk by the immense peaks, scanning the nearby ridges and trying to catch the avalanches that they heard regularly, usually before they could spot them. These avalanches would then crash down with a plume of powdery snow rising skyward. From the vantage point of their new camp, they could look down the length of the King Glacier where they had climbed. The camp was protected from the wind, but only in that it was near a slope of massive broken jumbles of ice covered in snow. Upon further ascending King Trench, to the crest of King Col, the mountaineers received a blow. They were confronted with an immense "mass of very steep and badly broken ice slopes covered with varying depths of snow" not spotted by earlier reconnaissance.[10] At least 1,000 feet separated them from the higher ice slopes of the Logan massif. They saw "a tremendous face of ice and snow, up which it appeared impossible to ascend."[11]

On an expedition of this kind, working far from a base of supplies, there has to be a lot of give and take. The leaders of the expedition will help your work as much as possible, and you will be expected to do the best you can to make a photographic record of the expedition. For this reason, the Department of Mines has secured the loan of a "Universal" motion picture camera from the Canadian Government Motion Picture Bureau, Department of Trade and Commerce, Ottawa, and is supplying 4,000 feet of negative film.

—L.L. Bolton

June 4 began in contrasting calm to the squall of the previous evening. Laing emerged from his tent to a day that was half clear. With his adventure of the day before in mind, he decided to stay in camp making skins, preparing collected specimens. His thoughts seemed to hang on the female raven and the nest left behind.

After a pancake breakfast, as Laing prepared to work, he detected a new call that had slowly begun to distinguish itself from the song of the common redpoll. He now suspected a pine siskin, a seed-eating nomad whose wheezy note usually consisted of a "Squee-e-e-e!" or a "Zree-e-e!" ascending in strength, distinct from the "Zrill!" of the redpoll.[12] The social gatherings of redpolls, crossbills and the siskins would generate a lot of chatter, but with patience, he found himself being able to distinguish each one.

Laing shot a healthy-looking male rabbit midday to spruce up his pantry, planning to eat him for dinner. While dispatching it, he had an idea. He placed the leftover rabbit offal on a nearby sandbar, and as he prepared skins, he looked up to see what might come for a pile of remains.[13] Later, while placing a cleaned skin on the drying rack, he heard the sound of something having touched down on the sand. Turning around, he saw a raven, a large male he thought, pecking at the offal. It raised its head, a piece of offal dangling from its beak, looked about, then lowered its head and continued its work. Laing sat down and watched in fascination. Could this be the dutiful father of the brood at the nest in the newly coined Raven Canyon? With a remaining chunk stuck in its beak, the raven bounced twice on its planned route then took to wing, in the direction of Laing's sortie of the day before.

Laing enjoyed the meal of pan-fried rabbit, the firelight flickering on his face as he ate with his hands. He had heard a few deep croaks from the canyon, and he smiled. As he ate, he noted none of the wasting in the hares observed on his rail journey was apparent in this one. In fact, there was a fair amount of fat on it.

Pleased with the amount of work accomplished the day before, Laing set off on June 5, a clear and cool morning, towards Barnard Glacier, across the sandbars in, what he now considered, a desperate search for the horned lark heard and briefly seen on May 17 while in that vicinity walking to Hubrick's Camp with the expedition.[14] He wanted to return to that location, on the gravel bars of the Short River near the camp previous to Hubrick's Camp. To get there, Laing took to the woods, using what he reckoned to be the old trail of the International Boundary Survey. He wondered what adventures the men had in their quest. What brought his thoughts back to his trail was that the recent dust storms had left evidence of their violence. The spruce trees were covered in material from the valley floor, and as he brushed past twigs, their recoil would generate clouds of dust that blanketed Laing. He would need a bath once he returned to camp. But for now, he wanted to get to Short River, and the increasing dust made him reconsider walking in the deep sand along the river. He changed course.

Before entering the clearing, at a place his notes identified as Teal Pond, Laing spotted an uncommon sight on a high branch—a flicker— and brought up his field glasses to confirm. Quickly he raised his rifle and fired, bringing the specimen down. He ran his fingers across the plumage, noticing it was male, and determined it was a typical flicker, but its throat feathers were mainly grey, an unexpected difference.[15] He made note of this and placed the specimen carefully in his pack.

Not long afterwards, out in the open and the direct sunlight, Laing came across tracks in the river sand in several places. Bending down to analyze them, he quickly determined by their size and even distribution between front and hind prints that they were of grizzly bear. These creatures, solitary souls by Laing's observance so far, managed to cover ground most effectively in their walks. But what would draw this one to peruse the gravel and sand? His passing study of what he believed to be grizzly scat during the walk along the Chitina with the expedition had contained a large quantity of rabbit remains. Another specimen showed the seeds of cranberry, silverberry and some other berries packed in with rabbit bones and fur.[16] There must be something of interest for them to explore here in the great expanse of the river valley.

Nearing Barnard Glacier and the location of Short River Camp, Laing prepared for his watch. Sitting down in the gravel, he closed his eyes and listened. It wouldn't be long before he heard something explosive. The "It-chit-chit-chit-chit-chit-chit-chit!" was not musical but denoted the business-like song of the Wilson's warbler. He hadn't heard it two days ago when he had secured a female. He listened to its urgency now, coming from the willows along the riverbank.[17]

Laing would wait for some time before hearing the tinkling song that soared over the valley. He brought his field glasses slowly up to his eyes, looking over the willows, and counted four horned larks, the distinctive black "horns" opposed by the downturned black plumage across the eyes on an otherwise white face. He put down the glasses. Taking decisive action, Laing brought his rifle to bear, leaned down on one knee and fired several times. When the fading report was reverberating up from the moraine of Barnard Glacier and across the valley, he gathered his equipment and went to the base of the willows. There he inspected the two specimens, relatively intact, both males and having bred for the season. His quest for specimens of the horned lark was over.[18] He placed them gingerly in his pack and set off for Hubrick's Camp.

After regaining his trail at pace along the river flat, at the edge of the woods, Laing spotted one more specimen within range, and without hesitation fired upon a common redpoll. He retrieved it and found, to his surprise, a nest about five feet from the ground, supported by the rough-barked trunk of a black poplar. Upon closer inspection, he noted the empty nest, composed of weed stems and tree fibres, was lined with hawk and ptarmigan feathers and willow cotton. It was ingeniously camouflaged to blend in with the tree bark, and it was by a miracle that Laing had spotted it. He guessed it may have been a second nesting, and unlike other breeding redpoll males he had secured, this one did not have the vibrant red breast and pink rump, its breast marked by a faint rosy tint that denoted, he concluded, a second winter plumage. However, this specimen may not have anything to do with this nest, he surmised. It was difficult at best to link males as the proprietor of a nest with any certainty.[19]

As he neared Hubrick's Camp close to 5:30 p.m., Laing glanced towards the hills behind the tent and saw that the Dall sheep in their various parties had merged into two large flocks. Fascinating. With his still camera, he took a photograph of this vantage point of his summer home, framing the large wood hide, the camp—at bottom and fitting in the mountains behind at top—and the various stages of spruce woods, thick at first then thinning out in layers until the bald expanse of rock laid bare on the peaks. Laing knew he still had much to explore up there, having only scratched the surface. He knew he would soon return to Raven Canyon. But after a thirty-mile hike, albeit buoyed by a successful outing, he was ready to have his planned meal of sheep stew and dumplings by the fire, wash some of the valley's dust from his face and have a good night's rest.

June 6 was spent preparing the skins from those specimens secured the day before. Laing was looking forward to this day; without a cloud in the sky, he had a clear view to the southeast of the Logan massif. He planned to use the still camera and Universal.

While having some bannock for breakfast, along with a little pan-fried bacon, Laing observed the ever-insistent whisky-jack, or Canada jay. A couple regularly came to Hubrick's Camp in search of a breakfast morsel to take away, Laing presumed, to the awaiting young beaks in the woods. He had seen the first young jays in the spruce woods on May 28.[20] Laing was beginning to lightheartedly refer to the little bird as the camp robber jay.

The clever, problem-solving whisky-jack wrestling with a ball of
bannock, in a frame from *The Conquest of Mount Logan*.
(COURTESY: LIBRARY AND ARCHIVES CANADA)

On this day, he wanted to make a special effort to confound the jays
and film the process. So, setting up the motion picture camera on its
tripod and framing his shot to include a small branch, which acted as a
perch fastened above a small square platform, he had made his challenge for them. He attached a small amount of elastic around a piece of
bannock, then fastened the other end to the perch so that it dangled
above the platform, not easily accessible from the perch or the platform.
With the jays at the nearby table, Laing knew he needed to roll film
soon, so he quickly moved behind the camera and began cranking. One
jay moved abruptly, realizing the hard biscuit had been left unattended.
The brainy bird observed the situation briefly then, after momentarily
hanging off the bannock, landed on the perch, leaned down and grabbed
it in its beak to bring it onto the perch. Using its body weight to flip it
over the perch so that it was now on a shorter tether, the jay grabbed the
piece whole and wrenched a bit off, proceeding to peck it mercilessly
until pieces flecked off and landed on the platform. Then the jay perched
on the bannock and pecked away at it, getting a fair reward by that

method as well. Laing knew he was getting invaluable material as he continued to crank away on what he saw as one of the cleverest of thieves who regularly visited his table. He concluded that the young must be dependent on the parents for some time, as he had not yet seen the young fend for themselves. But considering the tenacity of this pair, he decided to be patient and look for the little ones throughout the summer months.[21]

Drummond meadow-mouse was common near camp and seen at river level. Laing had set fourteen traps along the river's edge, the primary bait being bacon rind leftover from his breakfast. Successful bait through trial and error had been bacon or strong cheese. He found one mouse in his traps. He extracted it and placed in his pack. In another, he found a grey vole, possibly a mountain long-tailed vole that he would add to his morning's list of chores.

Although focused on preparing several skins for drying, Laing looked up at the new pile of offal he left on the sandbar. Then he set eyes upon the glorious sight of the Logan massif above the Logan Glacier on this clearest of days. Before long, he heard the telltale sound of something hopping and sinking on the sandbar and turned to see the dutiful father, the dark raven, rummaging through the offal, glancing up to see Laing looking at him from the camp. After some more pickings and gulps, the raven flew off to the left after a couple of more hops in the sand. Laing watched until he disappeared into the spruce woods.

Once the new skins were on the drying rack, Laing set up his still camera and tripod to capture Logan in all its glory. Lining up the shot to capture the peaks, he took a moment, looked at Logan and sighed.

His clock had stopped. When the sun had dipped as low as it got, he set it. But it was less and less of use lately.

He had Raven Canyon very much in mind for his outing the next day. He awoke at 6 a.m., according to his newly set clock. Hearing the deep croaks of a raven along with some accompanying chitterings, he had no need for an alarm clock with these early risers about.[22] No frost was on the tent, although it was, by all admittance, a cool morning. After pancakes, and some regular dealings with the jays, Laing packed up and was climbing up to the canyon before 8 a.m.

Once the canyon clearing emerged through the spruce woods, Laing picked up his pace, curious as to what he would see at the nest. Expecting it to be full of dependent young and a watchful father, he was surprised to find it had fewer than the five seen earlier. Could they have finally begun to leave the nest, to fly with their father? The ones left behind began to chitter away at a high pitch, a sound Laing likened more to that of sandhill cranes than the throaty, resonant croak he associated with ravens. So . . . where was father?

Laing recalled having seen pairs in flight over the valley as early as May 13 during the traverse to the Chitina River valley. This would either point to early nesting, and couples continuing their nuptial aerobatics after mating, or them creating their nest later in spring. At any rate, he was impressed with the wisdom of the raven parent. This was not an easy land to survive in. Back in McCarthy, he recalled ravens dipping into the feed of the tethered husky dogs. Locals said that the ravens knew the length of a dog chain right down to the link.[23]

Soon, father and remaining brood swooped in and returned to the nest. The young repeated their high-pitched plaintive noises, trying to be heard and seen, while father distributed, stuffing gaping beaks. The young appeared to be dependent for a while, preferring this mode of feeding to taking the initiative for themselves.[24] Father seemed to be getting on with it quite well.

Already it was promising to be a hot summer's day, the hill-slopes dry and dusty as Laing headed into them. He quickly secured an adult brown-headed chickadee, noticeably greyer and less brown than similar Hudsonian chickadees he knew from Ontario.[25] He had noted their relaxed "Si-da-daa!" had become a bit more common in the spruce woods of late, possibly because the young had left the nest; however, his specimen had two spiders in its beak.

The "Chit-it! Chit-it! Weet-weet-weet!" of the white-winged crossbill had become a regular song of the forest when a flock was about. However, Laing noticed something different today: above the forest canopy, flocks were heading down valley, westward.[26]

While observing the vicinity of the canyon, Laing heard the wheatear's jubilant flight song, probably the very bird he spotted June 3. He got down low, made his way to nearby clumps of willow trees and crouched down. Looking up, he made a sighting, high up on the canyon rim where only winged creatures could establish a nest. After some quiet observance, he decided some strategy was in order and made a few attempts to imitate the song. Before long, the bird, on a quick descent, gave a resonant "Wheet-eer!" and perched within range, bobbing curiously up and down.[27] Laing secured it, excited to have collected such a difficult to access creature with strategy,[28] knowing it would probably be his sole specimen.

Laing climbed a little higher and saw new activity among the ewes. Some had brought their lambs, now much nimbler, out into the open, each lamb following a ewe.[29]

Having waited out the daily dust event, Laing descended into camp at 7:30 p.m., exhausted, feet sore, knees giving in, almost ready to go to bed without his supper, when he noticed the camp wasn't as he had left it. A carton lay on the ground. Laing picked it up: hardtack gone. He dropped the carton and took fast hold of his rifle, beginning to reconnoiter for the culprit. Walking to the tent, slowly, he circled round, only to hear a rustling back where he dropped the carton. In a swift movement belying his exhaustion, Laing fired. The shot hit its mark. The Lake Bennett ground squirrel, its reddish colouring indicating a summer coat, had come back for the crumbs.

June 8, for the all-done-in Laing, was spent preparing the skins from his latest specimens, including his prize catch, the wheatear. But before starting this work, he loaded the Universal to continue chronicling the clever Canada jay couple. Now whisky-jack seemed especially perturbed when Laing supplied breakfast as mushy as boiled rice or oatmeal porridge because, even though they seemed to like it, carrying any more than a bill-full was problematic. He made a special dough, left over from pancake batter, to see their reaction. The jays went straight for it, chopping it into manageable bits, then carted them out to waiting beaks in the spruce woods. But it was other beaks Laing was thinking about feeding throughout his workday.

After preparing his skins, he disposed of the bird bodies and various mammal remains away from camp as usual, but this time brought it in a little closer, still on the sand. Laing felt that atonement was appropriately given to the hardworking father of five. As soon as the offering was put down and Laing stepped away, Father landed on the other side of it. What a keen scout he is![30] Then, behind him, two young appeared. Laing backed away, and then they set upon the pile.

CHAPTER 9

Splitting Up

The treacherous ice slopes of King Trench to the crest of the col may have dimmed the mountaineers' hopes for the planned route, but Mac-Carthy noted, on the opposite side of the trench, "the east shoulder of King Peak, rising a thousand feet or more above us, presented a steep face of perfect crampon snow."[1] From the col, they couldn't get a clear outlook on the massif above, but after gaining some altitude on the east arête (a narrow ridge) up King Peak, they had a bird's-eye view of the possibilities to conquer the barrier in front of them.

The party divided: Lambart took the second rope back to Observation Camp to prepare their evening meal and get ready for the next day, while the first rope of MacCarthy, Foster, Read and Morgan ascended the shoulder of King Peak (whose summit was known to be 17,130 feet) to its crest at 15,000 feet.[2] The altitude was beginning to have its effects on some of the mountaineers, although the reconnaissance was necessary if they were to have any hope of a plan. Driving the shafts further into the snow with every step was becoming more and more difficult. Once the first rope attained the shoulder, they turned around to study the slopes below the massif. After some discussion, they were satisfied they had located "the only feasible line of ascent to the upper reaches of slopes leading to an elevation of about 17,000 feet."[3] Their reconnaissance done, the men took in their surroundings.

To the south of us and 9,000 feet below lay the Seward and Columbus Glaciers with the magnificent St. Elias range rising in the purple sky beyond, showing between its peaks grand views of the mighty Malaspina Glacier with its myriads of moraines, while, fringing the crests, the blue Pacific outlined the whole panorama, a truly grand sight that was not excelled by any other view during the whole climb.[4]

Lambart and the rest of the party, settled in at Observation Camp, were reassured that it seemed possible to scale the intimidating ice slopes and were dazzled by the exhausted reconnaissance party's description of their views while on the east shoulder of King Peak. Beyond the vast glaciers lingered over, there were the peaks to the southeast, including "Alverstone, Hubbard, Vancouver, and, more to the south, the huge ghost-like mass of Mount Cook fill the scene, obscuring from view Disenchantment Bay on the coast and the Fairweather range beyond."[5] They remained spellbound as they told of the white expanse of

Excavating a tent site at King Col Camp, June 8.
(COURTESY: WHYTE MUSEUM OF THE CANADIAN ROCKIES, V14_AC0P_531)

the Seward Glacier around the southern base of Mount Logan. Past
Seward lay "the Mount Augusta-Mount Newton range; and off towards
its western extremity, separated only by the Newton Col, Mount St.
Elias rises like a huge shrouded sea lion, 26 miles distant."[6] The listing
of such a notable peak must have given the mountaineers renewed
vigour, their labours having placed them amid such illustrious and near-
mythological peaks. To Lambart's reckoning, much of the described
view had never been seen by human eyes.[7]

After this description, the positive news of the possible progress into
the crevassed slopes that lay before them above King Col was tempered
by the fact that they did not have a clear route. What lay ahead was a
"veritable jumble of ice blocks, séracs, and cliffs, all of huge dimensions."[8]
To this end, they decided that MacCarthy, Foster and Read, after a day's
rest for all on June 7 at Observation Camp and a day of relaying supplies up to King Col Camp on June 8, would set out on reconnaissance.[9]

Lambart described their "spot of life in this wilderness of snow" at
Observation Camp in his diary, assembled in "a little knot of 4 tents, 3
'Brownies' (alpine 7x8) and 1 green (7x6)," and added:

One brownie [sic] is the Cook tent, in which 3 little (3 1/2 lbs) Primus
are for many hours roaring per day. . . . Andy and . . . Bob Morgan are in
control. Our sugar and ham ration is not as great and would like to see
them & some times [sic] our meat supplies are too much to be good for
us and we might be suffering in consequence. . . . Our green tent Andy
& Morgan sleep upon 2 small cork & two small air mattresses besides 2
or 3 sheep skins and are very comfortable. In other 'Brownie' Hall, Carpe
& Read sleep 2 mattresses to 3 people. In another Brownie Mac, Billy &
I reside comfortable . . . the great event of the day being crawling into
our eiderdowns.[10]

Breakfast was served by 4 a.m. on June 8: porridge with milk and
brown sugar, bacon, eggs, hotcakes, tea and biscuits. The eight men pulled
out of camp just after 5:45 a.m., arriving three hours later, with a sled
load of 650 pounds, at the base of the icefalls. Individual loads were
taken up on their backs to the new camp at the col. MacCarthy, Foster
and Read settled in there while Lambart and the others descended to

accomplish more "jerk-necking" or hauling equipment by sled.[11] Mac-Carthy, who had served in the United States Navy for a decade, including during the Spanish-American War of 1898, empathized with the men destined to do the menial labour while his first rope team prepared for more mountaineering: "He that has not been in the support or the reserve forces in battle never can appreciate what it means in will power and endurance to do the drudgery while the others are enjoying the combat."[12]

In the thinner air, digging tent sites several feet into a snowbank, one for cooking and one for sleeping, was difficult. But the men managed to establish the tents and turned in early in preparation for the next day's physical labour.

MacCarthy would rely on the skills of Foster to remedy one eye, which had become uncomfortably painful, most likely causing a fitful sleep for the expedition leader.[13]

Although from a scientific standpoint specimens from Alaska are equally desirable, from our Museum's standpoint it is desirable to get as many records as possible within Canadian territory, and we trust that other things being equal, you will endeavour to use your time and other resources to get as much scientific material as possible from the Yukon side of the International Boundary. As the region in which you will work is virtually unknown biologically, any specimens from that general region will be interesting and valuable.

—L.L. Bolton

Laing's father had been an exceptional hunter, and young Mack had learned about the birds, mammals and insects that threatened the livestock at the family farm in Clearsprings, Manitoba. It was with a sense of pride that he took up a rifle at the age of eleven, given the responsibility of pest warden. He learned early on that by getting to know those creatures he hunted he would be most effective in maintaining this responsibility at the farm. His role as naturalist began with the rifle.[14]

Laing picked up his .32 auxiliary on the beautiful clear morning of

June 9 with his pack on his back and set off for Trail End. The eight-mile hike would allow him to inspect MacCarthy's cache, the food intended for the mountaineers returning after their assault. It was entirely possible that the cache, even though packaged thoroughly and hung on a high branch, could still be ravaged by the elements or wildlife.[15] Mac-Carthy clearly intended that the ample supply would prevent rationing, wanting "an abundance of food at all stages of the advance as well as the retreat."[16] The Trail End cache was small compared to the caches the mountaineers were redistributing currently, overseen by King Peak. However, as Laing was noticing grizzly bear trails, he knew it was prudent to keep a watch on the mountaineers' provisions.

As he walked towards the edge of timber, he planned to potentially move his camp to Trail End, at the lower end of the Chitina Glacier moraine, a field of rocky debris that Laing hoped would provide sightings of wildlife seldom encountered from his excursions around Hubrick's Camp. One possibility, the collared pika, occasionally seen among the rubble of slides, might appear in the debris ahead. He found none in the Barnard Glacier moraine, but he was keen to know whether a moraine above the treeline would bear fruit.[17] By Laing's reckoning, the pika was a strange little creature, an odd, shapeless bag of an animal, flea-ridden with a paper-like skin. He called them "hay-makers" because they stored gatherings of grasses in winter bunkers among rocky deposits.

While keeping his eyes sharp for pikas, Laing noticed another elusive creature, a grizzly, a half-mile ahead. His pace quickened to close the distance before losing sight of him. It was still a mystery what these large omnivores were doing prowling around the glacial streams of the valley. He continued to move as quickly as possible while still sinking into the sand with every step. The grizzly increased its speed to an awkward lumbering gallop, yet its pace seemed to be faster than Laing's. He now was holding the .32 with both hands, at a forty-five-degree angle to his chest, charging like a soldier going over the top; he was not going to lose the bruin again. Oddly, the bear spotted a glacial stream and began lifting its nose at the contents, slowing to a crawl. Laing got to within 200 yards and slowed right down before stopping to watch the bear as it continued to look down at the glacial stream. Laing whistled to him but got no reaction; perhaps the sound was drowned out by the water coursing down the channel. Then, just as suddenly as he had become transfixed by it, the bear crossed the stream and wobbled and shook his way in his ambling gallop up the bank and out of sight. Laing watched awestruck at the two front feet, followed by two hind feet, positioning that allowed it to cover ground at an astounding rate. He left the pursuit there and looked forward to his next experience with what he saw as a magnificent animal.

"Quick! Three Beers!" called the olive-sided flycatcher, distracting him from the earlier energetic encounter. The strident whistle, echoing across the expanse, kept him company as he strode across the sandbars, approaching the end of timber, nearing the Chitina moraine.

Investigating the debris for anything from pika to rabbit, Laing spotted a congregation of Dawson red-backed mice huddled around a clump of buffalo berry. He quickly levelled his .32 and fired, scattering the little ones, who, despite his diligent hunting about the sandbars and rocks, were not in a mood to reappear.[18]

Laing did add to his collection a female rabbit, a Mackenzie varying hare. Black was distinct on the back, the feet were whitish.[19] With no more to collect nearby, he reverted to his original plan of checking the goods cached in the spruce tree. As all canvas looked secure and untainted, Laing scouted the Trail End area for a future tent site, deciding to set up a secondary camp there the following month. He returned the way he had come, listening to his constant companion: "Quick! Three Beers!"

June 10 got off to an early start at Hubrick's Camp with the promise of a warm day. With a wake-up greeting from the young ravens, it was impossible to sleep late. After a rapid, meagre breakfast, Laing sprung towards Read's Slide and Tree Sparrow Point.

Laing heard a new sound, the rapid staccato of the young and the louder rattle of an adult male Arctic three-toed woodpecker, he suspected. Try as he might, he did not locate a nest at Read's Slide and decided to search again the next day, believing he was onto something. The warlike mosquitos may have helped him make the decision.

After the usual afternoon dust clouds, the evening wind carried some larger than Laing had ever seen in the valley. At 7:30 p.m., a great dust bank approached Hubrick's Camp with such ferocity and suddenness that he hardly had time to find shelter. While he was seeking protection in the upper area, the dust bank blew over his back and, he observed, continued up the mountainside. Inside the tent, Laing covered his eyes and waited out the wind that, before too long, dissipated and continued west. He noted in his diary how strange and wondrous these currents were that played in the valley.

The next day, Laing set out early towards Read's Slide in conditions that promised to be cooler and breezier than the previous morning. Among some windfall, he heard a woodpecker, and with sharp senses, searched out a male Arctic three-toed woodpecker. He examined it, seeing its sex organs were not very enlarged, indicating a non-breeding state. This surprised him considering he had heard the sounds of an active nest yesterday. He proceeded to climb towards Read's Slide.

Near a burn, he suddenly became aware of motion above—a three-toed on the wing! Raising his .32, he fired once. Down it fell, landing nearby. A quick examination indicated it was a female.[20] Laing looked up quickly, settled the female in his pack, shouldered the gun and ran off towards the burn. Within 100 metres, he slowed to a saunter, then stopped, listening. He was in a patch of burned spruce, a recovering zone from a recent fire, when he heard it: the staccato of the young and the near-bark of the father at the hole leading to the nest, about twenty-five feet from the ground. The pater was nearly shouting into the nest as if trying to settle down the noisy brood away from Laing's eyes. By his guess though, this late in the breeding season, the little ones must be quite grown. The loud chirp from the dad continued, reminding him of the bursts made by a red squirrel when on a tirade.[21] He made a mental note to watch this nest. The chirping faded as Laing walked slowly away toward the slide.

He soon heard a new voice, one that had him excited again, and clutched his .32. The red-breasted nuthatch was sending out his own sharp burst, a tone lower than that of the three-toed but still a piercing and unmistakable cry. By this time, Laing was enveloped again in the cover of the forest, but just as soon as he heard the song, it disappeared.[22] This would be another specimen to watch for.

On the descent into Hubrick's Camp, Laing secured one more adult olive-backed thrush, his last adult of seven collected since May 31. The tender rising song of the numerous thrushes continued to ring throughout the woods after the echoing shot died out and he descended to camp.

Laing sat in front of a small fire that evening, as the initial drops of rain fell, sizzling on contact with the embers. Reflecting on his day, he noted the new plants in bloom: *Amelanchier*, dwarf viburnum, mountain bluebells. Perhaps he needed to have a closer look at plant life; a flower day was in order.

The river was higher today than previously; this gave him pause as to its meaning. He no doubt would soon be chasing away another red squirrel keen as mustard to find a stray pilot biscuit. He listened to the thrushes and also to the ravens who had visited upon his arrival in camp. Father and children, accustomed to gifts soon after Laing finished making skins, bounced around in camp, keen to receive their supper. With his tasks completed, he took the offal down towards the sandbar, the cacophony from the family reaching a fever pitch, convincing him to not proceed as far out as usual before placing his neat offering in a pile for their acceptance. This was part intent, Laing curious as to how adventurous and tame the young would become in their maturity. Clearly, the family had now settled in the neighbourhood; the young ones commonly perched on the scaffold just ahead of the tent door.[23] Laing was now part of the family.

CHAPTER 10

The Prospect of a Rendezvous

The two tents were positioned in the sun next to the bunches of willow wands, sticking out of the snow in a row like an odd alpine crop that had missed harvest time by a long while. W.W. Foster, Norman Read and Albert MacCarthy emerged from their tents and prepared to set out, stepping into their snowshoes, beginning what promised to be a lengthy reconnaissance on this day, June 9.

While the reconnoitring party was searching for the best route into the heights of the massif, Lambart, Carpe, Hall, Morgan and Taylor continued relaying equipment from Observation Camp to King Col, resulting in the entire party being consolidated by the day's end.[1] Lambart detailed earlier that the "kitchen equipment twice as much as required. Heavy duplication of equipment . . . 12 crampons, fully 6 extra snow shoes and 6 extra ice axes." His sour mood might have been exacerbated by his poor sleep: "had a poor night—Carpe's 'bark' not agreeable and Morgan in grouching with the other two."[2] The quintet took down tents and left behind a small cache. With the sled well-loaded, Taylor alternating pushing and pulling, Morgan on the gee pole and Hall, Carpe and Lambart "as three dogs in harness," they started another day of toil.[3]

Foster, Read and MacCarthy snowshoed up the steep incline until the rough, jagged ice made switching to crampons necessary. The next

King Peak, June 9. The mountain was a dominant presence at King Col.
(COURTESY: WHYTE MUSEUM OF THE CANADIAN ROCKIES, V14_AC0P_535)

few hours introduced them to ice formations that took on nearly mythological status, a labyrinth that they had to navigate to find a route the
rest of the mountaineers were depending on to ascend the Logan massif. Perhaps it was the rarified air or the size of the ice behemoths, but
the men began to create names for these structures, should a rendezvous
be necessary in case of an emergency or foul weather. The first, a tower

of ice that dwarfed them, appeared unstable, but they had to pass under it. They christened it "Diamond Sérac." Following this, there was a passage, perhaps resembling a sill, or a window jutting through a roof, termed, with tongue in cheek, the "Dormer Window." Once over that, they encountered the "Cork Screw," an ice incline with a twist that the men faced down. Over the next few hours, they made their way through "Tent City," decided "Hog Back" was not the route to take and discovered "MacCarthy's Gap," which looked to be a treacherous passage, a snow bridge, a "sinister ridge to the stretches above." After traversing it, the men slowly negotiated the "Stage Coach," passed slowly and respectfully along the "Avenue of Blocks," and distinguishing itself from most unstable trenches in a glacier, the "Friendly Crevasse" took them on "a straight and narrow path to its secure bridge." Then it was simply a matter of taking a jagged downward path, digging in their ice axes at "Glissade Hill."[4]

They had done it. They had managed to cut a route through and around and over the clutter of ice cliffs, séracs and other intimidating structures they had viewed from the shoulder of King Peak at 15,000 feet a few days earlier. The men had travelled an estimated five miles over seven hours, rising to 16,500 feet.[5] And if they hadn't been working so hard to overcome it, they might have seen the environment they were in as staggeringly picturesque.

On the return down to King Col, the trio ensured that a campsite had been picked out at about 17,000 feet, where the double peak at the crest of the massif could be seen, then proceeded back the way they came, etching steps into the ice on the steeper slopes they anticipated would create the greatest challenge for men carrying significantly weighed backpacks.[6]

Lambart had led Carpe, Taylor, Morgan and Hall through a tiresome day beginning at 7:10, relaying to King Col. After pulling a heavy sled load to the bottom of the icefall, they slung 70-pound packs up to the col.[7] "Morgan and Andy preparing meal," Lambart recorded, "while rest put up 2 tents and get settled taking photographs as well."[8] With great anticipation, they saw the trio snowshoeing to camp at about 7:30 p.m. The expedition's future hung on their report.

MacCarthy, Foster and Read gave them much to be hopeful about: news of a practical route, although hazardous, that they had pieced together during their strenuous day. Crampons would be needed soon after the initial ascent from camp and certainly through the disorderly ice labyrinth. They told of confronting the various ice structures, climbing 1,000 feet, encountering a large fissure, down which, Lambart later recalled, "thousands of feet below, the rocky precipices of the south face could be seen." Lambart and the col crew all agreed that "MacCarthy's Gap" was an appropriate name for the snow bridge, leading across the "ice chasm" and through a slender entry, with more climbing and descending to the "upper plateaus" that promised continued progress to the summit.[9]

MacCarthy wrote in his diary: "Tomorrow day of rest—and work!" Considering the previous day's drudgery, June 10 would be more restful as they only had to relay "tents, grub, primus stoves, fuel, etc." from the caches below King Col Camp. Lambart wrote it would be "a day of preparation for the regions above." He noted how strict MacCarthy was being "on making up equipment and finding about weights." A decision was made by the leader and deputy leader. Four men would travel on two ropes. There would be three tents from now on; two green tents and a Brownie. There would be four eiderdown robes, four air mattresses and a pump, two Primus stoves, four pieces of cookery, three gallons of oil, six to eight pounds of food in the men's bags, eighteen pounds extra special food, one shovel and, last but not least, the willow wands.[10] The newly consolidated camp would now become a shelter should anything go wrong in the upper reaches.[11] Foster, Read and Carpe took up the load from the first hill on King Glacier, and Lambart, Hall, Taylor and Morgan took on the load from the cache above that.[12] In the coming days, they transferred equipment and provisions up into the newly discovered route, where they would test their knowledge of the bread crumbs in the form of the named ice structures leading to their next camp.

For your expenses on the expedition, the Department of Mines has allotted $1,300.00 of which $472.50 will be required for your salary for 4-1/2

months, beginning approximately April 15, 1925. The expedition has
agreed to supply you with subsistence and transportation from the time
the expedition leaves McCarthy until it returns to that place, computed
at sixty (60) days at six dollars ($6.00) per day, and you will pay this
amount ($360.00) in advance to the officer in charge of the expedition
from the money advanced to you. Steamer fares from Seattle to Cordova,
Alaska, including meals, are $78.00 each way, or $156.00 for the round
trip, and railway fares from Cordova to McCarthy, Alaska, $22.90, each
way, or $45.80 for the round trip. This leaves $265.70 for contingent expenses, including transportation and subsistence from Comox to Seattle
and return, subsistence at Seattle, Cordova and McCarthy both going
and returning, ammunition, films for your still camera, etc., purchased in
Seattle, expenses for instructions and development of films at Seattle and
incidental expenses beyond McCarthy. You will have to use your own
judgment as to the amount you will be able to expend for additional local
assistance in the field. Duplicate vouchers should be kept for all expendi-
tures, and returned with your account at the end of the season.

—L.L. Bolton

It had been a month since Laing and the expedition team had left
McCarthy and began their hike into the Chitina River valley, eventually
arriving at a remote camp named after an old prospector and his wife.[13]
In the light rain, Laing ruminated a little on the men and how they
might be progressing. Logan wasn't visible today, but he imagined they
were getting close, or perhaps they were on their way back, triumphant.
He was poking at the porridge pot hanging over the flames, rain sizzling
on the embers. Hubrick's Canyon was the destination today. He was on
time and ready to ascend for his self-prescribed flower day.

On the lower slopes, Laing's attention was first drawn to what he
considered the most glowing flower of the hills, the red-purple vetch,
growing in clumps a foot-and-a-half tall. Also in profusion was the
anemone.[14] He took samples of both for the plant press. Most evocative
though was the whiff of perfume from the patches of wolf willow, or
silverberry,[15] that took him back to his boyhood on the prairie.

In the woods, Laing was taken aback by something else: a goshawk.
It was a brown blur that swept in, flying low, apparently in the dive of
the predator seeking its next meal. A month before, at Young Creek, he

had seen one pack off a red squirrel as it soared away. Since then, the goshawk was seen regularly at Hubrick's Camp, but rarely did he witness one bolt out of the spruce like that.[16]

Another surprise awaited him, but one with less suddenness. Whereas his sightings of the Alaska porcupine had so far been in camp, having gnawed on charred wood, here was one, at the timberline, sitting on dead spruce twigs piled up against windfall. Laing had found evidence that this species worked away on the bark of smaller spruce, but he hadn't found one so contemplative and stolid. He raised his .32 in the pitter-patter of the falling rain and fired. On closer examination, this male was blackish and quite old. He compromised and collected only the skull from the wet specimen,[17] saving the remains for the raven family. It had been a flower day with little to note about birds, but perhaps he could capture the ravens' activity while they collected their regular offering.

Back at camp in the evening, while setting up the still camera, Laing's eyes were drawn by a motion eastward on Grizzly Point: a golden eagle. As usual, it was hunting low under heavy cloud cover that limited visibility in the upper reaches. He grabbed his .32 and aimed, but before he could get a clear shot, the trajectory of the hunter took it into the clouds. Although seeing golden eagles had become a daily occurrence, they usually hovered further up and over a flock of Dall sheep where the hunting was good. However, getting a clear view of one at river level was rare. In the few seconds Laing observed the eagle, most likely a male, he noticed the base of the tail from his upper side was white, plumage that reminded him of golden eagles at the Assiniboine River in Manitoba. He had also spotted this plumage on golden eagles seen with his friend and colleague Allan Brooks in the Okanagan three years previous, during the first half of the British Columbia field season.

The usual cacophony of the raven family rose to a crescendo as Laing placed the pile of porcupine remains a little nearer to camp. Not the types to turn down a free dinner, pater and the five young bounded into place while he ran back to photograph the gathering family. Father carved up the remnants and distributed them to his encouraging children. Laing was reminded further of that past field season when he and Brooks worked alongside Percy Taverner, Chief Ornithologist at the

Victoria Memorial Museum, and a summer student from Saskatchewan, D. Alan Sampson. He recalled how impressed he was with Brooks's
knowledge of British Columbia birds and how productive a bird painter
he was. Brooks, like Laing, was a skilled hunter as well as a naturalist,
who also had farming experience in Western Canada.[18] They had much
in common. Laing would have tales to tell him from this season.

After his own dinner, Laing settled at Grizzly Point and sat on a rock
waiting, rifle in hand. He had hoped for a return of the grizzly or indeed
the golden eagle, but instead, he sat in the drizzle, staring out into the
void. It was only as the mosquitos gathered in force and a territorial ram
got nasty, that Laing retreated to the safety of his tent.

June 13 looked much like the previous day: the clouds hung low, the
rain light but persistent. The ravens had him up and at 'em. After a rapid
breakfast, he departed at 9 a.m. for Read's Slide.

In the deep spruce woods, Laing discovered what looked to be an
eagle body, a juvenile, with no typical adult white rump, hung ten feet
up on a branch, and judging by its dilapidated state, may have been there
since the previous season. After noting the bare tarsus, he had made this
rough guess. Perhaps when salmon return to the Chitina, the eagles
come to feed. He thought it was a northern bald eagle, a bird he had not
seen since his railway journey from Cordova.[19]

On his return, Laing managed to flush out a common redpoll that
anxiously exclaimed "Swee-a-t!" Instead of swivelling to aim his firearm,
he thought this might indicate more than its own survival instinct. After searching in the burn, he spotted a nest on the charred remnant of a
willow. It was less than a foot from the ground, composed of the softest
of materials around—rabbit fur and willow cotton—and contained five
eggs. Considering the time of year, he judged it was probably a second
hatching. The eggs were light blue with pale brown and grey touches.[20]
It was a delicate and sensitive note to end a day's outing where the clouds
hung low.

The ravens. The ravens. The ravens! It was just after 4 a.m. when Laing
was up and around, and even the fifth of the young ones, the tardiest of
all, was there to remind him of his role as provider. They were all becoming quite bold. And if they weren't bold enough, the mosquitos were
bolder.

This day, with the sun beaming, would be a day of excellence; of that, Laing was sure. He had a great deal of energy and a drive to scale new heights. Perhaps then he would have escaped the mosquitos.

The common redpoll, such as the one Laing had observed the day before, was associated often with the pine siskin. Their calls were so close to each other that he found them hard to distinguish. Also, where the redpoll was so numerous, the pine siskin was much more rarely spotted. So when the long "Squee-e-e-e!" drew his eye up while in the deep woods, Laing instinctively lifted the .32 to meet it and fired. Seeing it was a female, perhaps of a late nest-building pair, he was pleased he had not mistaken it for a redpoll, or even a white-winged crossbill, which they closely resembled.[21] He settled the female in his pack, shouldered his rifle and pack and moved on at a quick pace.

Rapidly traversing up, through the muskeg of spruce, into the white poplar thickets, emerging into the open slopes worn smooth by the trampling of sheep, on through the willow and the black poplar woods, at nearly the end of timber, Laing slowed, raising his face to the sun, sweating from the pace. He heard a familiar slow rattle, his head turning to meet it with his gaze. He associated this sound not with higher altitudes but with the lower woods closer to camp, and he rushed to raise his rifle, dropped to one knee, aimed and fired. Shouldering the rifle while standing up, he drew closer to where the bird fell. It was an American three-toed woodpecker, a male, and the first that Laing had spotted so high up. Its back was distinctively white and like a hairy woodpecker, different than any specimen Laing was familiar with from the Yukon, British Columbia, Alberta and further east.[22] He nestled it safely in his pack before preparing to climb further.

He was above the treeline, past the slopes of low willow, around the cliffs, up the sweeping exposed alpine slopes to the ever-present snow. A quick spotting of a pipit followed, his glance guided by its squeaking, as it alighted then took off, a bird he'd not seen since May 27 at river level near Barnard Glacier.[23] Laing turned to see the valley laid out before him. The view was staggering: to the east a collection of peaks including those of the Logan massif, nearly clear but for an approaching darkness that looked as though it would envelop it entirely. Would the mountaineers be prepared for that approaching storm? He picked out a place in the sun, where an outcropping protected him from the cold breeze, to eat his lunch and take in this elevated point of view on the Chitina River valley.

Having had his fill of food and view, Laing resumed his naturalist's scrutiny, curious as to what he might find at this altitude, 5,500 feet, he estimated. Soon a flutter in his peripheral vision brought a horned lark into sight. He had seen these foragers delivering their tinkling flight song high over the valley, and so it made sense they would alight at such heights. Garnering stability from the rocks against his side, and resisting the mountain breeze as best he could, he aimed the .32 and secured two specimens. Climbing down, he collected them, quickly determining they were both females carrying nearly formed eggs, the last horned lark specimens collected for the Chitina River valley. Laing had decided that this mountain would be known in his notes and observations as Horned Lark Mountain.[24]

On his descent, the horned lark females still in mind, Laing came across a fascinating sight that stopped him in his tracks. At first, he must have struggled to classify what he saw. Laing had clapped eyes on a large whitish grizzly, sitting on a knoll on this breezy mountainside, admiring the view. It must have been even more of a staggering sight than the view of the valley from near the upper snowy reaches where he'd lunched. He did not reach for his weapon. As he observed, he started to reason why a grizzly, normally seen at river level, had adopted these heights as his preferred environment. The only similar colour he could compare the bear's fur with was the fleece of a mountain sheep. Certainly, his face (as Laing had made a best guess that this solitary figure was the odd man out, so to speak) and back fur seemed as yellow-creamy as that of Dall sheep but a burning question lingered for Laing: What was he doing here?

As the grizzly pawed away mosquitos, Laing began whistling and shouting in an attempt to move him. Although the bear was in no rush to leave his dominion, in good time he got up and ambled away. Laing noticed the whole torso shimmying with the motion of its unhurried gait; his whole coat, save its brown hind legs, appeared creamy. Slowly approaching the bear's domain, Laing soon developed an appreciation as to why the knoll was attractive to him: torn burrows indicated a prime hunting space for ground squirrels.[25]

The Lake Bennett ground squirrel was plentiful in these bald upper slopes, but Laing had also spotted them among the cliffs below the timberline and in the willow thickets. He decided these creatures had two major predators: the grizzly bear and the golden eagle. And whereas the grizzly found it hard to penetrate the rocky fortresses the squirrels had constructed to defend themselves, up in the higher reaches, their burrows were much shallower, perhaps due to frost close to the surface. At any rate, the bear had left evidence that a feast had preceded his lounging on the knoll.

Upon hearing a "Chit-i-git!" Laing sprang into action. He had secured several specimens but none from this altitude where the evidence seemed to point to an abundance of squirrels. In a flash, he levelled his .32 and fired, securing the last of four specimens. Its pelage showed remains of the greyish winter coat on the back, with a touch of silver on the neck and shoulders, but the underparts were starting to redden into the summer coat. The tail was blackish in the higher part and more reddish below.[26]

After adding the squirrel to his increasingly full pack, Laing became more determined to return to lower altitudes. Along the way, he collected several new flowers and pressed them securely into his full satchel. At about 4,000 feet he secured two female "hay-makers," collared pikas, one of which was carrying two large embryos, completing his collection of pikas from the Chitina region. He found it interesting that the usual cloud of fleas so prominent around the pikas' necks would disappear soon after death.[27]

His descent was hastened, as he worked his tired knees into the spruce woods, by the sight of his familiar whisky-jack. Keen to see their nest, he continued in their direction, but he became distracted by a myrtle warbler. He decided to secure it and, upon inspection, knew collecting the long-sought-after male adult was the best course of action.

Having unpacked after his busiest day yet based out of Hubrick's Camp, Laing wrote down a suitable title for the day's adventure, one that he might write about in future: *The Collector's Knapsack.*

CHAPTER 11

To the General Advance

Whereas the expedition's deputy leader, H.F. Lambart, recorded June 10 as relatively restful after the previous days, its leader, A.H. MacCarthy, described it as a light workday with caches being brought up and preparations made ahead of the advance. King Col Camp would be an anchor, a place the expedition members could retreat to should weather conditions deteriorate, as they were wont to do, or should another hardship befall them. It would serve as refuge.[1]

To illustrate the point, June 11 featured an intense snowstorm in the morning that kept the men huddled in their tents. Lambart described the three days ahead as "occupied in incessant packing." It was important that, with King Col Camp being established as their refuge prior to the further advance on the massif, remaining supplies be brought up to strengthen it as their safe haven in the days ahead. But those days would challenge the men to complete their consolidation work. "The weather was indescribably bad," Lambart later wrote, "and the incessant wind, the heavy snowfall, the cold, all added to our labour."[2] In his diary, he also admitted to being "a little short of breath last night."[3] The altitude was also beginning to hamper their efforts.

At 10:50 a.m., MacCarthy, Lambart, Foster and Hall set out to attack the upper levels, to reach the next campsite carrying forty-pound packs of equipment and rations, with dense clouds above them.[4] That left Carpe, Read, Morgan and Taylor to travel to the icefalls and bring the rest of the cache to King Col. Carpe rolled some film in camp, capturing Read slinging a sack over his shoulder and Foster packing another. But with the poor weather those days, little else was documented visually. However, Lambart snapped some photographs of the group waiting at MacCarthy's Gap. MacCarthy's rope soon noted that the snowstorm had obliterated the evidence of the earlier reconnaissance route, and they were glad to have a trail of willow wands to guide them, especially when the fog descended and a storm raged later. The thinning air continued to make progress hard going. Hog Back was as far as they could get, depositing their loads at about 15,400 feet, before turning back to King Col Camp.[5] Arriving at the camp by 7:15 p.m., they reunited with Read, Taylor, Carpe and Morgan. Lambart noted their exhaustion: "They just staggered into camp tired and done up with the heavy loads.... Mac had bad eyes which are being treated by Billy.... Morgan sick tonight & threw up his lunch. Carpe sick to stomach often. Grub lay out anything but right—All very tired and over done." Lambart seemed to be at the end of his tether: "If Mac doesn't let up there are a few that will not get through who otherwise could have done so."[6]

Due to the heavy snowfall and fog, they spent the next two days in camp, the first being an important day of rest, especially for those badly affected by the altitude and exertion. Lambart noted that the other tent's occupants "are going without breakfast" but that his tent was having "an orgy of food in which I am not much inclined to take part with sore eyes last night & headache."[7] June 13 featured a hearty breakfast of flapjacks, porridge, sausage and bacon, MacCarthy having established that they would have full rations the next eighteen days. MacCarthy took advantage of a sudden change to bright and sunny weather, and six of the party hurriedly marched down to the cache "for all grub there, gas and a few odds & ends," Lambart recalled. After a quick lunch, they returned at 6 p.m. to a "gorgeous spread" of Vegex, chicken, rice, stewed fruit, tea, jam and biscuits.[8] That evening, Hall recorded, "it cleared and a great sea of clouds below us to the north gradually thinned out. The sky was deep blue overhead."[9] The men, like a steel trap, were ready to spring on the treacherous route above, and "by the night of the 13th we were ready for a further advance."[10]

The next day, packs of about forty-five pounds were slung. Ice axes were in hands, sheathed now by two wool mittens covered by a leather outer mitten, some sheathed in a big windproof outer mitten with an extended gauntlet.[11] The men wore up to three wool shirts over heavy wool underwear, windproof and waterproof Duxbak canvas trousers, topped off by hooded drill-cloth parkas that reached below the knees for protection in the anticipated freezing wind and storms.[12] Snow glasses, some climbers favouring the amber glass option over smoked, Fieuzal and Crookes glass for its ability to allow more light in while still protecting the eyes, were worn, along with one or two woollen balaclava helmets.[13] The sun shone on King Peak and King Col Camp. The shoepacs were soon to be a thing of the past, with dry-tanned moccasins over feet swathed in at least four pairs of woollen socks with an inner fleece-like lining that helped ensure better circulation by allowing for friction. These were sometimes bound to what Hall considered the ideal snowshoe for walking and climbing in hard or soft snow: the "bearpaw shoe" that featured a "hinged toe-piece made by Sprague in Boston."[14] The last of the mountaineers quietly left their refuge, one rope departing at 6 a.m., the other at 7:15 a.m., setting out in the soft snow; the whole expedition proceeding on what looked to be a favourable day. MacCarthy was concerned that the new snowfall would make for greater avalanche risk on the steep slopes, but no sudden booms occurred.

MacCarthy observed that the soft snow ranged in depth from four inches to two feet, with a surface crust of about half an inch that allowed for some resistance before a man's weight punctured through.[15] But as Lambart lamented, progress was not rapid as they were soon enveloped in a storm that blinded them in snowfall: "At one point we made only a few hundred feet in forty minutes."[16] When the poor weather subsided, they continued to make distance.

The men who hadn't been on the reconnaissance mission remarked upon the size and scope of the ice formations, and as they slowly manoeuvred, step by step, up the tortuously steep route, they gradually covered ground via Diamond Sérac, Dormer Window, Cork Screw and

Tent City, until reaching the site of the Hog Back deposit, made by MacCarthy and the men on June 11, at about 15,400 feet.[17] There the expedition sat down for a brief rest and luncheon at noon, marvelling at the glacial world around them. Views of the peaks of Cook, Augusta and Saint Elias and the immensity of Seward Glacier appeared, and they watched fog form over the distant sea.[18]

The Hog Back cache was distributed among the men. Slow progress was made. Allen Carpe occasionally stopped to set up the Filmo on its tripod to capture moments where mountaineers, shrouded and dark against the pristine whiteness, slowly trudged through deep snow around large blocks of ice, leaning heavily on their ice axes, willow wands and snowshoes sticking out from their packsacks. The men encountered MacCarthy's Gap, a narrow gateway between towering chunks of ice leaning forward at a sharp angle, which promised to lead them to the upper reaches of the Logan massif. Carpe again delayed his own progress by setting up the Filmo to catch a wide shot of a trio of mountaineers entering the passage. Moving to a location closer to the gap itself, he rolled film to capture moments of exhausted mountaineers, plunging their ice axes several feet into deep snow and struggling over a step, before reaching the other side. He then tilted the camera upwards to show the peak far above, before securing the camera and tripod on his packsack and making his own struggle over the gap. On the other side, he set them up to film the remaining men emerging from the gap, grappling with ice axes pumping, as they came triumphantly through a near-arch that appeared like a structure from mythology, carved out by the natural world, a world gradually being conquered by the expedition team. Eventually, as the men edged further past the "colossal masses of ice" that surrounded them, they cleared the Avenue of Blocks after negotiating several hours of trudging through deep snow.[19]

Carpe continued to roll film at points of exhaustion where men sat down, collapsing under the burden of their packsacks, in several feet of snow, surrounded by enormous ice structures. He captured the ice structures on an ascent, then he rolled film again on the men as they ascended on their rope. One wide shot featured three of the mountaineers, in a static shot, the weather clearly deteriorating, as they slowly passed a sheer ice cliff, rising perhaps fifty feet or more to their right, appearing to supervise them in their plight. Several times he filmed the variety of ice structures: a sheer ice wall, a peak with three steep ridges, a cone-like shape or perhaps a cornice. These shots demonstrate a kind of frenzy in the man held accountable for capturing the conquering of Mount Logan, a man responsible for documenting the extraordinary environment that had never been seen before. It was a pioneering effort, a struggle beyond the climb, to frame the expedition in its triumph.

However, the deteriorating weather eventually pushed the mountaineers to stop, with even the veteran MacCarthy calling it a day as the snowstorm enveloped them in powerful, chilling winds and gusting snow at 5:30 p.m.[20] Lambart noted that, by 6:15 p.m., they had established camp, two Brownies and the green tent, on an open plateau that they named Ice Cliff Camp, just below 16,000 feet. His diary entry described: "Changing into dry as possible socks, & thoroughly cold and miserably fogged up completely & here we are camping at this height."[21] Despite the poor weather and the men's exhausted state, Lambart believed the expedition was "well content with the day's progress, since we had succeeded on bringing to this point three tents and sufficient provisions for four days."[22]

<hr>

Mr. Lambart, on behalf of the expedition, engages to see that you get all possible help from the expedition to enable you to make your collections complete, as long as your work does not conflict with the main purpose of the expedition; to arrange for your subsistence from the time the expedition leaves McCarthy until its return to that place, and to transport your photographic equipment and a reasonable amount of personal equipment during the same time. Owing to the difficulties of transportation and the shortage of pack-horses in the region, it is expected that you will limit your baggage to the minimum needed for efficient work in your lines.

—L.L. Bolton

His *Collector's Knapsack* day behind him, Laing spent a rainy morning in camp on June 15 with plans to make skins from the proliferation of specimens collected the day before. It was so cool that he felt the need to warm his tent, setting a low fire inside it. During the process of cleaning his specimens and hanging them outside in the shade to dry, he would frequently provide for the increasingly comfortable raven family. He placed the offal remains closer and closer to where he was working on this day. They took the bait when offered, becoming progressively bolder. After one meal, the family went for a high-altitude flight across the valley, soaring over the river.

Early on June 16, Laing looked out his tent door and spotted his old friend, the creamy-coated grizzly, meandering over the foot of Read's Slide. He watched him until he was out of sight, noting again how his hind legs were brown. The ravens were as vocal as ever.

It was approximately 9 a.m. when Laing headed for Hubrick's Canyon. While travelling up a cliff, he noticed it was covered in red flowers, so he named it Columbine Cliff, in honour of budding wild red columbine.

Above the cliff, perched high up on a spruce, there was a new songbird. Listening more carefully, Laing heard its "Tink!" establishing territory, distinguishing it from the "Peet!" of an olive-backed thrush. It was a male Townsend's solitaire and was an unusual songbird sighting. Upon establishing its identity, he raised his .32 and secured it for the collection. The satisfaction he had in finding this specimen nearly rivalled that of finding the wheatear. He later described its lively song as suggestive of "western tanager, robin, and rose-breasted grosbeak all in one."[23] He would not gather too many of these, he surmised, as he shouldered his firearm and packed it safely away.

On the return downhill, as his knees screamed in defiance of frequent climbs into higher altitudes and then strenuous descents, Laing noticed the passage of another elusive creature: the pigeon hawk. What an interesting little falcon! As it darted, too fast for Laing to take aim, he noticed how they showed little difference in appearance throughout the seasons and maintained their complete autumn plumage. Also, he was not able to locate their nest.[24]

The ravens seemed to have relocated. Could it be they had turned their backs on the nest and made Hubrick's Camp their headquarters?

Laing would spend an enjoyable evening with the family that adopted him. It was clearly a family of six now. Laing marvelled at the ambition of the patriarch. It was also clear that the youngsters knew where to find the evening's grub and watched for it with zeal: such intelligence! Laing noted that they did not fear him one jot as he brought out offal, and on this evening, he produced a new treat. He had shot a ground squirrel, and having removed its head and slit open the belly considered it ready to be served. Placing it not far away, he watched as father landed, flitted about a little, then, without further ado, pounced upon the remains, attempting to fly off with them in his beak. The squirrel body weighing, by Laing's estimation, about a pound, father soon realized the idealism in such a difficult, yet ambitious, enterprise. Perhaps he had watched a pigeon hawk or golden eagle pack away its prey in its talons, but he could not accomplish the same feat. So, he set to work unpacking the little corpse, unloading viscera, making quick work of it, swallowing a little for good measure. Then, he tried to fly off with the lighter remains but dropped them on a nearby bank. Landing by his prize again, he tore into the squirrel with renewed vigour and removed more guts. By this time, one of his progeny had landed near this curious dismembering, looking on, no doubt wishing for a morsel. His little wings beat and lowered to the ground, with his beak stuck out as he made his needs heard. But father was having none of it this evening, deciding it best to get as much out of this gift as he could, taking off with the lighter remains, with junior in pursuit after rummaging around in the leftovers. Laing liked to believe that the fledgling got his share.[25]

Although June 17 began in cold, Laing ventured out early, leaving camp before 8 a.m. He intended to find a red-tailed hawk in the woods between Hubrick's Canyon and Raven Canyon, knowing they nested there and most likely hunted under a canopy of spruce, unlike other winged predators that searched for prey out in the open in the higher alpine country.[26]

He had a first sighting of a fledgling slate-coloured junco, secured a female golden-crowned kinglet and found two new orchids in bloom, collecting a specimen of each among the moss at Grizzly Point while checking out an unidentified woodpecker's drumming. There were no new flowers or birds to report.[27] It had been a gloomy and disappointing day.

The ravens often woke him up early, and in the ever-present daylight, it was about 4 a.m. on June 18 when Laing decided to check the morning's temperature: 43°F (just over 6°C). The world was quite silent, save for his raven family and the occasional twitter of crossbill or common redpoll. The clouds hung low, and rain fell on Hubrick's Camp until around 9 a.m. when Laing set out towards Tree Sparrow Point. He still hoped to catch sight of a red-tailed hawk, but there were no birds. Seeing as how there was little to report in that regard, he switched to botanizing.

With flowers appearing more consistently than birds on this downcast morning, Laing directed his attention to a colony of a red-brown orchid that grew in a mix of rotting spruce needles. He collected several, intending to press later in camp. Looking towards the upper reaches where the flower fields were very prolific, when the sun broke through around noon, he saw new snow there. Discouraged from further collecting, he decided to return to camp.

Awaiting the usual dust storm, at around 2 p.m., Laing was in the tent when he felt a different disturbance: an approaching rumbling that seemed to culminate in something resembling a large gunpowder blast that pushed the earth under him. The stove, pipes and other belongings rattled, and the very ground shook. When it faded, he emerged and looked about the valley. After a time of eerie quiet, some faint tremors grew slowly in intensity and then faded off. Laing initially suspected a nearby rock slide, a large one. But as he ruminated on what he had felt, he realized he had just experienced an earthquake.

Anticipating further aftershocks, he tried to turn his attention to the specimens collected that morning. He switched from his usual skin preparing for his bird and mammal collection, and became more familiar with another piece of equipment: the plant press. He had found his first green orchid, a *Habenaria*, that had sprouted near his food cache. His thoughts turned to photography, as the noisy ravens had returned, expecting a meal from him. Laing decided to relent and depressed the shutter again and again, as the family ate. It seemed the father trusted him little this day, edging in once he had cleared away. The brood kept watch for food, waiting until father brought it to them, then they tore into it voraciously. It was time Laing prepared himself something to eat.

After supper, he took a walk with his rifle to keep an eye out for grizzly. His focus was redirected by the view of the slope leading up to the Logan massif. Although the day had been mainly overcast, the heights seemed to rise above it. It must be very cold up there. Laing had spent one month alone, and in the evening, he noted that milestone, the afternoon earthquake and his first mountain coyote secured earlier that day on the river flat. He determined it was an aged female that was clearly in a nursing state, indicating young somewhere nearby. But it was the sight of flat white worms exiting the wound, what Laing judged to be tapeworms, that made him curious.[28]

The next day, a clear one with the occasional high cloud, was mainly spent in camp, after a morning photographing typical flowers in Hubrick's Canyon.

Laing recalled yesterday's examination of the coyote's body, the cavity riddled with tapeworm. The stomach contents interested him: an entire Mackenzie varying hare. Large pieces had been quickly bolted down. Young, when nursing, do not ordinarily eat meat in pieces, but if they were, the mother would have brought them some of the carcass. Laing had never heard any coyote howling in the valley.[29]

The coyote was one of only a handful he had seen since leaving McCarthy. Townsfolk stated that coyote had been unknown to them until 1915, when, Laing would later report, "it appeared and took up residence." The pack train had met up with one at Bryson's Cabin back on May 15; and while Laing was making his way up Hubrick's Canyon on May 29, he saw a coyote below him on the other side of the canyon, barking defensively. He reported later that he thought it "to be a female near den, and this (was) borne out later when tracks of a family of young found on sand at edge of woods." He also concluded that the coyote here weren't much of an influence on mountain sheep numbers, as he had not seen any above the timberline, and indeed they seemed to be uninterested in climbing into the hills. Few coyote tracks had been found up to this point on the sheep highways. They seemed to prefer ranging the lower areas, perhaps capturing sheep in the winter when they were at lower levels.[30]

Laing also pondered on this clear, warmer day that it took two seconds to secure a coyote and several hours to prepare it for the drying board. His assignment today: to clean the skin and skull. While preparing the skin, he noted it was still the summer pelage, faded and worn out. The skull was quite large for a specimen of this mammal.[31] As for the remains: he had a plan for those.

Laing offered the skinned body of the coyote to the raven family, who had been making their presence felt, as usual. He placed it close to camp on a sandbar and prepared to document the occasion with the still camera on the tripod, at the ready. The little ones shouted encouragement to father, who began by carving it into smaller portions. But the ravens refused to eat what was offered, and with Laing patiently waiting behind the camera to capture the family meal![32] Perhaps coyote was an acquired taste.

June 20 was a much cooler day, and the cloud cover promised it would be a gloomy one. Nonetheless, Laing was off by 8 a.m., determined to investigate the area between Turn Again Canyon and Raven Canyon. Here he encountered a little ram, a yearling that seemed to have his old coat still clinging to him. It was not what he considered a handsome specimen of Dall, but Laing was drawn in by the solitary creature. He named him Napoleon, which seemed to suit him, perhaps because of his diminutive stature. "Come on," Laing called to the ram in as persuasive a voice he could muster. To his delight, Napoleon came up a few steps, fidgeted a little, then with renewed vigour closed the distance between them. Laing continued to talk to him, and Napoleon seemed to enjoy it. Suddenly he was within twenty-five feet and made eye contact with him, a connection that lasted a few minutes. Laing smiled, enjoying this link with a wild creature, before Napoleon disengaged and walked down into the canyon. He realized that the ram looked somewhat unwell, his coat all ragged, but noted his legs were clean.

Laing proceeded into the spruce woods, where he investigated some orchids, finding a dozen blooms in the moss. The new flower was welcomed into his collection.

Sudden motion high above Hubrick's Camp caught Laing's attention. A hawk owl! It was flying in from the valley, from the direction of the Chitina moraine. He raised his .32 and fired. The descent was so pronounced that he considered it for a moment to be that of a falcon. Retrieving the specimen, he discovered to his satisfaction that it was an American hawk owl that had in its talons another specimen, a recently caught slate-coloured junco, a fledgling.[33] Laing had regularly heard this junco's trill that featured such a variety of songs, but its capture by the hawk owl seemed to point out how hard life is, even for the most jubilant of creatures. After scanning the immediate vicinity, he located a junco nest containing one egg. It was on a steep slope, a beautiful construction lined with sheep hair, nestled in a hole within a bearberry patch. The egg had a bluish tint on white, with some tiny brownish spots on the larger end.[34] Such beauty, so delicate.

Even though the clouds hung low, Laing deemed June 21 an ideal day to be out and about. By 8 a.m., he was already en route to Aspen Bluff, not too far away from Short River. He intended to rendezvous with a red-tailed hawk. As fate would have it, he did not encounter one but did secure three other birds that would help round out his collection.

An eerie ringing whistle brought him to bear on a varied thrush. Laing had seen several in May at Cordova, McCarthy and Young Creek during the march into the Chitina River valley. He knew they bred here: he could hear that haunting, solid-note song. He had found his final specimen in the spruce woods, where that echoing tone resonated among the tall trees. Doubtless, he'd continue to hear but not see thrushes well into midsummer.[35]

At the edge of the woods, he had a first encounter with a bohemian waxwing. Indeed, he had found a small flock, a half dozen in a twittering band up on a high burned bluff, securing one adult male for the collection.[36] Still within the woods, virtually at river level, there was a lakelet, a pond really, where Laing observed with field glasses a gathering of green-winged teal males, their splash of green around the eye, on a warm brown head, giving them away. True to form the little ducks were congregated on a small shallow body of fresh water. He had briefly sighted one at the pond back on May 25, but he took his time and secured one of the males here, naming the body of water, as a result, Teal Pond.[37]

It would also be an important day for the plant collection, with Laing gathering some mountain avens along the muskeg trail. More successful colonies grew further up in the hills, but he collected several of the white-petalled flowers here for pressing at the camp.[38]

The "moskeets" were up early on June 22. They were almost as prolific as the ravens. Laing mainly spent the day in camp, working on his specimens. In the morning, he walked into the woods, glimpsing a Townsend's solitaire and hearing several bohemian waxwings. Finally, he was given a tantalizing hint that red-tailed hawks were still active in the forest when he heard one scream.

On an evening stroll up to Raven Canyon, Laing spotted six mountain sheep. Inspired to head out on a movie day, he returned to camp and loaded film in the Universal with the intent to record them.

June 23 began with the ravens calling, white-winged crossbills joining in at breakfast with their staccato chattering. It was a clear morning with little cloud, a promising day to make some movies. With a few offerings left behind for his familial dependents, Laing set out at 8:30 a.m. to try for Raven Canyon, hoping to find sheep where he had run into Napoleon. That was easier said than done as he was carrying, by his own admission, a brutal load of a movie camera, tripod and rifle.

Later, with the camera set on the tripod, partly camouflaged and focused where the sheep were the previous evening, he rested on a cushion of bearberry on the ridge, waiting for something interesting to happen. He recalled once having seen the creamy grizzly from here and wondered where he was ambling these days. He wrote notes, and looked up at his surroundings occasionally, deciding that no country could compare with the beauty of the landscapes in this green and blue terrain of the Chitina River valley.

From his bearberry base, Laing scanned miles of range with his field glasses over the next few hours and saw not a sheep. But there was some consolation in spotting two golden eagles sweeping along the edge of the bench of cliffs below. Their wide wingspans illustrated their strength and hunting confidence. It was common for them to hunt in pairs: did this mean the young were hatched and the parents were searching for food? The rabbits and ground squirrels were no doubt cowering beneath their shadows. The eagles were extraordinary creatures to watch on the hunt.

Rain began as a sprinkle and increased, sending a defeated Laing back to camp to protect the camera, stumbling in at 5:30 p.m. burdened with his gear and rifle in the heaviest downpour he had encountered in the Chitina River valley. He would return to Raven Canyon again to try to film the sheep stronghold, but he was flustered with their absence today.

Laing was amused, once the rain let up, watching the ravens as they again addressed the coyote body. In addition to father carving the remnants, the brood began to make their way in and carve up their own portions. He watched the family eat, admiring how the young had learned.

CHAPTER 12

The Conquest

"The anxiety caused by a delay," H.F. Lambart would later write in his report for the Royal Geographical Society, "is often worse than the facing of difficulties themselves."[1]

Dense fog and a relentless storm restricted the mountaineers to Ice Cliff Camp on June 15. The howling winds and heavy snowfall confined them to tents, with nothing to do and, indeed, the promise of nothing being accomplished for the time being: "all manner of alternative plans suggested themselves by which we could utilize the time to the best advantage," Lambart mused, "but in the end we held tight and prayed for a change."[2]

Checking the thermometer early the next morning in improved conditions, the temperature sitting at −3°F (about −19°C), they determined to make an advance. By eight a.m., the two ropes were breakfasted, packed, galvanized and on the way to climb from 15,000 feet and pursue the route to Windy Camp, the limits of the reconnaissance party's travels a week before. "We made steady progress till noon," Lambart later recalled, "when a sudden wall of fog blocked out all vision."[3] This would have paralyzed any progress, but luckily, with the knowledge that MacCarthy, Foster and Read had of the route ahead, after luncheon, the mountaineers followed with confidence. As MacCarthy reported: "Reached upper slopes of Glissade Hill in fog, everything obscure, snow

Windy Camp, with the Logan massif in the background.
(COURTESY: WHYTE MUSEUM OF THE CANADIAN ROCKIES, V14_AC0P_540)

very heavy and glare on snow strong."[4] After that, it was an impressive afternoon, as Lambart later commented on the achievement of the reconnaissance party, they "with amazing accuracy, picked out a route through a chaos of ice blocks and across an immense crevasse which barred the way."[5] The day's efforts by the team of mountaineers had both ropes reaching just short of 17,000 feet and, at 6:30 p.m., establishing Windy Camp. But for MacCarthy, the reconnaissance information spent and the unknown ahead, he recruited Foster and Lambart to "get a clear view of the whole route above. At 8 p.m. temperature was 27 degrees [Fahrenheit] below and the minimum recorded during the night 33 below, warming to 20 below at 3:30 a.m. Party all in fair shape but not strong for the work to be done."[6] It was clear that the altitude and climbing were taking a toll on the mountaineers.

It could have been that the next day started clear as a bell or that MacCarthy had decided the entire party would do the next reconnaissance work, but spirits started to pick up. The irrepressible Andy Taylor was up at 3:30 a.m. to make breakfast. Lambart had a good night's sleep until 4 a.m. in the eiderdown robe "& nearly every thing I possess on."[7] Carpe even started rolling with the Filmo again, getting some footage of the tents and scattered snowshoes stuck deep in the snow, panning across Windy Camp, to reveal Mount Saint Elias some twenty-five miles distant. Some hoped that they might even glimpse the summit. MacCarthy considered the day's climb "easy and slow going," but they sunk willow wands throughout the route, establishing their beacons in case the weather turned sour again. The climbing party positioned themselves looking east, having "reached the steep stretches on the back side of the double peak and then the saddle at about 18,800 feet and waited half an hour for view."[8] Their glimpse of the Logan massif didn't happen as the "ferocity of the storm and driving snow" obscured it. Some of the mountaineers descended, but others remained steadfast, determined to get their sighting of their objective, "hoping," as Lambart observed, "that from a point farther to the north-west and on the other side of the double peak which rose above us, a better view could be obtained if the weather should clear."[9] The opportunity never presented itself, and although some remained for an hour more, all eventually went back to Windy Camp and turned in at 8 p.m. Hall reported his exhaustion at the heights reached: "[I] felt altitude with slight headache and weariness, though I think the latter was mainly due to poor sleeping last three nights, for a quadruple sleeping-bag allows almost no relaxation."[10]

MacCarthy and Lambart came to a sobering understanding at this point. The mountaineers had provisions for only one more day. Most of their supplies were back at King Col Camp. They didn't have a complete grasp of where the peak was or what conditions were like past 18,500 feet altitude. Thus, MacCarthy had a difficult decision to make as leader. "Mr. MacCarthy rightly decided that the party should split," Lambart later recalled, "and while some brought up provisions from the lower camp at the King Col, the others should again proceed to the 18,500 level." From there, they could not only determine the location of the summit but also ascertain conditions and estimate how many more camps would be required.[11] So, on June 18, MacCarthy sent Lambart, Carpe,

Hall, Morgan and Taylor back down "to Col Camp for a good night's rest and thence to bring up big loads of provisions."[12] Then it was up to MacCarthy, Foster and Read to climb the double peak. After much lung-punishing toil, they reached the saddle where they had been the day before. But the winds were too strong and did not allow for much of a view of what lay beyond. However, they managed to get fleeting views of yet another double peak. MacCarthy's assessment was that "this evidently was the real double peak shown on the map to be north-west of the main peak and next in height to it, but nothing was visible beyond it."[13] The three mountaineers were left to speculate, while lying flat, looking over the edge of the saddle, shouting over the din, as to what lay ahead. Different opinions were offered, one insisting the double peak was their goal, another thinking that a struggle still lay beyond it before they reached the true summit. It was an extraordinary junction to reach, prone in the snow: the men were not entirely certain what the true summit was among the peaks of the Logan massif. It had to be addressed. Having exceeded all previous reconnaissance, they had to determine their own route. MacCarthy recalled, "we felt, if at all possible, the two highest peaks of the massif should be climbed, in order to be certain of setting foot on the highest point of the mountain."[14]

The trio's work was not yet done at those heights. They called the peak they found themselves on "False Double Peak," and further studied the terrain to the south. It appeared to be a jumble of very precipitous and fragmented faces, and was so in the direction of both peaks to the southeast and to the limits of their vision downwards. This was, as the men were learning, representative of the Logan massif east of King Col, and may have to be accepted as what would confront them ahead. The men were settling on this realization as they trudged towards the north side of the massif. While doing so, at 18,500 feet, they plodded over "the main ridge of Mt. Logan by a saddle" and made a startling discovery. MacCarthy, Foster and Read saw to the east "steep though smooth ice and snow slopes leading down toward the north shoulder of Double Peak beyond, an easy route for us to take and a good camp site at the base of this north shoulder."[15]

Lambart summed up how, through the course of June 18, many of the expedition's worries were smoothed out, and plans were made that would see them that much closer to their conquest of Mount Logan. "The reconnaissance of the heights beyond 18,500 feet was made under the most severe weather conditions," Lambart wrote in thanks to MacCarthy, Foster and Read, "but by making a long day of it, the party succeeded in securing a fairly clear knowledge of the nature of the ground ahead of us."[16] However, the knowledge of the trio's discovery was unknown to "the carrying party" that was spending the night back at King Col Camp, with the mercury dipping down to the lowest temperature of the expedition: −33°F (over −36°C). At Windy Camp, MacCarthy read −32°F when the reconnaissance party arrived at 11 p.m. Their discovery of a clear route and future campsite was significant, but also on MacCarthy's mind were the unknowns of whether there was a discernable "final peak" and how much further it was. However, it was clear to him that at least another camp beyond Windy Camp would be necessary to get there.[17]

June 19 would be a "day of never-to-be-forgotten toil."[18] Although heavy snow had fallen overnight, the day began clear and without wind at King Col Camp. "Andy up at 5," Lambart scribbled in his diary, "and breakfast at 6 a perfect feast of sweet things which we greatly lacked above."[19] The carrying party pushed themselves to their limits in deep snow and continued snowfall, bringing up the provisions that would sustain the entire party in the final days to the summit. The snowfall was particularly ferocious, and it was "an immense relief to all" when they met up at Stage Coach with MacCarthy, Foster and Read, who had come down from Windy Camp to help the exhausted carrying party with their burden.[20] Upon dividing the heavy loads equally among the mountaineers, the second rope led upwards. Although MacCarthy remarked that, during the hour that passed, "the temperature had been mild and visibility fair with occasional rays of hot sunshine," at the exposed slopes past Glissade Hill a storm descended upon them, dispensing a fury they had hitherto not experienced. Veteran climber MacCarthy described the change as "a piercing cold wind that blew the soft snow into a veritable blizzard and in a moment changed conditions from mild summer to arctic winter."[21] Lambart would go beyond MacCarthy's description, relating how, just past the site of Ice Cliff Camp, "the storm reached the height of its fury. Blind with the driving snow, every step an agony by reason of the depth of the snow and the labour of drawing breath at that altitude, we struggled on." This day tested all the mountaineers of the Mount Logan Expedition, having them dig deep within themselves to push on in the worst of the sudden weather changes the region was throwing at them. "We had reached the limits of our endurance," Lambart admitted, "we were at the point of retreating; but summoning the last ounces of our strength we laboured forward, and at 9 p.m. reached Windy Camp."[22]

After their ordeal, they had to dig out their camp from the deep snow before they could settle into their eiderdown robes and air mattresses. With the tents flattened, "several fingers were frosted in re-pitching them."[23] But once done, the exhausted expedition party turned in. Henry S. Hall Jr., in his paper "Notes on Equipment" published in the *Canadian Alpine Journal*, described the sleeping gear used in the low temperatures at this stage of the expedition. The robes MacCarthy and Lambart often referred to were "sleeping bags made by the Woods Manufacturing Co., of Ottawa, [which] consisted of two eiderdown quilts, a camel's hair blanket, a waterproof cover and a ground cloth."[24] In March, Lambart wrote a letter to the Woods Manufacturing Company expressing "the satisfaction I have always had in the use of the Woods Eiderdown sleeping robe. As you know we have used these many years and on no occasion have they proved more servicable [sic], than in connection with the surveys of the International Boundary line between the Yukon and Alaska where weight, warmth, and protection were the chief factors."[25] MacCarthy certainly was grateful for the warmth these enclosures promised when camp was dug out, and he mentioned the speed in which the others headed for the sack, with "all hands turning in by ten o'clock to secure the protection of our heavy eiderdown robes from the intense cold."[26] Hall further described the outer cover of these bags, "joined at the edge by clasps," that allowed for another bag to be clasped into it for extra warmth; one such bag was six feet wide, and "four men slept in it for twelve days, above 14,000 feet." But perhaps as an acknowledgement to the lack of privacy the men were experiencing at these heights, he wrote that this sleeping configuration "gave added warmth but allowed less than normal relaxation." Hall also pointed out that their eiderdown envelopes wouldn't have been as warm without the air mattresses that buffered the sleeping men from the ice. In the absence of these protective layers, he wrote, "it would have been difficult to have kept warm, so persistent is the chill emanating from an icy bed even through the waterproof tent floor."[27] So, the men gladly retreated to be enveloped in these many covers on that cold night, as they wrapped up the exhausting day of June 19, 1925.

Unfortunately, Morgan had sustained frostbite on several fingers during that day, perhaps exposed for too long while attaching footgear or refastening packs, but his feet had suffered the lion's share of the frost. "The sun lower down had caused snow to melt into the leather uppers of the shoe-pacs," Hall noted. When temperatures returned to freezing later, "it was found later that Morgan's feet were frozen."[28] Several years previous, his feet had been severely frozen, and so, as Lambart had noted, "Morgan especially had had great difficulty in keeping his feet in condition."[29] And now his previous injury had come back to haunt him, at what may have been, for him as a mountaineer, the worst time. Hall had also suffered from exposure and exhaustion. MacCarthy was convinced, with this new revelation, that the mountaineers "had reached the limit for safe or comfortable use of rubber shoe packs or oiled leather foot gear and must change to dry-tanned moccasins with an abundance of heavy socks."[30]

With Morgan's ability to proceed now very much in doubt, and the next day promising more drudgery to move camp forward from Windy Camp, a decision had to be made. By the time June 20 introduced itself with more extreme cold and stormy conditions, Morgan had made his choice. He would not proceed to the next camp as the two ropes progressed, but would descend. This must have been a difficult pronouncement, and its impact on the team must have been heavy news. It was perhaps with mixed feelings that they heard of Hall's decision to accompany Morgan back down, as "these men had worked magnificently" and had become an integral part of the team, but for Hall to volunteer to support his fellow mountaineer and countryman was a generous act.[31] As a parting gesture, Hall "insisted that he be allowed to take the

The team huddles from stormy weather at 18,500 feet, June 20.
(COURTESY: LIBRARY AND ARCHIVES CANADA)

heaviest of our packs on the relay of equipment and supplies to the next camp site which we decided should be on the plateau near the base of Double Peak," MacCarthy recalled.[32]

The mountaineers hoped that a great deal of progress would be made bringing supplies further up, making for an attempt to attain a new campsite, but the weather's deterioration meant more waiting. It was 2 p.m. before conditions favoured any travel, so thirty minutes later, while the skies looked threatening, they started off with supplies, leaving Morgan behind. MacCarthy thought this late departure did not bode well, but "it was imperative that we should make distance forward as rapidly as possible."[33] However, by 5 p.m., having reached 18,500 feet, they could go no further as the storm had returned, but they had successfully cached their supplies, ten days' worth, in a rock saddle among the "upper group of peaks where our feet touched open rock for the first time since leaving Quartz Ridge."[34] The crew, including Hall, who had made his last foray upwards with his fellow expedition members, arrived back at Windy Camp at 7 p.m., under a sombre sky in the faint evening light; all turned in at 10 p.m.

As Lambart wrote later, Sunday, June 21, was a day "not of holy calm but of fiendish storm."[35] "The longest day of the year," his diary recorded, "celebrated by the worst blizzards and storms we have ever had."[36] Overnight it resulted in heavy snowfall, with equally forceful winds continuing into the morning. At 10 a.m., MacCarthy noted the temperature holding at −5°F (about −20°C). Before considering taking hold of their ice axes, the crew had to hold a solemn observance, a little ceremony for the two departing members. MacCarthy made note of their contributions as "Hall and Morgan set off on their 150-foot rope down the trail with its first willow just visible, and soon they were swallowed up in the fog and flying snow, leaving us to reap the benefit of their many days of arduous labor [sic]."[37] Of their progress in the maelstrom, their comrades would only have guessed. But Hall would pick up their story of retreat in his own account of the expedition, expressing with gratitude that their progress through the blinding snow was only possible because of the markers: "The only thing which made this possible was the row of willow twigs, at intervals of about the length our rope, all the way down the mountain, which we had carried up and put in place during the ascent." They made it to King Col Camp late that afternoon.[38]

The fury outside the tents at Windy Camp continued, while the men slept. But at 3 p.m., "the sun suddenly shone out, the wind died away, leaving a world of dazzling white."[39] The calm woke the men up, a peace settled upon the white-scape with sun bathing the newly fallen snow. "All hands rise and shine, lash and carry!" came the call from their leader, and a sudden frenzy of activity took place.[40] It was time to advance, and soon the mountaineers were snowshoeing their way up, intending to set up camp at 18,500 feet, at their cache of the day before. Allen Carpe rolled some brief bursts of film, capturing the oxygen-starved efforts of the men, few willow wands strapped to their packs now, relying all the more on their ice axes for support, climbing in glorious sunshine through deep snow. By 9:30 p.m., they reached the site, put up their tents, and "after a wonderful meal prepared by the indefatigable Andy Taylor, we crawled into our bed rolls for a night of warm rest."[41] The accomplishment of "185 Camp" was not lost on the mountaineers, who had tucked into their dinner at their two tents with the knowledge that, at that altitude, it was "probably the highest regular camp ever pitched on the

North American Continent," as MacCarthy flaunted.[42] However, this knowledge was tempered by the fact that, at this elevation, every motion was difficult. The cold was one challenge, with the mercury dipping to −17.5°F (−27.5°C). Lambart was content, "warm with all on & my feet finally coming to life by putting on my mittens."[43] But, as he reflected on this part of the ascent, he wrote "respiration was laboured, and consequently our movements were slow to distraction. It was wearing on our spirits to see our route above us and yet not be able to do more than crawl interminably forward."[44] Perhaps his understanding of the men's limitations at this height seasoned MacCarthy's clipped diary entry: "Day not lost, fine trip, a bit cold but comfortable and camp alongside food cache, but not close enough for final dash if at all possible to make one more camp, preferably beyond Double Peak."[45] He recalled having slept soundly, as though he were sleeping at a much lower altitude, odd considering it was a day of relatively little work. Perhaps it was for this, and the general sense the others had a similar satisfying rest, that he would be grateful because the expedition leader knew the next day would most likely test them to the full.

Just past 11 a.m. on June 22, the men got underway. "This looks as if it were going to be 'the' day," Lambart wrote optimistically in his diary.[46] They left behind a two-day bag of provisions, but carried what they thought they would need: "eight days' provisions and our camp equipment."[47] Lambart recalled their packs being especially heavy, even though they actually descended 1,000 feet. "Vitality very low," he later scrawled in his diary, "and feeling this altitude."[48] They traversed a massive ice dome that would later be known as Hurricane Hill. MacCarthy remembered the snow being far lighter than during the previous day's slog: "the going was fairly good on snow shoes for about a mile and a half, and then the snow became soft and deep, so that at 2:30 p.m. we were forced to stop and rig Plateau Camp at about 17,800 feet."[49] Although this early settling might have seemed like a disappointment at the time, with only a little more than four miles traversed, soon a fierce, sudden wind buffeted them, surrounding them in a snowstorm that eliminated visibility and continued through the night. They set up their two tents at the edge of an expansive plateau of snow that descended to the north.[50] Unceremoniously getting into their eiderdown robes that evening, listening to the snowstorm whipping their tents howling outside, the men settled to their rest. MacCarthy contemplated their chances, with the ample provisions on their backs giving them a good opportunity for success, but the uncertainty of the expedition's completion was very much on his mind. His diary read:

> Had supper at 4 p.m., discussed plans with all hands and decided to take the first good chance for mountain. Have eight days grub and fuel for venture; could hold out for ten or twelve days on grub available, but do not think strength of all members of the party would last that long, for task ahead—probably two peaks to make—will be severe strain; must push and push fast as possible and then *some more*.[51]

June 23 began in a storm, the same chaos that surrounded their tents all night. The men peeked outside in the small hours, disheartened by what they saw. But by eight a.m., the wind diminished and a period of calm soon surrounded the camp. "We were wakened, however," Lambart later recalled, "again at eight by Mac's cheery voice outside saying that it looked as if this was to be 'the day.'" The thermometer read 15°F (a little below –9°C), up from –15°F (a little below –26°C) overnight.[52] The sun shone and preparations were made for an advance. It would be a day of exploration, for even the seasoned Lambart of the Geodetic Survey of Canada did not know what lay ahead. As the calm continued during the morning's preparations, "leaving us in a deep blanket of soft snow and a dense fog which enveloped us until about 10 a.m.," the men were deep in thought about the steps that lay ahead.[53] To harden their resolve, they prepared themselves with "emergency rations, a supply of extra clothing, our cameras and aneroid barometer" before pushing on from Plateau Camp, at about 11 a.m.[54] The sun now poked through the fog, and its bright light reflecting off surrounding slopes proved to be too much for MacCarthy's eyes, previously affected by the snow's glare, despite his use of two sets of snow glasses. With the leader severely compromised by his weakened state, "Foster took the lead, thus meeting an emergency as he did scores of times during the campaign when progress was slow or conditions became serious, for he was our sheet anchor no matter what the difficulty."[55] Lambart, remembering the tension that permeated the mood on departure, their goal out there somewhere, tenuous, as the view of the final summit had been obscured, later wrote: "Buried in our own thoughts we moved along, our gait the slow rolling movement of progress on snowshoes."[56]

After following the outline of a massive snow basin, tracing an ice ridge that had them descending slightly, they got within sight of Double Peak within an hour. Then, their course took them back up. The comparatively easy snowshoeing of the morning was now forgotten, as they climbed, "until we reached the base of the final slopes that led to the saddle between the two domes."[57] They rested, ate a little while sitting in the snow and put on their crampons, somewhat delayed when Read had some difficulties with his. MacCarthy felt able here to take the lead from Foster.

He set out on a course that took the mountaineers on the western side of the shoulder, going after a high peak within sight, about two miles distant. Without data to determine which peak was indeed higher, MacCarthy knew that both peaks would most likely have to be climbed to be sure. He recalled during his 1924 reconnaissance of the approach route, with Andy Taylor and Miles Atkinson, he had determined that one peak was maybe higher than the other by as little as fifty feet:

> I had studied the high peaks on the massif through my glasses from afar, and on alternate days had assigned the glory of being the topmost pinnacle to each of these two peaks; thus in spite of the map I was yet to be convinced by level observations from the top of one to the other before I conceded the honour to either peak.[58]

MacCarthy had worried over which peak would be higher, and now, so close to the prize, to the conquest, it came down to a guess. He consoled himself with the focus on diligence: one had to be higher; if necessary, both would be climbed.[59]

They climbed a half-mile on the western side of the shoulder. A willow trail was diligently established. At this point, with the steepness increasing, and the cutting of ice steps becoming necessary, it was a reminder of how important the ropes were for safety. Although the snow was ideal for crampons, the spikes holding fast on the incline, one slip at this angle of ascent could have meant the whole rope could have a long fall. Steel scraped against ice as the men moved, relentlessly, hopefully, upward. Lambart recorded in his diary: "I would judge the climb was under 1200 feet. There were two tops. We came over the first which was an ice hogsback and then dropped slightly to small ice plateau with little rook battlements on E. side. From here we crossed over something into a little ice col." While Read was fixing his crampons, the sun came out in a dramatic fashion, bathing Mount Saint Elias to the south. Lambart, struck with the view, instinctively dug out his Ross camera, struggling to free his hand. "My finger started to freeze immediately in the cold wind," he recalled, "& it was a frightful business adjusting shutter on to lens. I don't know what I got, I don't think any at all really."[60]

The sunshine beamed down on them, the sky almost clear, as one by one, the six men reached the summit of Double Peak, attaining 19,800 feet, "the highest any member of the party had ever been above sea level on foot," MacCarthy observed.[61] Foster and Read had got higher in the relatively new technology, the airplane. Once they all attained the peak, they got their bearings. The view was astonishing: before them lay the entire eastern section of the Logan massif, completely unobstructed, along with the immense Seward Glacier and Mount Saint Elias range to the south and southwest.[62] But a glimpse to the southeast was most revealing: there rose a peak slightly higher than where they now stood. "There, two miles away," MacCarthy wrote later, "with a 1000-foot drop between the peaks, towered the real summit of Mt. Logan, a sight on the levelling instrument confirming the supposition that the peak beyond must be a 100 or more feet higher than where we stood."[63] Lambart wrote in his diary: "On what we thought to be the summit we saw straight off east about 3 miles the real summit of Logan which up to this time I don't think any of us had seen before."[64] Now, with this realization, the men paid little heed to the staggering view and sprung into action. It was 4:20 p.m., and time was of the essence to cross that chasm to reach their goal. They would have to split up. The second rope of Lambart, Read and Taylor would have to follow the willow trail to retrieve a cache left where they had begun their ascent. Meanwhile, the

North summit, 19,800 feet, June 23. It was from this peak
the mountaineers spotted the true summit of Mount Logan.
(PHOTO: ALLEN CARPE, COURTESY: AMERICAN ALPINE CLUB LIBRARY)

lead rope of MacCarthy, Foster and Carpe would make as much of a
direct assault on the true summit as possible, descending in an easterly
direction to achieve the saddle between the two peaks. All told, they
had spent less than a minute on the peak. The second rope soon redis-
covered their cache, sat on the rocks, extracted their iron-fortified rations and munched while at "the bottom of the depression between the
two peaks . . . dangling our feet over the edge of the steep slopes which
dropped away towards the south, right to the surface of the Seward
Glacier, thousands of feet below."[65] The surrounding vistas were not
truly taken in, the food merely being ingested to fortify the final stage
of the conquest within their grasp. They finished eating and stashed
away their snowshoes and any additional unnecessary weight just above
their resting spot before pushing on with increasing urgency to meet the
other three mountaineers.

MacCarthy, Foster and Carpe were at the spot that their leader, during his reconnaissance trip in the summer of 1924, had determined

from a distance would make an ideal camp prior to the summit. It would not materialize as such but would make for a rendezvous. They waited in the shadow of the distinctive rocky outcrop that makes up the brunt of the summit ridge of the Mount Logan massif. The second rope, with Read getting increasingly impatient, "found rope one in the bottom of the valley resting along the edges of the rocks dropping through down to the Seward," Lambart wrote.[66] "In half an hour," MacCarthy noted, "we were again one party and the final assault began."[67] After caching their snowshoes and anything else they could part with, they marched across the hard windblown snow. Lambart remembered an icescape of ancient wind-carved forms, chiselled over time immemorial by punishing, sudden gusts. Through this fantastic realm, the men trudged, led by MacCarthy, using his experience in this land of hard ice, choosing their path, employing every opportunity to gain a foothold in the natural etchings of the ice, weaving back and forth to avoid ice structures that blocked their path. They had found an arête, an easterly narrow ridge, making progress along this less steep route, descended into a dip and gained ground along another narrow ridge leading to the true summit of Mount Logan. At 8 p.m., suddenly, without fanfare or ceremony, with "a strange feeling of unconcern, almost of unreality," they had reached the final steps of conquering the tallest mountain in the Dominion of Canada. However, a mysterious phenomenon now took place. Lambart recalled later in *The Geographical Journal*, "we were met with the strange apparition of 'the spectre of the Brocken.'"[68]

All natural history specimens and negatives taken on the expedition are to be the property of the Department of Mines, (subject only to such agreements regarding motion picture film as may be made between the Department of Mines and the expedition leaders), and are to be shipped as promptly as possibly [sic] to me here. Field negatives of a purely personal nature are not to be retained by the Department, and will be returned to you as soon as possible under the same regulations which you have agreed to in previous field seasons of work for the Victoria Memorial Museum.

—L.L. Bolton

Laing headed for Teal Pond again on June 24. It was early, about 8 a.m. He had hawks in mind.

He found the valley cooler and cloudier, and the abundant mosquitos were unpleasant company. Late June had certainly not disappointed when it came to finding new plant life for his collection. On the half-mile of old trail that took Laing into muskeg, not far from camp, he came across an orchid that featured a large, whitish, fringed lip that was dotted with red, by his account, a showy one, so from here on, he would call it showy orchid. After collecting some, more commonly known as white lady's slipper, he moved along and found that the area had become a neighbourhood for hundreds of this orchid in bud.[69] Interspersed among his showy orchid were other orchids of green, brown and yellow, but it was the lady's slipper that demanded the most attention.

Along the way, close to the river, Laing saw something he had not witnessed since McCarthy: a solitary sandpiper was stepping through the gravel. Could this be its breeding ground? What would bring this single one so far east?[70]

Laing secured a juvenile and a rosy, adult male redpoll.[71]

Not long after arrival at Teal Pond, he observed six sheep. What brought them this far down the mountain's back? Did the cold get to them? For much of the spring, they had been progressively climbing to higher altitudes, hunting for new vegetation, including mountain avens found above the timberline.[72] The cold must have been quite sharp and sudden to bring them down to Teal Pond.

Upon closer observation, it became clear to Laing that a beaver was also using the pond environment. There were willow branch cuttings, some with healthy leaves still attached. Although he saw none present, he noticed the chewed branches, as well as a hole dug in one side of the pond, evidence that would keep him searching at Teal Pond in the days to come for the beaver.[73]

After supper, Laing made his way back up to Raven Canyon with the movie camera, hoping to catch sight of the sheep. He found it quite cold and saw no sign of them either at the canyon or further up the mountainside. Where were they riding out the cold that evening?

With the temperature very much in mind, Laing decided early on June 25 to waylay the idea of an upper-levels expedition and set out for

Read's Slide instead. He regretted this soon after departure as the clouds parted at about 9 a.m.

During this outing, Laing revisited the nest of the Arctic three-toed woodpecker he had seen on June 11. After determining the noisy brood had indeed left, he felled the nest tree, a sickly burned spruce. His first impression was that, for such a relatively large bird, the nest was small, wedged into a hole in the tree, twenty-five feet up. The door measured 1-7/8 inches in diameter, wasn't round, and was larger than the passage. The parents had excavated 12-1/4 inches into the wood to accommodate the nest. The widest part of the passage, 4-3/4 inches, led to a layer of powdered wood and the skin sloughs of the departed young. After noting his measurements, Laing saw another burned spruce, and carved into it, about five feet from the ground, an aperture that led to a nest, perhaps used by the same couple to rear their young a season previous.[74]

Later, back in camp, Laing busied himself with making two skins, then rolled film on the ravens feeding from the leftover offal. After dinner, he returned to Raven Canyon for one more desperate attempt with the movie camera to capture the sheep. Fresh prints indicated a large ram had been by earlier. A northern hairy woodpecker distracted him, flitting in a stunted poplar stand about twenty-five feet away.[75] He lost hope of filming the sheep by 7:30 p.m., or so he thought, realizing his watch had stopped. He reset it by the low point of the sun for 10:30 p.m.

Laing was setting his sights on alpine country on June 26, again heading out early; the sun had not yet touched the floor of the river valley. The morning sunlight splashed across the range on the opposite side of the valley, and he had never seen Mount Logan so clearly outlined.

Stopping in Raven Canyon to look for any signs of sheep, Laing saw a ram had obscured his own recent prints. It seemed that the sheep had gone into hiding in the continuing cool conditions. Following a path he called Sheep Boulevard, he discovered a new lower pathway, which he tramped along until he crossed over an ice bridge, and jumped from rock to rock before finding a further sheep path.

Eventually, this led to the upper alpine slopes, and, lying there without a care in the world, at about 5,500 feet, was the creamy-coloured grizzly. Laing had taken to calling him Ephraim, or Eph for short, and despite his having whistled, hooted and hollered to get his attention, the bear did not even flinch. The knoll he lay on seemed to be his breezy spot to take in the air and sun, occasionally brushing away mosquitos. Laing kept his distance at about 150 yards away. Soon Laing moved off, and poking around the slope found fresh diggings where Eph had no doubt been uncovering ground squirrels. He seemed to be in a post-meal repose.[76]

Later, while finding his own alpine perch, Laing took in the pleasant breeze and studied his surroundings. During that hour, while the valley was clear, and Logan, like a companion over his shoulder, gleamed in the sunlight, the world was good. Then, suddenly the breeze picked up and became cooler, and slowly a haze obscured Logan's face, and the regular dust clouds made their way up the valley with the usual winds. The valley darkened. Laing descended.

In true Chitina River valley fashion, a land proving to be one of contrasts, heavy rain overnight ceased abruptly at dawn. Hearing a northern hairy woodpecker, Laing rose suddenly at 5 a.m. and, while still in his tent, shot the bird off the top of the tripod (the spruce poles leaning against one another, used as a food cache). He retrieved it from the woods behind the tent.

Once he was up, Laing, on that cold and ugly June 27, went up to Raven Canyon, where he had left the camera, covered, set up for future attempts to film the sheep. The camera was dry overall, with just a few beads of moisture, but he feared the rain would have damaged it and decided to pack it back down to camp level. He thought, superstitiously, that once he had brought the camera down, then the sheep would take the opportunity to frolic about the canyon again.

On his way back to camp, Laing decided to take advantage of a vista of the valley and set up the camera and tripod, rolling film while panning across it. When doing so, he realized the tripod's head was loose and worried that all previous filming would appear uneven or jolted with his cranking. Back at camp, he set to work on it, taking out some paper shimming in the mount, unsure what it was for, and reassembled it with a handy small screwdriver.

That afternoon, while making skins of a ground squirrel and two red voles, Laing wondered about what he could only term as "Alaskan moments." Freshwater gathered from the increasing streams trickling their way through the river valley usually meant clear-as-a-bell pristine liquid. But on this day, he got a viscous silt and mud mixture of the consistency of pea soup, perhaps gathered from a melting period of the Chitina Glacier to the east.

June 28 was notable for more than Laing's securing of a hermit thrush at the timberline, his only specimen from his time in the Chitina River valley.[77] In what seemed like an ordinary evening, he heard something that took him by surprise: a yodel and a shout. Two men staggered down the valley and into Hubrick's Camp. As he encountered them, they were almost unrecognizable as the men he had seen marching with their ice axes confidently aloft from Trail End. Morgan and Hall had thinned down considerably and appeared haggard. Their faces were sunburned, their gait suggested frostbitten feet, and they were starving.

As Laing would hear in an evening full of tales, while he kept the kettle going and hot food coming, the caches so carefully laid for the return home had been ravaged by bears. Morgan and Hall had been without food for three days. In between mouthfuls, they told of their parting from the mountaineers on June 21 in the bewildering snowstorm that had them on either end of a 150-foot rope following the willow twig markers. By their estimation, those simple twigs were the only way they were able to retrace their steps to the camps previously established. By the following evening, they had reached Cascades, stopping two days there to recover and tend to their injuries. It took them four more days, in which they had found the disappointing sights of several food caches destroyed, to finally reunite with Laing at Hubrick's Camp.[78] He marvelled at the amount of grub they were packing away.

On the morning of June 29, Laing left his guests to rest, while he continued to work the poplar flats for a northern hairy woodpecker, hearing its "Brrrrr!" It would be the last he would hear of this drum roll in the Chitina. He secured a male golden-crowned kinglet by luring it down with his own call.

The next day, Laing was up with the ravens at 5:30 a.m., looking forward to showing Horned Lark Mountain to Hall. It was a cool and cloudy start to the day, but as the weather seemed likely to deteriorate, they postponed their plans.

Laing, however, pursued his work in Read's Slide country, hearing another golden-crowned kinglet, spotting a Hudsonian chickadee and listening to its "Si-da-daa! Si-da-daa!" finding a female spruce grouse and her little ones in a burn just above Hubrick's, watching as two myrtle warblers acted injured to distract him, perhaps from their nest in the spruce woods, and seeing two young hares "as large as two fists."[79]

CHAPTER 13

Visitors

MacCarthy saw directly in front of him "a most startling and wonderful spectacle—the reflection of myself in the centre of a small and completely circular rainbow."[1] He had just cleared the north ridge leading to the summit, and whereas Lambart recalled witnessing this strange phenomenon at the summit, MacCarthy wrote about having seen it while still climbing to reach the true summit.

For days prior, the mountaineers had clearly been suffering the effects of altitude as they pushed their bodies to their limits, where light-headedness had been common and each step had felt like a major undertaking. MacCarthy had made the final cuts in the ice and reached the top of the ridge, where, feeling unsteady from his exertions, he was confronted with what appeared, or could be interpreted, to be a delusional sight. It was immediately apparent to him that "now I was possibly seeing the unreal, perhaps one of Nature's brilliant hoops through which I must jump when legs and feet felt like lead after their long ordeal."[2] As he stared out into the circular rainbow, Carpe and Foster arrived behind him, and upon spotting the spectacle, Carpe said, to the relief of the exhausted MacCarthy: "That is the Brocken Spectre with a halo." Foster confirmed this explanation of what they saw.[3]

Lambart described the men: "all appeared like little capishawned elf-men & it was hard to tell one from the other."[4] He offered no further details of the Spectre, but MacCarthy, despite his initial misconception, was enthused and felt privileged to have observed it, especially once other mountaineers described seeing it themselves. "This was a rare treat for all of us," MacCarthy later wrote, "for I believe it is the first time it has been seen on this continent or, at least, has been recorded." It was possible, however, that A.O. Wheeler saw a similar phenomenon on Sentinel Mountain, in Alberta, as recorded in the *Canadian Alpine Journal* in 1917.[5] Confirming that the whole party had made this sighting, MacCarthy later wrote that Lambart's rope had seen the same phenomenon, "each his own reflection in the circular rainbow."[6]

Breaking from this sight, MacCarthy saw some uncertainty ahead, with a fifty-foot drop visible in the ridge that led to the top. Would his route get them there? Would some unforeseen problem stop them so close to their goal? He remembered it as follows:

> The drop was steep on our side to the crack that opened at its bottom which, although presenting an open face, fortunately was securely bridged. The rise, however, on the other side, of perhaps a hundred yards, although almost knife edge, seemed easy to negotiate with our crampons after all the trials we had been through, and in a few minutes landed us on the summit at 8 p.m., where we all shook hands and were foolishly happy in the success of our venture and the thought that our troubles were at an end.[7]

In the National Museum of Canada film *The Conquest of Mount Logan*, just past the thirty-four minute mark, text holds for eighteen seconds, as if for emphasis, stating:

> Look out for this brief picture, the climax of the story. It took two years of planning and toil and endurance for these six men to stand for a moment at 8 p.m. on June 23rd, 1925, on the highest peak in the Dominion of Canada.

During the twenty-five minutes that the mountaineers spent on the true summit of Mount Logan, Allen Carpe used the Bell & Howell Filmo to record the men, indistinguishable from one another. The film

The mountaineers atop the true summit of Mount Logan, captured by Carpe.
(COURTESY: LIBRARY AND ARCHIVES CANADA)

speed makes it seem as though they are moving at twice normal speed, all covered in a layer of frost, the high winds buffeting their parkas, ice axes in hand, faces obscured and black in appearance, with the distance fading into a white void, one mountaineer clapping his hands furiously, perhaps to get his circulation going or perhaps out of enthusiasm for the moment. A brief shot shows four men standing as a fierce wind whips across them. Another is composed of three mountaineers, from midsection to head; one, perhaps Lambart, with a completely frosted beard; another hooded, smaller, looks at the camera; and to the right, a thinner figure stares at the camera, right hand tight to body. And within ten seconds, Carpe filmed the summit event that appears in the final cut of *The Conquest of Mount Logan*. Lambart went on at length to congratulate and thank Norman Read for capturing the environment with "a small vest-pocket Kodak, when the use of a larger camera was entirely too difficult." He noted also that "Bill proposed making Andy an honorary member of the Alpine Club which I heartily endorsed."[8] But he gave Allen Carpe the greatest of compliments: "Mr. Carpe has at all times and under all conditions made cinematographic records of the movement of the expedition under circumstances of great difficulty and hardship to himself."[9]

In this forbidding landscape, with cliffs plunging down thousands of feet to the Seward Glacier, MacCarthy took stock of the stages of their ascent viewable from where they stood, writing: "We veritably seemed to be standing on the top of the world with King Peak and many others that had looked like insurmountable heights now lying below us and appearing in the vast sea of foam as a mere speck of flotsam."[10] The men stood close to one another, still needing to do a few tasks before departure after photographs and handshakes. The large aneroid barometer, an instrument comprising a low-pressure range to use at the highest peak of Logan, that had been specially made by Short & Mason of London for the expedition by order of the Canadian government, calibrated by the Physical Testing Laboratory in Ottawa, still needed to be placed, and its readings noted.[11] Andy Taylor pointed out with increasing urgency that an intense storm was imminent. Carpe deposited a small brass tube, no bigger than a thumb, into the snow that contained the record of their names and the date, June 23, 1925.[12] They began the descent. A thermometer exposed briefly at the summit had read 4°F (about −15°C).[13]

Although the panoramic view was spellbinding, the clouds coming in between Mount Saint Elias and Mount Augusta indicated that another sharp change in the weather would soon confront the mountaineers. It was 8:20 p.m., according to MacCarthy, when they departed, Lambart in the lead of the second rope.[14] Using the steps MacCarthy had cut in the steep gradient, the men descended the ridge, eventually reuniting with their snowshoes. It was here that the anticipated storm unleashed itself with full fury upon them. Lambart wrote that they had stopped placing willow wands as they had run out of the markers prior to "reaching the summit of the first peak early in the afternoon, and now we groped along guided only by the general slope of the ground; we continued thus stumbling forward for upwards of an hour, though the time might have been much longer, in a fruitless effort to locate the end of the trail."[15]

Fog enveloped them, and powerful bone-chilling gusts of wind now increased the threat of exposure in the freezing conditions. "The situation looks hopeless," Lambart later wrote in his diary, "when we make a quick decision—about the only one left, namely to Bivouac!"[16] MacCarthy recalled it was at about 19,000 feet, approximately 1:30 a.m. on June 24, that they began, exhausted as they were, to use ice axes and snowshoes to dig into a snowbank, in a last-ditch effort to hole up in a snow cave, to wait out the deadly storm. "The storm continued during the night and the temperature dropped until the air was penetratingly cold," MacCarthy wrote, "the last reading of the thermometer before it was lost in the snow showing 12 degrees below."[17] The mountaineers later eschewed their work in digging shelters to bivouac for the night. "Foster, Mac & Carpe have a shelter into which they can get part of their bodies with their legs protruding," Lambart recalled in his diary. "By an unfortunate episode Read & I are thrown together in a similar burrow and Andy is alone in a smaller hole but a better hole along side."[18] While they had an inconsistent rest overnight and into the late morning, the storm diminishing into a calm snowfall, the mountaineers' extremities were getting frostbitten, and snow blindness was affecting all.[19] In his diary, Lambart described his great discomfort that night: "I did not rest long & had to sit up frequently gasping for breath finally I had to stand up to get relief & to kick some life back into my feet which were gradually becoming senseless." He had a growing concern that his feet were freezing, lamenting: "The 4 pair of socks had restricted my circulation and this night was the means of putting my feet in a frightful state for the whole of the journey back to Hubrick making me into a frightful cripple."[20]

With light somewhat less intense, but the heavy snowfall continuing, MacCarthy estimated that, by noon, the mountaineers' visibility was no further than fifty feet. How were they to ascertain where they were? Where were they going once they set out? The expanse of snow ahead was just a stretch of whiteness, making getting their bearings uncertain. What was certain was that the storm was not appearing to relent. Even with the men in such poor shape, MacCarthy felt they had to press on and, perhaps somewhere along the way, find one of the willow markers.

It was a risk, but staying partially huddled in the harsh cold was even riskier.[21]

In Lambart's view, it was clear that, by noon of June 24, staying as exposed as they were was not an option. As he recalled, "the conditions had not changed, and it was a question of hazarding another night in the open or striking out into the snow and fog, hoping against hope that just one little willow twig might show itself."[22] Around 1 p.m., they emerged from the "bear caves" where they had bivouacked the night away, and by 2 p.m. pushed on, carefully stepping downward, keeping higher ground on their left, crossing the slope. Andy Taylor had taken the lead.

To MacCarthy, their chances of finding willow markers were fair. He knew the second rope had deposited them between their cache at the base of Double Peak and a point en route to the true summit where they had run out. He estimated they would have required 100 more in order to have completely traced their route. If they could attain a point where they rejoined their trail up as they had pushed on to the true summit, they may come across one.[23]

Taylor cautiously moved along, taking deep steps with his snowshoes into light new snow. MacCarthy was buoyed by the fact the party was moving again, and that in getting the blood circulation going, and making these small efforts to get down from the higher altitude, they were making progress. He dared not think about what would happen if they were to tarry for much longer in these freezing conditions. He knew, though, that caution was necessary, remembering from the ascent that they were in a potentially dangerous place. Lives were now at stake, and as MacCarthy later wrote, "the greatest caution was necessary to avoid the steep slopes and cliffs we knew lay below and between us and the valley between the two peaks."[24] So caution, yet urgency, was required, and as Taylor stretched out, feeling his way across the surface of a glacier, suddenly he disappeared.

Before them was just a rope stretching out into a white void, but no Andy Taylor. Lambart and Read hung back, stopped in their tracks. Lambart recalled, "I will never forget the tired helplessness of the bunch, none seemed to care what hapened [sic] next, the ropes were all amongst our feet and we all moved like people doped."[25] MacCarthy, Foster and

Carpe, on their rope, moved ahead and looked into the expanse Taylor had fallen into. They could see him "some 10 or 15 feet below the surface we were standing on, and was safe."[26] With help from MacCarthy, Taylor was led up a slope to the right and brought up to the level of his rope with Lambart and Read, and they continued on.

Encouraged by the fact that their capable guide, Andy Taylor, was not harmed by his fall, MacCarthy recalled ribbing him a little by reminding him of mountaineering etiquette: "that it was not considered good form to leave other members of a rope without warning." Almost in response to his playful comment, not long after MacCarthy led his rope to blindly search for the proper route in the whiteout conditions, the team leader disappeared into the void himself, falling fifteen feet "over a snow bank with a proper rib-breaking check administered by Carpe and Foster to correct my own error." MacCarthy was startled but soon able to continue with his rope.[27]

The group was climbing on a slope when Read suddenly found what they were looking for: a single willow wand sticking out of the snow. "It appeared to us like a huge telegraph pole," Lambart later recalled. "Our joy was unbounded, and no words could describe the ecstasy of spirits which filled us all."[28] In this situation where lives were at stake, a very palpable reality if they had got lost in this raw, increasingly terrible environment, the discovery of such a simple, familiar and sought-after object as a twig brought about a kind of mirth MacCarthy believed was missing in them. "We knew deliverance from our world of cold, dreary unreality was at hand," he recalled later, "and we could again enjoy these things so long as we followed the line of our little black beacons in the limitless sea of white expanse."[29]

But this deliverance would still have to be fought for, as the winds kept apace and the sleet smote them with a terrible force, the men were at the limits of their physical abilities. Visibility was so limited that, although the willow wands were only separated by 100 feet, they still struggled to find each subsequent marker. And even though, as Lambart recalled, the practice became "not daring to allow the last man on the rope to leave the back one until the forward one had been found," MacCarthy's rope, after stopping to fix a pack, went off the route and became

separated from Lambart's rope, alternately led now by Taylor and
Read.[30] The storm seemed to have redoubled its efforts, enveloped Mac-
Carthy's rope and disoriented all three, forcing them to try retracing
their steps for over an hour. Their own snowshoe prints were erased in
an instant in the wind. It seemed MacCarthy's rope was on their own
and lost.[31]

Lambart's woes continued; his condition described in his diary:

> With no feeling in my feet & my finger tips stiff & general weakening it
> was tough for me, often having to stop for breath. Snow also a trouble &
> I delayed at times the rope quite a bit. My glasses were dark and the scene
> ahead was of two figures constantly silhouetted against a dead whiteness
> where ground and sky were one.[32]

At this point, on June 24, the men, taxed to the limit, began to lose
their grip on reality. Although neither mentioned anyone's names, Mac-
Carthy and Lambart both recorded, in their accounts of the expedition,
that members began hallucinating. The illusions put in their path by
their minds, perhaps grappling in their sleep-deprived states with previously known environments, would include the sudden appearance of a
wall of snow, seeming very real and palpable, but when they attempted
to touch it, nothing physical was there. Lambart described how "a wild
procession of fencing, barns, and houses seemed to be following our trail
on the right side, so realistic that looking at them one doubted one's
senses."[33]

Even though the ropes were separated, both had experienced similar
visions. On MacCarthy's rope, it was Carpe who suggested that they
not keep the rise of the slope on their right, but on the left, if they
wished to reverse their course and get to Plateau Camp. His advice was
taken in and agreed upon. By MacCarthy's estimation, it took possibly
more than two hours to correct themselves and "finally resulted in our
groping along throughout the whole night in a world of dreary reality."
It was here, perhaps with their minds searching for sleep, that Mac-
Carthy's rope also started seeing barns and shelters, structures of various
kinds that were not there and could not shelter them for the night.
Illusions of impossible-to-breach ice cliffs would appear suddenly in
their path, and they would simply pass through them. Inevitably, the

need for rest won out, and MacCarthy, Carpe and Foster were forced to take "two restless naps in miserable little holes we scooped out for ourselves."[34]

Lambart, Read and Taylor had stumbled to the two tents of Plateau Camp by about 7 p.m.[35] Awaiting MacCarthy, Carpe and Foster, they turned to fitful rest, with Taylor eventually setting to work firing up the Primus stoves in the small hours of June 25 and preparing their breakfast, but also with sufficient portions of boned chicken, granulated potatoes au gratin and Ovaltine for the trio still struggling to Plateau Camp.[36]

Increasing light brought out the surrounding peaks as the morning progressed. MacCarthy, Carpe and Foster rose, shook the snow from their parkas and continued trudging along, now with much better visibility and a willow wand trail to follow. Lambart recorded that the trio reached camp at 3:30 a.m.[37] MacCarthy, however, recalled his rope getting to Plateau Camp at 5 a.m., "glad to end our 34-hour ordeal with a fine breakfast prepared by Andy" and no doubt as warm a welcome as could be mustered.[38]

"In comparing notes," Lambart wrote, "we found that the other rope had experienced exactly the same thing." Their discussion after filling their bellies and recovering somewhat must have been full of the wonders, not only of their harrowing descent to Plateau Camp but also of the sights, real and conjured, that they saw.[39] "At 6 a.m.," MacCarthy wrote, "we turned in for a real rest, and it was not until 4 p.m. that the next meal was served, soon after which we all turned in again for an early start next morning."[40] Although Lambart reported, in a little more detail, that June 25 was "a glorious day of rest" but one "in which we could see to our injuries, and the storm having cleared during the night we had bright skies in which to take some photographs."[41]

In contrast, June 26 was a day of action, inspired by increasing desperation to get off the mountain. The skies and the mares' tails clouds indicated to MacCarthy, with foreboding, that soon the harsh weather of their descent into Plateau Camp would be upon them again, and although he recalled the party being awake at 6 a.m., the mountaineers were still not fully able to depart until closer to 11 a.m., perhaps because of their previous ordeal. Their goal for the day's efforts was to reach King

Col Camp, traversing 185 Camp and Windy Camp in the process. It was ambitious, but with the weather promising more harsh freezing conditions, the motivation was strong to put as much distance behind them and get to lower camps. And so, without much fanfare, the men abandoned "two brownie tents, mattresses, spare clothing, provisions and all other spare articles to the fate of Mt. Logan's merciless vengeance."[42] The campaign now seemed to be one, not of conquest, but of survival from the mountain's relentless punishment.

Lambart's second rope set off on snowshoes, following their willow trail. The forewarned storm was soon lashing them with hurricane force. This hit them while negotiating a climb on sheer ice to reach their former 185 Camp, or Ridge Camp, changing from snowshoes to crampons to traverse the hard wind-carved surface of the steep dome just below the ridge. Lambart recalled that "as we approached the snow shoulder (which was afterward called Hurricane Ridge) it started to blow up and fog up and when we commenced the ascent of the ridge leading to the 185 Col the wind increased in fury and the surface snow was driven along the surface of the snow at 60 MPH"[43] The drop in temperature was tremendous, catching some of the men as they exposed their hands as briefly as possible, to fasten what MacCarthy referred to as "their long, senseless, frozen tape lashings."[44] The sandy texture of the snow was quite punishing as it blew against the men in thick belts, almost like waves. This fierce sleet whipping against them, along with exhaustion, the effects of snow blindness and the increasing of frostbite, was making the experience atop what MacCarthy called Hurricane Hill an unforgettable one. "I am sure that terrible ordeal on Hurricane Hill," he later recalled, "will long remain in the recollection of every member of the party as the most dangerous menace to life and limb the expedition offered."[45] For the time being, the men were exposed, and with Lambart's rope slightly ahead of MacCarthy's, the second-in-command of the expedition looked back and created a mental photograph of the men at their darkest point:

MacCarthy, Carpe, and Foster could be seen struggling, so disfigured with ice as to be quite unrecognizable. Frozen to their beards and helmets protruded long icicles, tinged red in one case from sore and bleeding lips; they looked like huge pelicans beating against the storm.[46]

Although it may have seemed like many hours, by 3 p.m. all expedition members had found shelter in the protected location behind their former camp at 18,500 feet elevation. They still had far to go in their ambitious itinerary. After resting for a time in relative safety from the relentless blowing snow, they continued down the southern slopes, protected in the lee of a ridge. The storm conditions abated, and the sheer icy surface became deep snow, with the tops of willow wands guiding them towards an altitude that made breathing easier. It was time to remove the crampons and put on snowshoes, a simple act that must have been very difficult with several more frostbitten fingers between them.[47] There still were hours of toil ahead before King Col.

Lambart, feeling as "weak as a cat" with his hands and feet touched with frost and difficulty breathing, was beginning to falter. The ropes were now hundreds of feet apart, by his estimation, and the wind's fury continued. He recalled "ice formed about our faces and we had to tear it away to see." The hard snow developed a steep angle, and Lambart began stumbling, pulling Taylor with him. He recovered but Read, getting impatient and cold, suddenly detached himself from the rope and moved on. With no feeling in his hands, Lambart couldn't remove his snowshoes. Taylor was already cutting steps, and Lambart had no choice but to follow him on his knees. As they got over an ice edge and into a depression, he managed to extract his frozen feet from the snowshoes, staggering on, attempting to increase his pace but now too weak to keep going. Taylor held him up at many points. Lambart admitted in his expedition diary, "Mac said afterwards that I owed my life to Andy & perhaps I do." They soon reconnected with Read and met the other rope resting in a little rock col.[48]

At 2:30 p.m., the men found Windy Camp under snow, but despite everything that had been left in their previous shelter—among them a green tent, clothes and some food stores—all they were interested in digging out of a corner of the tent was footwear: the shoe-pacs or "barker boots" that could be laced up for later use after their days spent on the ice.[49] Some might have said this act was, in and of itself, tremendously optimistic, as they had many miles of ice to cross before reaching a point when they would not be fastening snowshoes and would be marching across rock or gravel. Their safe passage was far from guaranteed.

The Logan massif continued to fight against any optimism the men might have had at Windy Camp, plunging them into more intense snowfall and thick fog.[50] Any kind of spring in their steps shown in the early days departing from Trail End had been reduced to a kind of stumbling and flailing down the deep snowy slopes above Ice Cliff Camp.[51] Now came the stage of travelling the labyrinth once again, through the features diligently named by MacCarthy in his reconnaissance, when their clear passage to the further reaches of the massif was in serious doubt. This time, the effort seemed to be to cross as soon as possible through the zone of crevasses, during which, they removed and fastened snowshoes and crampons several times. MacCarthy recalled this test of the men's endurance, one they all silently knew, would get them tantalizingly close to their goal, as the hours passed into night.

> Passing down, along Friendly Crevasse, sliding the lower bit of Glissade Hill, wallowing along the Avenue of Blocks and passing Stage Coach as it seemed to be *diligence complète*, we were soon through the [MacCarthy's] Gap, had circled the Hog Back, passed the Avenue of Tents, and, carefully working our way through a new avalanche of ice, heeled down the Corkscrew and around Dormer Window and "mushed" rapidly along until we were clear of Diamond Sérac when, greatly to our relief of mind, we saw far below us our three brownie tents at King Col Camp all standing, although half buried in snow.[52]

Even a beautifully outlined silhouetted view of Mount Vancouver, Mount Cook, Mount Augusta and Mount Saint Elias a little earlier could not have distracted the six men from their descent into King Col.[53] They plowed forward in a desperate attempt to attain shelter, arriving at the three partially buried tents about 1:30 a.m. on June 27. The men investigated the tents to see how best to enter them "without expending too much labour in removing snow that had crushed in the sides and blocked the entrances."[54] The capable Andy Taylor, who had managed to somehow escape the confines of the rope with Lambart and Read to reach King Col Camp ahead of the higgledy-piggledy group, had already prepared the camp and set up for meals. The deep feeling of relief the expedition had getting to King Col Camp for some rest and rehabilitation, having completed a seemingly endless day of perseverance, suffering and determination against all odds, was almost as immense as the Logan massif they had just traversed.[55]

June 27 was a day of rest, one that revealed the damage inflicted on the men's bodies in the previous days. W.W. Foster began the unpleasant work of seeing to the men's frostbite.[56] Later on, accomplished mountaineer A.O. Wheeler wrote about the difficult work Foster did to mend these injuries:

> His comrades tell of how Foster, at the end of a day or night of such gruelling travel, would first of all set to work to doctor the frost-bites of fellow-sufferers; and how his cheery self-sacrificing manner did much to relieve tension created by the long continued and almost unbearable conditions of cold and fatigue.[57]

MacCarthy reported that they rested at King Col Camp for thirty-six hours. Foster made his way from man to man, taking care and bandaging frozen fingers and toes. He himself had two fingers and a big toe frozen. Taylor had one finger frozen, and Carpe had frostbite on two toes and two fingers, even with having not filmed much since the summit. The expedition leader himself noted how all the first joints on his fingers and thumbs were turning black. All of Lambart's toes were frozen.[58] Many of the transitions from snowshoes to crampons, fastened with exposed fingers, had clearly taken their toll. Wheeler further praised second-in-command Lambart for his optimism and inner strength "while suffering from feet so badly frozen that the skin had come off and the raw flesh was protruding."[59]

With the men barely able to backpack, they abandoned three Brownie tents and other items in King Col Camp that would not be required.

They knew that Cascades Camp, their comparatively luxurious base camp, would probably have food stores cached away for consumption on the return journey.

Their route now was directly down the King Glacier that would bring them back to a very useful bit of equipment cached on the ascent some three weeks previous. At the King icefall, the expedition dug out the Yukon sled, in increasingly deteriorating weather conditions.[60] In the intense snowfall, Allen Carpe managed to mount the Filmo on the tripod and captured five men, in their parkas, extracting the equipment from the deep snow, as a punishing wind pushed flakes across from screen right to left at a forty-five-degree angle. Using cached provisions, the men sipped strong tea from their thermos bottles and ate a cold luncheon.[61] They managed to get the sled upright and piled on their packs, taking a burden of weight off their damaged feet. Travel was good to Observation Camp, last seen June 9, where the men rapidly gathered up a few more items, including Lambart's bag containing a diary, and then, without ceremony, left the site, in anticipation of reaching the snow dome.[62] After a mile of trudging through deep snow, they arrived at the dome above Quartz Ridge. Due to the deep soft snow, they once again abandoned the sled and returned packs to their backs, having left several items that were no longer deemed essential. They reached the summit of Quartz Ridge by 9 p.m.; the sight of the tents below at Cascades Camp was welcomed by all. Two hours later, after descending 1,000 feet through deep, soft new-fallen snow, they arrived at the collapsed and scattered campsite at the head of the Ogilvie Glacier. Almost to accentuate their unstable surroundings, the men found the tents, equipment and provisions within were on pillars of ice, the surrounding ice surface having caved in. By the wee hours of June 29, the camp was in new-found order, tents repitched, with the cook tent prioritized, provisions found and "appalling quantities of food" consumed.[63] "With the two Colemans going," Lambart later wrote, "& this mansion of a tent about us (as it seemed after our life in the little fellow above) seemed heaven." MacCarthy had been sick to his stomach and was weak. Lambart recalled, "all miserably tired but realy [sic] happy at the thought of being where we were."[64] Read and Taylor turned in surrounded by the pots and pans in the kitchen tent. Carpe and Lambart slept in the cache tent "among the food boxes and dunnage bags."[65] MacCarthy and Foster crawled into a Brownie tent. Settling into their slumber at the old base camp, the men felt somewhat relieved knowing they were officially no longer on the mountain they sought so aggressively to conquer. However, that relief was tempered by the fact that they still had to walk fifty miles over ice and moraine, not to mention the nearly ninety miles after that to return to McCarthy, the end of steel. But for now, they could rest two days safe in the knowledge that they had accomplished what they set out to do, and the mountain had not claimed them.[66]

It is understood that the expedition is to build boats to float down the river on the return journey, and returned equipment and specimens may be taken down in that way to the railway, and then sent by freight collect to Ottawa. Mr. Lambart has agreed to pay express on Camera from Ottawa to Seattle and will carry such field equipment, traps, etc., as we are sending from Ottawa as personal baggage when he leaves Ottawa for Seattle on April 18th.

—L.L. Bolton

His ravens woke him early, and with light being as constant as it was lately, Laing was up for the day at 4 a.m. on July 1. While still in camp, he had managed to secure a northern hairy woodpecker. Examining its tail feathers, he saw that they were worn back considerably, perhaps three-quarters of an inch more than those of previous specimens. Laing believed this was due to movement against burnt wood. He had found that the woodpecker was a common presence in the burns of the lower hillsides near camp, as well as in stands of stunted black poplar. The only breeding pair Laing had encountered, though, was in a burn almost level with camp, but he had never seen a juvenile. It was interesting indeed that they were so numerous, but certainly not as much as the American three-toed woodpecker. He could tell them apart from their call notes and drum roll: the three-toed had a more musical call, and the hairy woodpecker had a quicker rhythm.[67]

After Morgan and Hall staggered into Hubrick's Camp, Laing had left them to their own devices, and recovery, and on July 2, he proceeded apace, departing on a search for recently heard, but not seen, Townsend's solitaire. Since securing one specimen on June 16, he had been unsuccessful in capturing another, but had heard the song, a "Tink! Tink!" that implied a combination of western tanager, robin and rose-breasted grosbeak.[68] He spotted young slate-coloured juncos, the first seen without parental supervision.[69] Through field glasses, Laing detected a sight exclusive to the southern slopes above the timberline, opposite Barnard Glacier: mountain goats.

It had been a perfect, clear day in Laing's view. So picturesque that, upon returning to Hubrick's Camp, he rounded up his motion picture and still photography equipment and spent some time capturing flowers near camp. The floral life was extraordinary here, with new additions to the collection being gathered almost every day. From anemones to fireweed to dryas, the upper Chitina River valley was a glorious mix of colours, whether in the burns, along the riverbank or in the canyon.[70] Laing rolled film moving up from the third to the fourth bench of the canyon, before stopping the camera and taking in his surroundings. The air had a clarity on this day that rivalled any he had experienced, with a hint of autumn in it.

The next day was also clear, and Hall asked Laing to join him in searching for timber, not finding a woodpecker's nest, which would have been Laing's routine, but to find material to construct watercraft. Boats could be a means to travel by river to McCarthy, and although the water levels had risen, they were not high enough for a deep-draft vessel. Hall conferred with Laing about where to look for sturdy planks. After breakfast, they marched to what Laing called Tree Sparrow Point and the Cutoff Trail. Hall was impressed, aware of Laing's knowledge of the region and the names attributed to landmarks that he was clearly well-acquainted with. Laing in turn would learn that Hall became keen about mountaineering on a visit to Switzerland while still in his teens, was an infantry officer in World War 1 and became a member of the American Alpine Club at war's end.

Hiking Cutoff Trail took them past glorious collections of little white lady's slipper orchids in bloom, but as Laing showed off his plant knowledge and pointed out the diverse profusion of flowers, he noted no new species. They pressed on along the trail that brought them to Teal Pond, where he would impress Hall with its variety of birds and animals. It did not disappoint, as Laing saw the pond was inhabited this morning. This was an opportunity not only to gather more specimens for Laing's collection but also to show Hall what he did while the mountaineers had been engaged in their assault on the massif. Crouching down, Laing pointed out a white-winged scoter, an auspicious start to his tour for Hall's benefit. Without further ado, Laing raised his .32 and shot it, proclaiming the rarity of this find, his first encounter with the species. Laing and Hall rounded the lake to retrieve what would prove to be an aging female. But as Laing showed Hall, this was a well-fed specimen, with a longer than usual bill on an almost completely black head, with a few light spots adding some colour.[71] He stowed his specimen away, and as Hall looked on, said that he would make a skin of her back at Hubrick's Camp. Before long Laing had made similar finds, securing a lesser yellowlegs adult male and a juvenile female sandpiper, impressing Hall with his marksmanship and ornithological knowledge.[72]

Unfortunately, the search for boat construction material did not impress Hall as much. As they returned to camp, the "quittering" heard off in the woods somewhere that Laing cheerfully mentioned was found to be from an American three-toed woodpecker, Hall brooded on the time and labour required to fell and create lumber and then construct a vessel that could transport himself and the beleaguered Morgan back to the civilization of McCarthy. Perhaps with some more rest, Morgan might be well enough to hike through the valley.

As Laing demonstrated to Hall and Morgan his process of making skins, this time for the fat scoter, the usual afternoon dust cloud careened down the valley, interrupting the sunny day.

On July 4, Laing left Hall with Morgan. Clouds hung about the mountains on the south slope, and he set out with determination for Wheatear Mountain. The red-tailed hawk was a gaping hole in his collection, one he intended to fill. But beyond securing a young white-crowned sparrow and a Townsend's solitaire, a bird that he found quite a challenge to locate and capture, he had very little to report.

The following day, warmer and mostly clear, Laing set out early to once again reach the three-toed woodpecker nest he examined near Tree Sparrow Point. His searching eye found a cornucopia of birds: whisky-jacks, various thrushes, white-winged crossbills, myrtle warblers, redpolls and pine siskin.

The evening's search near the river would feature a memorable moment in Laing's time in the valley. After spotting a red-tail, he fired his .32, securing what he determined was an adult female, still with the brown tail of a juvenile's plumage. Although the specimen was part of a pair hunting over the lower slopes near Hubrick's, Laing's analysis confirmed the bird was not breeding. He scribbled down a description of its colours: "Iris rich brown. No yellow in bill; tip blackish, base more bluish, cere and gape greenish. Toes and tarsus pale yellowish grey—not strongly yellow."[73] Laing packed his notebook and prize securely in his pack, shouldered his rifle and strode back to camp.

In his determination to capture the prize red-tail, it had slipped his mind that Hall and Morgan were leaving on foot in the morning, and he found them in the midst of their packing for the return to civilization. He interrupted them long enough to scribble down their addresses: Henry S. Hall Jr., 472 Beacon St., Boston and Robert M. Morgan, 619 Downer St., Mill.

They had a long journey ahead of them. Had they recovered sufficiently to take in the rough miles to McCarthy?

On July 6, all were up at 4 a.m. with the ravens, and in the perpetual light, Laing, Hall and Morgan prepared for the day ahead. They took to the trail at 8 a.m., arriving soon at the beginning of Cutoff Trail where, among a scattering of juncos and redpolls, Laing spotted a family of brown-headed chickadees, and he quickly secured an adult specimen. On stowing it, he reflected on having seen these chickadees in camp that morning and several more besides.

The trio marched across the burned ridge above Teal Pond, and almost as though to signal the time for parting, a red-tailed hawk flew by at close range, screaming its familiar call. Laing shook hands with both men, who seemed to be weathering their injuries with aplomb and resolve, wished them luck and watched them go. Morgan's pack looked particularly heavy considering the severity of the frostbite on his feet. He hoped they could find shelter at Short River before evening.

On his way back to camp, at Tree Sparrow Point, Laing heard two shots echo through the valley. His head jerked at the sound that had come from the east. He doubled-timed it back towards Hubrick's Camp. What he saw as he approached took him by surprise, especially because he had just set two of the mountaineers off on their trek to McCarthy.

It was Norman Read.

And he was alone.

CHAPTER 14

Putting the Ice Behind Them

As on all expeditions of this kind into regions far from civilization, many contingencies can not be foreseen, and success depends upon loyalty and co-operation between the members of the expedition and the leaders. You will accordingly be subject to the orders of the leader of the expedition or his deputed authority, subject to mutual understandings exchanged between the Department of Mines and the expedition that the expedition assist you in collecting natural history specimens and that you act as photographer for the expedition.

—L.L. Bolton

The mountaineers could now afford to allow themselves the comfort they had earned, and they celebrated having escaped Logan's wrath. June 29 and 30 were days of rest and recuperation, at Cascades Camp, a place of relative luxury compared to what they had encountered on their descent. There were times the men warmed themselves in the sun, like cats purring on a windowsill. There were times they were tended to by Foster, their intrepid medic, who saw not only to Lambart's severely frostbitten toes but also to MacCarthy's snow-blinded eyes, which were giving him pain. They all got back into the practice of washing themselves in the morning. They drank copious amounts of water as they had access to their larger oil stoves for melting snow. As Lambart later wrote,

Foster dressing Carpe's frozen fingers at Cascades Camp.
MacCarthy awaiting treatment for his snow-blinded eyes. June 29-30.
(COURTESY: WHYTE MUSEUM OF THE CANADIAN ROCKIES, V14_AC0P_550)

they "celebrated in royal style the conquest of Mount Logan: the celebra-
tion consisted in dining largely upon almost every conceivable delicacy
that the genius of man has contrived to put up in a can, and in sleeping
at great length."[1] But to Foster, a disciplined lieutenant-colonel who
had accompanied the now-beleaguered expedition leader MacCarthy
up Mount Robson, the mountain had not allowed them to escape unscathed, that much was certain.[2] They needed more medical attention,
especially MacCarthy and Lambart, once they reached McCarthy. The
trek before them involved traversing glaciers, and although MacCarthy
and Foster exchanged light-hearted comments about their situation, the
two military men knew the reality of the next few difficult days.

However, with Foster's care and after two days' rest, the mountaineers
felt renewed confidence they could make the remaining miles to get them
off the ice. Before departure, to cheer everyone up, Lambart snapped a

photograph of five of them in the cook tent, with Coleman and Primus stoves working and the food boxes. Any cheer, though, was dulled by Lambart's ongoing pain. "My feet terribly sore and of little use to others."[3] Fog delayed their departure from Advance Base Camp, but by 8 a.m., they left, sliding two loaded sleds. Along their travels on that Dominion Day, they found meltwater, and the sight of a bird was cause to stop a moment and marvel at seeing another living thing.[4] At 6:20 p.m., they had reached the rocks of the moraine at Turn Camp, an extraordinary vista for the mountaineers who had spent so much time on the snow and ice.[5] This also meant a distinct shift in direction, a westward course that would bring them back into Alaska at Boundary Camp and eventually Trail End and Hubrick's Camp where the biologist Laing was stationed.

Lambart was woken up by a raven croaking at the door of the eight-by-ten silk tent also occupied by Carpe, Taylor and Read. MacCarthy and Foster were in a Brownie. "Clear beautiful, warm day," Lambart wrote in his diary, "and most of it spent asleep in the sun on mattress spread out on moraine." Even while recuperating, he reported his "feet terribly bad."[6] In increasingly wet conditions, they determined that travel during the day was not safe on the Logan Glacier. After Taylor brought them in for supper at 6 p.m., they cleared up and cached the sleeping robes, snowshoes, food for eight for a week, large tent and stoves that Taylor planned to salvage later. It wasn't until 9 p.m. on July 2 that the mountaineers departed Turn Camp, continuing to use the sleds across the crust formed on the snow in colder temperatures. Although this was easier to traverse, some toil was required as the sleds could not negotiate the rock and debris of the moraines, forcing the mountaineers to relay loads.

Stopping was necessary at about noon on July 3 as pulling the sleds across the Logan Glacier was deemed to be impossible.[7] "Mac pretty low," Lambart wrote, "sleeping on sled until ready to start."[8] They had to abandon the sleds and shoulder their packs, leaving behind an oil stove and other pieces of equipment too difficult to carry. After a brief rest, the afternoon featured more travel down the glacier to where they would bivouac "a mile beyond the end of the Boundary mountain point."[9]

MacCarthy, Carpe and Foster resting after their ordeal,
Cascades Camp, June 29-30. They did not escape unscathed.
(COURTESY: WHYTE MUSEUM OF THE CANADIAN ROCKIES, V14_AC0P_553)

Travel had been slow, and even without sleds, would continue to be slow
with additional weight supported on frostbitten feet. However, they
knew a cache with food stored for the return trip would be reachable by
the next day at Fraser Baldwin Cache.

Trudging along the glacier, the mountaineers were disappointed with
what they saw by noon. A bear, or bears, had apparently managed to
break into the bear-proof cache the men had been looking forward to
accessing; only a basic meal could be salvaged from leftovers.[10] Read,
who had arrived the previous evening, was warming himself over a fire.
The mountaineers spent four hours at this site, hopeful that the next
cache, at Chitina Point (Walsh Camp), would still be intact. But before
getting there, Foster acknowledged their accomplishment observable in
the changing surroundings and surface that they walked on: "tremendous pleasure was obtained in stepping off the glacier to the green carpet

of vegetation at its side, the first seen after forty-four days spent upon ice."[11] Lambart also wrote with feeling about finally being on terra firma: "The ecstasy of being once more amongst the green shrubbery and of feeling the soft turf underfoot cannot be understood except by those who have had a similar experience."[12]

After a while they stopped for a meagre helping of the remaining sardines, veal loaf and tea.

Unfortunately, the enjoyment of being officially off the ice was reduced by the sight of yet another wrecked food and supply cache: another bear, or bears, had destroyed the carefully laid and protected cache that MacCarthy's freighting expedition had left for their return journey. It was 1 a.m. on July 5. Exhausted, the mountaineers rested, only resuming their westward journey at noon. Hungry and increasingly desperate, frostbitten feet aching from the relentless pressure, the men hoped against hope that a cache at Trail End would be intact. "Although the journey being only 6 miles it was a long & dreary pull," Lambart later wrote, "and at the same time having a sneaking feeling that Laing may not have left food there for us."[13] At about 7:30 p.m., they slowly approached Trail End and saw, to their immense relief, dangling from the tree branch, the food cache that Laing had placed there.[14]

After a warm meal in their bellies, and the luxury of a campfire, the mountaineers enjoyed the kind of deep sleep they could only have dreamt of but a few days ago. The relative safety of Hubrick's Camp was only eight miles away.[15]

Later in the morning of July 6, the men roused themselves back onto their feet and committed themselves to the hike along the sandbars of the Chitina River valley. Norman Read, a man lighter since departing Hubrick's Camp on May 18 but still athletically built and lanky, took to the trail before Taylor, Carpe and Lambart were awake. MacCarthy and Foster had made their breakfast quietly and were ready to depart. Lambart, who was clearly suffering from frostbite, needed more time but, supported by Taylor and Carpe, departed by 11 a.m.

Like a man wanting to finish strong in a 100-yard dash, Read got to Hubrick's Camp first, looking for Laing. Knowing of his ability with a firearm and a shared fondness for the hunt, Read tracked down his rifle,

H.F. Lambart at Hubrick's Camp, July 7.
(COURTESY: WHYTE MUSEUM OF THE CANADIAN ROCKIES, V14_ACOP_571)

checked it was loaded and fired into the air. After reloading, he fired again, the sudden blasts reverberating through the valley.

Laing saw the fit, strong profile of Read and quickened his pace. They were soon shaking hands, and Read thanked him for placing the cache at Trail End. He told of the two previous caches destroyed by bears and how Laing's efforts allowed for better chances for the expedition. But where was the rest of the team? Read began telling him of their ordeal while they sat down in camp.

As if to confirm Read's words, at about 1 p.m., MacCarthy and Foster arrived, looking to Laing much the worse for wear. Much trimmer and exhausted, the men had clearly had a terrible experience and lived to tell the tale. Before long they were all seated, and Foster asked about Morgan and Hall. Laing replied that they had spent several days in camp recuperating, with Hall having briefly researched building boats to travel the remaining distance to McCarthy, but they had set out on foot that very morning! Happy to hear that their two teammates had made it down the mountain, Read, MacCarthy and Foster breathed a little easier. But Foster continued to tell Laing how frostbite had affected the expedition's return, especially for Lambart, who was being supported by Taylor and Carpe. It was quite possible Lambart could go no further on foot, and the men set to discussing getting to McCarthy, still eighty miles away. Laing relayed Hall's determination that building boats was not practical. The mountaineers agreed due to the time and labour needed. What, however, if they were to build rafts?

At 5 p.m., Laing spotted what he thought of as the rear guard, Lambart, Carpe and Taylor, slowly making their way across the sandbars and gravel. Lambart was clearly in a bad way, and Carpe and Taylor, who were not without their own ailments, assisted him into camp. Carpe's frozen toes were giving him trouble, but Lambart was not fit to continue on foot.

Lambart wrote in *The Geographical Journal* that "material and tools had been left for whip-sawing lumber and building two boats to take us down the swift stream of the Chitina River," but that, in the end, "it was decided to abandon any idea of the boats, and instead to trust ourselves to the mercies of two rafts."[16] This would be the subject of much discussion in the camp.

But before the evening meal, which Laing helped prepare, he suggested a shot of the six returning to camp. The men agreed to do it for posterity, and with brave faces, set off to a point further east, and with MacCarthy in the lead, walked past the camera one by one, with little

Andy Taylor at Hubrick's Camp, July 7.
(COURTESY: WHYTE MUSEUM OF THE CANADIAN ROCKIES, V14_AC0P_570)

sign of the limping and staggering that Laing had witnessed earlier that day.

Later Laing would request the gang get together for a group movie, in front of the sizable wooden hide tripod and the site's large tent. Lambart, Foster, Read, MacCarthy, Carpe and Taylor lined up left to right and chatted with one another. In the shot, a strong wind blew in from the valley, perhaps promising the regular afternoon dust, buffeting their hat brims. In the final cut of the film *The Conquest of Mount Logan*, a card introduces individual shots of the successful mountaineers, reading "Six reached the summit. As they appeared on July 6th after getting back to the timbered camp at Hubricks [sic]."

First up: "Albert H. MacCarthy, Wilmer B.C., Leader." A man is seen from the waist up, a double-pocketed shirt over a diminished frame, a short-brimmed hat worn above eyes bespectacled, squinting to slits, lips chapped and a trim grey beard. A smile is attempted but not really achieved. Foliage in the background blows to and fro. "H.F. Lambart, Geodetic Survey of Canada, Ottawa, Ont., Deputy Leader." A taller bearded man steps into the same frame, wearing a bright collared, three-button shirt and a short-brimmed hat. He makes a self-conscious smile, chatting jovially with somebody to his left, off-camera. Perhaps in response to a suggestion, he adjusts the brim of his hat, removing it then putting it back on, to allow for the sunlight to reach his eyes. "Allen Carpe, New York City, USA, American Alpine Club Representative." A man, wearing a similar three-button shirt, goggles around his neck, steps into frame from the left. When a gust of wind lifts the brim of his hat, we can see his bright eyes and easy smile. He holds a folded piece of paper and lifts it up to read it. He speaks directly to camera, perhaps mentioning what he had read. Could it be a letter? "Lt. Col. W.W. Foster, DSO, ADC, Vancouver, B.C., Official Recorder." Like MacCarthy, this man appears much diminished, with slumping shoulders underneath his collared coat. His long bearded face, nose and squinting eyes are topped by a bright hat with a crumpled brim. He speaks briefly, directly to Laing perhaps, while gazing at the camera. "A.M. Taylor, Ottawa, Ont., Trail Guide." A bearded man wearing a collared shirt, pants with suspenders and a short-brimmed hat looks directly and patiently at the camera (Carpe is to his right, partially out of frame, reading his folded paper). He stoically waits for Laing to indicate he has ended the shot. "N.H. Read, New York, USA" Here a man, in a dark collared shirt, with broad shoulders, grey hair blowing in the breeze, smiles and speaks to someone off-camera to his left, as though perhaps self-conscious of this moment of stillness before the motion picture camera. He squints into the distance, keen to move away, his tanned face break-

Hamilton Mack Laing at Hubrick's Camp, July 7.
(COURTESY: WHYTE MUSEUM OF THE CANADIAN ROCKIES, V14_AC0P_575)

ing into a broad smile. The next text card appears: "Building the rafts."

During the morning of July 7, they hung around the camp discussing ideas about ways to build rafts and use them to get the men to McCarthy. Laing waited as plans and counter plans for the exit from the valley to civilization were entertained. Under the low clouds and light rain, he was itching to get out of camp.

Laing found a sympathetic ear with Norman Read, and the two snuck out of camp around noon to practice a common interest, hunting, intending to find sheep. Read, tired of the rationed meals, or lack of them, thought finding a sheep to feast on was quite an attractive possibility. Laing led him to Raven Canyon, where he had sometimes seen them. As they ascended the canyon the light rain became heavier, with no sign of sheep.

Read lightened the mood by telling the naturalist what they had seen on their return. On June 28, they'd seen a small bird at Cascades, just outside a tent. Laing was curious and asked for more detail. After all, this was at the Ogilvie Glacier, where ice was dominant. Why would a small bird appear there? Nevertheless, Read indicated it was a pleasant sight, reminding the mountaineers that they were on course to where living things could thrive. He added that they saw either a bee or a wasp just below Cascades. The same day, they had spotted a mosquito on the ice.

Read mentioned to an increasingly curious Laing that, at Turn Camp, when transitioning from the Ogilvie to Logan Glacier, they had found a group of ravens. Perhaps a family? This was indeed something of a revelation to Laing: Why would ravens have appeared in such an inhospitable place? Was the presence of the men attracting them? Laing had already described his own adoption by the ravens at Hubrick's. Concluding his report, Read told Laing of seeing sheep close to the Alaska/Yukon border while still on the Logan Glacier.

Their luck at finding sheep for dinner seeming to have run out, Laing decided, as the rain continued to fall, to get out of the open. Read fell behind as Laing hurried down the canyon, crossed it, then climbed across Sheep Boulevard.

At this point, Laing noticed some movement ahead, a black figure rolling over rocks. Instinctively, he raised his .32 and pulled the trigger. What Laing quickly realized was a black bear rolled down about 100 feet. Upon reaching it, he recognized the specimen as a large male that had partly shed. Concerned about the bear's tumble, he closely examined it and determined it was an ideal specimen with perfect intact teeth. Measuring it, he remembered seeing a black bear the day before on an open slope just above Hubrick's. Could this be the same one? He had been somewhat confounded that, in his absences, the bear had not discovered the camp and ravaged it for edibles. It would appear Laing had struck first.[17]

Laing picked a nearby spot under a spruce tree, built a fire and prepared to skin the bear, as it was not feasible to drag his newest specimen to camp. Also, he knew the mountaineers would be deep in planning their return to civilization. He enjoyed the change of scenery for what had become a routine act, preparing an excellent specimen for the collection. By 6:30 p.m., he arrived in camp, carrying what he could, including a skull.

It rained all night and continued when Laing got up at 6 a.m. Shortly after, he made a surprise discovery upon hearing a new song. The sweet whistling was unmistakably from a yellow warbler. Rushing to look out the door for confirmation, he saw its bright yellow against the sand and gravel. Before he could do anything about it though, the bird flew.[18] He would have liked to pursue it, but July 8 was spoken for, to take the expedition party to Teal Pond in search of timber.

By 8 a.m., Laing set off, Carpe, Read and MacCarthy in tow, with ropes, axes and saws. Laing had described touring the area with Hall, showing him its spruce. Having seen what was on offer, MacCarthy took action and gave instructions to Carpe, Read and Laing. Soon ten trees were felled, their branches pruned. They had decided to construct two rafts, each eighteen feet long. As the rain fell, the men worked into the afternoon, planning to return the next day.

Laing took the opportunity to finish preparing the black bear. While skinning the paws, the five-toed front and hind feet, he noted they appeared very similar to human hands.

Again, overnight it rained heavily, and Laing emerged on July 9 to low clouds obscuring the mountains beyond, flattening the landscape.

Read had seen a gull chased by ravens. Laing grabbed his .32 and headed for the hills. He discovered a herring gull eating the carcass of a porcupine, competing with Laing's raven family. This was surely a wanderer, very far inland from where it should be. Nevertheless, he raised his rifle and secured his only specimen, an adult female gull, for the collection.[19] With much work to do that day, he returned to camp.

Under light rain, the men once again left at 8:30 a.m. for Teal Pond.

At Cutoff Trail, Laing spotted a three-toed woodpecker, but he had to put his routines aside; it was a day for raft building.

They felled more trees and sawed them before hauling the timber down to river level, where they would do more sawing and fitting. Lambart and MacCarthy rested in camp, cooking and reading. Lambart, updating his diary, wrote that they planned for the two rafts to be "five logs in width and 16 feet long" and would "carry three men each, with the dunnage lashed on an elevated rack in the centre."[20]

The rain turned into the heaviest Laing had experienced at Hubrick's. The men returned to camp by 6 p.m. The clouds were slowly climbing the hills. The promise of a drier day made the men hopeful it would be productive in building the rafts to take them to McCarthy. First, they brought the logs closer to the water, where most of the construction would take place.

Laing had brought the Universal and began filming the men at midday, intending to capture the rafts' construction. A bundle of six logs lay on two smaller ones laid perpendicular and underneath to elevate them from the gravel floor. Foster hacked away at one end of the rightmost log with an axe. Carpe took a long wedge of wood and placed it neatly into a gap made in the leftmost log, checking that it fit snugly. Read and Taylor sawed logs to ensure they were all a uniform length. Laing changed angles to roll film on the wooded edge of the valley's south side, Taylor working another set of logs at the far end of the shot, doctoring a log end for some purpose, while Read continued to toil vigorously with a four-foot saw. Laing again switched angles. With Taylor now in the foreground seated on the log being worked on, legs wide open, he hammered something into its end, creating a gap or wedging something inside, eventually looking at the camera and smiling. The next shot revealed what his work was intended to accomplish: the four men, carrying light poles with rope in the centre attached to the ends of a log, walked it with ease out into the valley, towards what Laing knew as the middle channel of the river.

At the river, Laing continued to roll film. Now there were six logs, also arranged perpendicularly across two supporting poles, with the river flowing freely. The camera faced west, showing the mass of Gibraltar

Rock standing in the middle of the valley. Taylor, at left, whittled away at a chunk of wood with his axe, creating a sweep. Carpe brought in two logs about four feet long and six inches in diameter onto the raft. In Laing's next shot at a new angle, we see where these two logs were intended to go: fastened onto the centre of the raft to make a raised platform, with several even thinner straight branches laid across those in line with the logs. The other piece of superstructure visible is a small tripod at the stern of the craft, a sweep holder, to support a sweep, used in navigating the raft down the channel of the river. As Laing looked south, panning slowly from right to left, we see Taylor, with an axe in his right hand, taking away the sweep meant for just that purpose in his left hand. He walks away from camera, looked briefly into the distance and drops the sweep to the ground. Carpe stands to the left, speaking to the men who are working on a second raft near him. In the distance is a hint that the mountaineers are planning to depart sooner rather than later: their gear lay in packs scattered across the rocky riverbank, ready for loading onto the rafts' racks. The men were racing against time.

In one more shot, filmed at a distance, focused on all the men, save Lambart, who was looking after his feet, having a hot bath, and cooking a meal, they worked hard to fabricate the finishing touches on the structures, in which they had placed much hope and effort.[21] In the late afternoon light, the slopes of the southern side of the valley were visible in a haze. The shot clearly shows the rafts now have sweep holders at both ends. The men hammer away in an idyllic scene that belied their wishes: to return to civilization. Laing stopped rolling film, having got what he needed, and looked on to the hardworking men, the fading sunlight on his face.

After completing the rafts around 6 p.m., the men returned to camp and informed Lambart they were ready for departure the next day.

With Laing staying behind, it was once again a time for goodbyes. Foster, who had been tending to Lambart's feet and working on the rafts, wrote later: "Laing elected to remain until the condition of the valley would permit a pack train to be sent in for himself and the fine collection he had secured, so that three persons were to go on each raft."[22]

As with Morgan and Hall who had left mere days before, addresses were exchanged and promises to write proclaimed. They had all developed a mutual respect for one another in meeting yet another challenge, labouring at it and seeing it through. Laing scribbled the following in his diary: Allen Carpe, 135 W. 58th St. NYC, 195 Broadway; Col. W.W. Foster, Pacific Bldg. Van.; Norman H. Read, 7 E. 40th St. NYC; Capt. A.H. MacCarthy, Wilmer, B.C.

In the grey and dour evening, as rain began to fall, the men went silent.

July 11 began with a late breakfast. Laing assisted Taylor in dismantling the tent and packing it down, taking it to the river. Although the sun soon burst through, some dark storm clouds were seen clustering around some mountaintops, making MacCarthy and Lambart wonder about how the day might end and what lay ahead in the crossing of over eighty miles via two conveyances that had not really been tested yet. However, Laing revelled at the clearer sky revealing the lovely new snow on the mountaintops, where the sun shone. If he believed in omens, that may have been a good one for the voyage ahead. Also, Laing remarked on some Dall sheep spotted on the southern slopes across the valley. Lambart later ruminated on the significance of their departure from Hubrick's Camp, noting that they were about to risk themselves and their possessions "to an unknown river" that would hopefully carry the six mountaineers forty-five miles that day.

Just after noon, the two rafts were prepared and ready for departure. Laing watched the gang have a last meal by the river's edge and then prepared the Universal for filming. A plan had been hatched to have a sweep operated by a man at the bow and a man at the stern, with another seated on the elevated platform with gear able to operate a pole to further direct the watercraft. With an added touch of humour to what was a daunting venture into the unknown, the Alpine Club of Canada rafts were named *Logan* (to carry Taylor, Read and Lambart) and *Loganette* (carrying MacCarthy, Carpe and Foster).[23] In order to launch the loaded rafts, all hands were on the channel's edges. Carpe and Read did the heavy lifting, each handling a pole placed under the raft and prying it along two logs acting as rollers. Foster joined in, with Mac-

Carthy and Taylor on either side helping with poles to encourage the raft into the quick, cold, silty waters of the middle channel. As Laing rolled film on this launching, eventually most of the craft was in the water, with only a bit holding fast to the wooden roller, while Taylor held onto the raft to secure it. There was nothing left to do but leave. After Laing shook hands with each man, he walked further along the shore to allow for some lead time to film the passing rafts from three angles, leaving the mountaineers to their own devices. He planted the tripod firmly into the gravel and prepared himself for some rapid actions.

In *The Conquest of Mount Logan*, text appears prior to the passing of the two rafts. In a final good-humoured nod to Canada's roots, and the support of the Alpine Club in England, the card read: "A new version of the Oxford-Cambridge boat race—8 miles an hour down the Chitina to McCarthy—to civilization and home."

The shot features the high peaks in the south of the valley, with the channel coursing to the right of camera. The *Logan* appears from the left, slowly making its way into the centre of the frame. At the bow, Lambart adeptly pushes his pole on the starboard side against the channel's bottom, propelling the raft along, Read is seated in the middle, and Taylor at the stern pushes his pole on the port side.

Laing quickly swivelled the camera, so as to get a direct shot of the rafts passing from left to right. The *Logan* enters the frame, and we see Lambart's sweep at rest in the holder, with him pushing his pole on the starboard side, Read seated squarely in the middle, and Taylor pushing his pole on the starboard side, and switching it to the other side, in the moment captured before they exit right. We watch the waters feeding the Chitina River's power flow by before the *Loganette* appears. The bow sweep is resting as well. Foster is at its side pushing his pole to starboard. Carpe is seated on the rack, taking the pole Foster hands back to him before he takes up the bow sweep, using his pole to steady the craft before laying it on his lap. MacCarthy is using his sweep to direct the raft, looking to the bow before adjusting course with it. The craft exits the frame on the right.

Laing swivels the camera again, the lens now following the *Logan* in the distance as it turns in the water's course. The *Loganette* comes into frame from the left, as we continue to see MacCarthy making course corrections with the sweep, turning to look where the craft is heading, ensuring it follows his guidance. He takes a moment to wave at Laing and the camera, doffs and waves his hat enthusiastically before replacing it and taking the helm once again of the *Loganette*. Carpe waves too.

Laing waved back at them, still cranking the film, and admired the watercraft. When *Logan* got caught in the shallows, Taylor stepped into the water and tried to pry the craft loose. Eventually, Read and Lambart join him in his efforts. The *Loganette* also appears to slow down at the same point but continued with some prying of poles. A quick cut shows both crafts moving again. This is where the film displays "THE END." After stopping the camera, Laing watched the rafts continue to sweep downstream for a while until they were out of sight.

He returned to Hubrick's by 2 p.m. to what he could only describe as the filthiest camp he ever saw. The mountaineers had left what they could spare, with the intent of Laing using it or it being hauled out when the pack train came in August. For example, Laing came across two extra pounds of sugar. After spending seven hours tidying up, he made himself a late supper.

Sitting by the fire, feeling a little lonely, but savouring the quiet, Laing looked out at the valley, taking stock of the last six days' excitement. Poking at the fire with a stick left over from the raft building, he ruminated on the charms of solitude.

CHAPTER 15

The Return Home

Lambart estimated it was 1:15 p.m. when they began their journey on the *Logan* and the *Loganette*. There were some sudden groundings on the gravel bars when a turn was underestimated, but overall, the rafts enjoyed a swift run down-current. As he explained, though, they had to make some adjustments as, all except Taylor, who called McCarthy home and was very familiar with the character of local rivers, were inexperienced. Lambart wrote how the "Alaskan glacial stream is a power to be dealt with in no trifling manner. It is quite unlike other streams. Excessively cold and carrying in suspension great quantities of silt, the water has a decidedly thick appearance, and the Chitina River careers down the wide open valley at 6 miles per hour in treacherous constantly changing channels."[1] He recalled not long after departure the *Loganette*, with Carpe, Foster and MacCarthy on board were in jovial spirits because of the distance being covered, in a wide channel parallel to that of the *Logan*. It was exhilarating to move down the river so quickly and to feel that the Mount Logan experience was behind them. "We stopped and had something to nibble once," Lambart wrote in his diary. "Few points on the old trail I recognized. The wooded points & Gibraltar Rock of course but little else except where the glaciers and streams we knew came in."[2] At one point, the *Loganette* actually passed the *Logan* in a broad channel. Lambart lost track of their position.[3] But steering the *Logan* had become all-encompassing as Taylor, Read and Lambart closed the distance between themselves and McCarthy.

As the sun dipped low in the land of perpetual light, Taylor gently piloted them to a stop, where they had a meal. He soon had them pushing off again. At no time did they spot the *Loganette*.

The fate of the *Loganette* was in line with their worst fears. By Foster's account, the craft he, MacCarthy and Carpe were navigating had entered the rapid current of the main channel of the Chitina River, where the waters became rough, near the junction with Short River. Rapids, like they hadn't experienced, jostled the raft and eventually, according to Foster, about eighteen miles from Hubrick's Camp, overturned it, throwing the men and all their belongings into the frigid waters. This was somewhat ironic, as Lambart's diary records that "Mac took the best raft" and that "just before we took to the rafts I told Mac that he had all the strong men on the one raft & suggested a change but he spurned my offer."[4] As the soaked men struggled to regain contact with what was left of their upside-down vessel, it was with "some difficulty and using the upturned raft, a landing was finally made, and what could be salvaged from the water-soaked baggage was cached in trees trusting that it could be picked up when the pack train went back for the naturalist later on."[5] The men were not harmed, just thoroughly soaked, and while they grabbed what they could from the upset craft, Carpe let out a cry of exasperation as he acknowledged the many waterlogged film cartridges. Thankfully, some were not soaked, and it appeared that the visual record of their ascent of Logan was not completely wiped out.[6] However, their hopes were dashed of continuing on the *Loganette*, which was no longer river-worthy. With the salvaged gear secure and dripping in the high cache, Foster, MacCarthy and Carpe, in their bedraggled state, faced the prospect of a hike of seventy miles.[7]

By contrast, in a bit of navigation by Taylor that Lambart considered "a fine piece of work," the *Logan* was smoothly guided into Rush Pond, a lagoon that was their destination. Taylor knew once they had reached a "depression in the contour of the hills indicating the spot where we should land," that it was time to edge away from the current and settle into where they would camp for the night. By Lambart's estimation,

The indefatigable Andy Taylor, preparing breakfast at Rush Pond, July 12.
(COURTESY: WHYTE MUSEUM OF THE CANADIAN ROCKIES, V14_AC0P_582)

they had travelled sixty miles on board the *Logan*.[8] From there onwards, it was on foot.

Taylor's keen eye and expertise had brought them to a place of comfort, where they sat before a roaring fire, often wondering what had become of Foster, MacCarthy and Carpe and hoping to be reunited the next day. They settled into their tents for the sleep they would need prior to hiking to McCarthy, a journey of just over thirty miles.[9]

The weather on July 12 was ideal for beginning the walk from Rush Pond. Lambart's bandaged toes were giving him some dull pain that he knew would have to be addressed in McCarthy. Taylor was as spry and enthusiastic as ever, up early making eggs, bacon, hotcakes, and providing jam and tea.[10] Read's athleticism gave him an extra push that made the trio confident they would cover the miles. To better accomplish this, they had left most of what came off the raft for later retrieval by horse, carrying all they needed for a couple of days of walking. Following a horse trail, they climbed to the top of a ridge at the junction of the valleys carved out of the landscape by the Chitina and Nizina rivers. It was a bittersweet experience for Read and Lambart to look back on the valley where they had spent so much time, guiding them towards the Logan massif and now out, towards home.[11]

Lambart later wrote in his diary about this latter part of the expedition:

> My feet were in terrible shape but the trail soon pounded any feeling there was out & I got along remarkably well. In fact nothing much mattered now, we were on the absolutely last home stretch & the last link in this whole Logan Expedition which saying the least & kindest thing about it—the strangest venture of my life.[12]

Soon the trio was moving downhill through trees razed in a wildfire. By evening, they reached the Nizina bridge, hoping to find a telephone so Taylor could call to McCarthy for a vehicle to pick them up. But when they arrived "the road gang had moved out," and the area was bereft of human beings, forcing them to walk the remaining eleven miles into town. The road was a mess, muddy to an extreme, convincing the men that a car journey may have proven worse than the march.[13]

What appeared to be perhaps a hallucination, not unlike the ones on their perilous descent from the Logan massif, was a new roadhouse, ready to take in travellers, near the other side of the bridge. The three men accepted the hospitality of a retired Texas rancher they called Dad Wakefield, who distracted them from worrying about their missing friends with tales of olden days spent hunting buffalo. To their dismay, he had not seen any sign of Foster, Carpe or their leader, MacCarthy. Having supped at the road house, the men were fortified enough to set off at 11 p.m. Read and Taylor competed with each other as though racing the final stretch. "I followed in the wake of my two stumps doing pretty well," Lambart later wrote, "at times right behind and again quite a bit behind."[14] They arrived at McCarthy at 1:30 a.m. on July 13.[15]

Soon afterwards, Lambart initiated sending out the news of the

"Conquest of Logan."[16] Upon getting in touch with local Jack O'Neill, who had a prepared dispatch written by Foster, he instructed him to take it immediately to the telegraph agent, who wired its contents to the *Vancouver Daily Province.*[17] It was a bittersweet announcement, without the team leader, Foster and Carpe present, their whereabouts and condition unknown. But Lambart, needing treatment for his frozen toes, went in haste to nearby Kennicott Hospital.[18]

Lambart, Read and Taylor heard that they had just missed Hall and Morgan, who had arrived July 11 and taken the first train out to Cordova.[19] All going well, they would be on a steamer heading south sometime in the days ahead. This made for something of an anti-climactic return to civilization, in this jumbled way.

Lambart recalls his time in McCarthy with appreciation. Taylor parted from Read and Lambart on arrival and said he'd see them in the morning. Lambart wrote about how a "splendid little fellow (S. Wold) looked after us like a prince, got us rooms & oh what a bath I had before turning in." The state of his toes hadn't changed: "My feet were bad and I didn't do a great deal of sleeping but it was glorious getting into a real bed again."[20] He later added that they "were most kindly treated by the citizens of the little town, and in particular by Mr. Douglas, of the Kennecott Copper Mines, and Mr. J.B. O'Neill."[21]

Read, by far the fittest expedition member, was already preparing to take the train to Cordova. "Read . . . leaves at 1 p.m. for Cordova," Lambart wrote, "to catch the boat leaving tonight for the south. We're glad to get rid of him but parted cordially."[22] He left before knowing the fate of MacCarthy, Foster and Carpe.[23] In regards to these three, Lambart was somewhat reticent: "We were worried, or at least I was, about the other three, but what was the use, we were in no way to blame for any of their moves & they were masters of their own situation."[24]

Taylor was back home, although *The Conquest of Mount Logan* credits him as being from Ottawa, Ontario, maybe because his pay came from the federal centre. He was already preparing a search party on July 13, organizing more hands and a pack train, in hopes of finding MacCarthy, Foster and Carpe alive.[25] That same day, Lambart took a car ride to the hospital at Kennicott with Taylor and Jack O'Neill's daughter, Molly, along the Kennicott moraine "where I could shake my fist and say 'no more of you old boy.'"[26]

A Mr. Douglas, the mine manager, and a doctor greeted him, and an examination took place right away. "The verdict was not cheerful, immediate rest, dressings daily—suggests staying at hospital," Lambart's diary reported. His feet would give him trouble for six months, the doctor informed him.[27]

On the morning of July 15, when the relief party was about to set out led by the indefatigable Andy Taylor, with another guide and four horses, they received news from the trail. MacCarthy, Foster and Carpe were seen walking towards and would be in McCarthy by noon![28] In a phone call from them, Lambart finally learned what delayed them and heard about the soaked film cartridges and water damage to Carpe's cameras.

Lambart and Taylor were both very relieved to see them again. Lambart was complimentary towards their guide, Taylor, describing how by "his unselfishness and courage, by his unwearying [sic] efforts for the common good of the expedition, and his loyal friendship, he had won the admiration of the whole party."[29]

W.W. Foster, despite the setbacks caused by bear-ravaged caches and an overturned raft, lauded MacCarthy. He wrote about his thorough preparation, in getting to know the conditions that the team of mountaineers would face and stowing away equipment and food in advance. The groundwork and wisdom he brought to the expedition meant that "the fundamental matters of supply and transportation were thoroughly organized and, owing to his appreciation of the terrain, caches and stopping places en route and even the camping points on the massif were selected ahead and an itinerary planned which, except for variation on the actual climb, attributable to extreme weather conditions, was observed throughout."[30]

MacCarthy, Lambart, Foster and Carpe remained at McCarthy but would soon catch the train.[31] Lambart was up and around and attended by his doctor "dressing my feet & giving last words of wisdom regarding the dressings."[32] He paid his bill and said goodbye to the doctor and nurses who had looked after him. Regretting having to part from friends in Kennicott and McCarthy, especially their tireless guide, Andy Taylor,

they took the train departing July 18, staying in Chitina overnight, before arrival at Cordova and a quiet stay there, then boarded the SS *Yukon*
on July 22, settling into the comparative luxury the vessel offered.[33] The
next day in the Gulf of Alaska, the men looked towards Mount Saint
Elias, saw the Logan massif emerge from behind it and stared in silence.

Foster summed up the overall importance behind the expedition in
his *Canadian Alpine Journal* article:

> The spectacular part of the expedition was naturally the conquest of the
> mountain but, in addition, the geographical and meteorological infor-
> mation obtained is of considerable magnitude; and the contribution to
> mountaineering lore, the beauty of still and moving photographs and the
> research and fine collection of the naturalist in the Chitina Valley has
> added considerably to the store of human knowledge; and it is hoped
> these features will in due course be recorded in book form, to amplify and
> consolidate the many fine articles that have already appeared in scientific
> and other journals.[34]

> A full and complete copy or transcript of field notes on the natural
> history work done by you on the expedition will be furnished to the
> Department as soon as possible after your return from the field.

> —L.L. Bolton

On July 12, Laing looked about the valley and saw a perfect day, where
it felt like the previous rain had cleaned the air. He had been busy collecting two brown-headed, or Hudsonian, chickadees in camp, their
"Si-da-daa!" much more common since the young left the nest. These
two juveniles, he noted, were much greyer than those of northern Ontario. These were the last chickadees he would secure in the Chitina.[35]

He spent the rest of the day working around the camp and preparing
the bearskin. Attracted to the carcass, flies were everywhere. They even
swarmed around the pot where the cleaned head was boiling.

Laing consolidated his food stores with what the mountaineers had
left behind. He also cut some wood, tidied the tent, mended his pants
with a little canvas and constructed a new drying rack, making three

new skins on it. In an effort to clean up, he did three loads of washing, and, in the evening, a fourth. He hadn't even noticed the dust wafting down the valley. He still had to pack up both cameras. At the end of the day, he looked about the camp. With some disdain, he had to admit that, for all his efforts, the camp didn't look any better.

The next day, another perfect morning, Laing set off for Teal Pond. At Cutoff Trail, he collected tiny polygonum, which seemed to be an "early outpost of the more teeming colonies on the hills."[36] He realized that, with the season of bloom ending, there was nothing new to see. The eerie whistle of a varied thrush pierced the air, the last he would hear in the valley.[37]

At the pond, he secured a lesser yellowlegs, a juvenile female that completed his collection, considerably larger than the adult male captured on July 3.[38] A Barrow's golden-eye duck, brown head on a grey body, appeared on the water. The adult non-breeding female, the only one he'd secure, would add to Hoyes Lloyd's adult male secured in November 1922 at McCarthy.[39] There was time to pass by the nest of the American three-toed woodpecker, the source of the "quittering" Laing had pointed out to Hall on July 3 when hunting for timber. Laing had seen it as a vibrant nest, full of young, noisy and petulant, with the father clinging to its entrance, adding to the clamour, but on this day, it was empty, devoid of any sound, dead.[40] He noted the dimensions of the nest, its barrel appearing quite cylindrical. No sign of the young appeared.

Back at Hubrick's Camp, Laing made two more skins, hung them on the new drying rack, and swept his hand to clear the blowflies away from the bearskin. He placed the offal on the gravel bar, the raven family swooping down to enjoy their meal, noisily croaking their way to settle on the meat.

Laing sat down in the gravel and looked across the overcast valley, a breeze picked up, and he watched the dust storm rush up the far side of the valley. Turning away from it, he began packing the collection in anticipation of the pack train's arrival in August.

Laing would live for another month in the Chitina River valley collecting plant, bird and mammal specimens. On the evening of August 15, while wrapping up his collection, he saw a pack train coming from the west. Leading it was the familiar figure of Andy Taylor, who grinned upon seeing him. Laing waved, relieved to see a human being again.

It required a four-horse load to cart away all of Laing's collection from the Chitina River valley. Unfortunately, they only had three horses, so he spent much of August 16 packing and repacking to get everything loaded up. What made it more difficult was that it rained all day. The usual birds flitted about camp—juncos, myrtle warblers, chickadees— but he would miss the ravens; there had always been the ravens.

Andy Taylor checked with Laing that they had everything. They did. Laing turned his back on Hubrick's Camp, and they kept a slow but constant pace, crunching along gravel, on the walk alongside the flow of the Chitina, towards McCarthy.

Afterword

⬤

In *Birds of Western Canada*, one of his major books, Percy A. Taverner, who had begun his work at the National Museum of Canada as staff ornithologist in 1910, acknowledges the contributions of Hamilton Mack Laing.[1] After lauding Major Allan Brooks, Mr. Hoyes Lloyd and Mr. Louis Agassiz Fuertes, Taverner thanks "Mr. Hamilton M. Laing, who supplied much information on the ducks of the prairies, especially from the sportsman's standpoint. The quotations under those species are from his pen."[2] This classic reference book of bird classification, published in 1926, contained information gathered during Laing's previous five years of fieldwork.[3] Taverner and Rudolph Martin Anderson, a respected zoologist who headed up the biology department at the museum had recruited Laing, as a naturalist, to accompany the 1925 expedition aiming to make the first ascent of Mount Logan. With these two men, he shared authorship of his findings published in the museum's annual report for 1927.

Within the introduction of Taverner's book, the modern reader can learn much about the methodology of the field naturalist, explaining Laing's use of a .32 auxiliary to collect specimens, regulated by the Migratory Birds Convention Act that had received royal assent in 1917 and was signed into law in the U.S. in 1918. After being careful to qualify his words with an acknowledgement that "in the delicate balance of nature, birds should be respected" and that a "serious word should be said on the much discussed question of the collection of specimens as a method of bird study," Taverner points out that "it is no more possible for one to obtain accurate and comprehensive knowledge of birds than of plants or insects without collecting or at least handling specimens."[4] He makes it clear that his book would not be possible "without constant access to complete or extensive series of specimens."[5] Considering the recent strides that had been taken in wildlife conservation up to the late 1920s, a movement Taverner had taken part in, he established that the right to collect bird specimens covered within the Act, "cannot be distributed too freely."[6] Laing, in Taverner's view, was a privileged ornithological scientist, and in a world where public opinion had been gathering in both Canada and the United States to support wildlife conservation, it was a privilege that could not be taken for granted. In his influential book's introduction, Taverner seems to be making his argument, aware of growing public concern about birdlife depletion at the hands of unethical sportsmen, that Laing's use of a firearm to collect specimens could have been perceived as a campaign against wildlife, when by his reasoning "the scientific collector is sympathetic towards the principles of wild-life conservation."[7]

During the Mount Logan Expedition of 1925 and, indeed, for some time afterwards, terms such as "conquest," "assault" and "campaign" were used to describe what the mountaineers were setting out to do in the Yukon, in climbing the tallest mountain in the Dominion of Canada. Reading of Hamilton Mack Laing "securing" his specimens with his .32 auxiliary in his day-to-day biological work as a naturalist representing the National Museum of Canada might be difficult to fully understand and accept by today's standards, but he had set out to understand the greater natural world, to better our understanding of it, by capturing it and studying it. Whether by tracking down an elusive wheatear flitting in a canyon or by attempting to subdue the mysterious, powerful grizzly, Laing was on his own "conquest." He found himself to be a sportsman on the hunt in the Chitina River valley, at times facing the wilderness on an adversarial level, on a visceral quest to locate his targets, even though the end result for the skins, the specimens, was scientific.

But much like the way the mountaineers became a part of their un-predictable and fierce surroundings, their impeccably planned campaign unravelled by forces unleashed by previously unknown factors, Laing in time ceased to be merely a hunter or a scientist. He became something other than an individual on the fringes of a natural world seeking out his specimens; he became part of the environment in which he sought objectivity, an environment made up of interdependent elements. One feature that made the expedition innovative was the inclusion of not only still photography but also motion picture photography to capture living things in their environment, to show to an audience wishing to learn of natural habitat, a practice that was increasingly popular in the scientific community.

Laing, in his life's trajectory, would gradually be introduced to, and follow a path toward, conservation, and be sought out by others who also wanted to protect wildlife.

In reading Laing's diaries, I must admit passages that involved secur-ing specimens with a firearm were difficult to read and accept by my own twenty-first century sensibilities, but I understood that, historically, he was placed in a particular context during the rise of conservation. Much had been done prior to the Mount Logan Expedition of 1925 when it came to conservation; it's important to know where he fell on the trajectory of that movement.

To understand where Laing was in 1925, on the timeline of develop-ing interests in conservation, we need to look back to the late nineteenth century. Although he may not have wished it so, Hamilton Mack Laing was born in Ontario. Laing strongly felt he was a pioneer, a frontiers-man, the eldest son of a family of first-generation Manitobans. His parents, William and Rachel, had settled in Clearsprings, Manitoba, where they ran a farm. However, in February 1883, on a family visit to the Mack homestead in Hensall, his mother gave birth in the log house where she was born. In Laing's early years, the untilled prairie still fea-tured buffalo skulls, evidence of the excessive hunting that drove away the vast herds that had roamed there and generated the first calls to conserve wildlife.[8]

Laing's parents kept a herd of Scottish shorthorns for their beef, as well as some sheep and chickens. In the pioneer land of Clearsprings, Laing developed an early interest in birds, learning to identify them, noting their traits and habits and coveting first sightings of unusual birds. However, he acquired far more practical expertise from his father, as a skilled hunter, who brought up his eldest son to be the farm's game warden. As a preschooler, Laing was already adept in the use of traps and snares to capture or exterminate the insects, birds or mammals considered a threat. By 1894, at the age of eleven, he was using a rifle to keep predators and pests away. When a hawk was discovered in the chicken yard, he asked before grabbing his father's Remington and taking aim at the offending predator, earning his approval for collecting such a threat to the family's livelihood.

This early acceptance of man's value as game warden supported his belief that nature was not something meant to balance itself. This spilled over into his later work as a naturalist. Laing made it his business to understand and learn the habits of the predators and pests, becoming more adept in his role. His was a paradigm borne from the utilitarian existence of the farmer: an overabundance of predators and pests such as wolves, coyotes, eagles, hawks and owls would be given free rein to kill nesting birds, destroy crops and livestock. This, to him, simply, would not do.[9]

During Laing's upbringing in Clearsprings, there was a predominant belief in Canada in the abundance, or even the superabundance, of natural resources, including wildlife. As Roderick Haig-Brown noted at Canada's centenary, settlement was fashioned on the "discovery and exploitation of natural resources." Whether it was on the frontier of Canada or the United States, "early history of resource use everywhere on the continent was one of ruthless exploitation, based on what has been called 'the myth of abundance'—the belief that water, soil, forests, wildlife, and fisheries were inexhaustible."[10] In the United States, in "the early years of the eighteenth century," Stewart L. Udall wrote, "there grew up a vision of an agrarian paradise that would one day stretch to the western sea . . . [and] saw the beginnings of the Myth of Superabundance that would plunge us headlong into a century of land plunder and land abuse."[11] In Canada, Sir John A. Macdonald's government's

national policy hinged on this premise: the development of natural resources and the promise of a transcontinental railway "built to open up
new resource areas." In other words, it was "a set of economic policies
and programs designed to develop a national economy based upon the
use of Canada's natural resources."[12] Laing and his father's values would
have reflected the challenges met on a landscape where settlement was
only beginning. As naturalist Janet Foster argued:

> An uninhabited frontier, the myth of superabundance, and era of exploi-
> tation and lack of knowledge about wildlife, the political climate of the
> National Policy and the division of powers under the British North
> America Act—all of these factors and attitudes within government and
> among the Canadian people generally, obstructed and delayed the advent
> of wildlife conservation in Canada.[13]

With settlement came the destruction of wildlife habitat in favour of
clearing forests for farms, roads and railways. By 1885, the Canadian
Pacific Railway had been completed, and by that time, the wild buffalo
herds that had once spanned the prairie were gone, replaced by the sun-
bleached bones of the creatures that had been hunted to excess.[14] There
was a slow but building movement to conserve wilderness and wildlife,
with these being seen as natural resources that required protection. But
Canada went about it differently than did their neighbours to the south.

In Canada, we had to take our example from the United States and
its creation of national parks in an era of reckless hunting and destruc-
tive habitat loss. By 1872, they had established Yellowstone National
Park, the first national park anywhere. It had been created not only with
preservation in mind, the setting aside of all its natural resources from
being exploited commercially, but also as a place where people could
enjoy wilderness. The Yellowstone Park Act also protected the wildlife
within its boundaries from the "wanton destruction" of fish and game,
but it did not rule out hunting, as the park was wilderness, and it was
assumed visitors would have to hunt and fish to survive in a challenging
landscape. No railway accessed the park, and it was far from settlement,
which would be some chief differences between it and Canada's first
national park.[15]

In 1887, Rocky Mountains National Park, now known as Banff National Park, was created, but it wasn't intended to preserve wildlife in the same way as Yellowstone. The park was accessed by the railway that would lead to a resort that featured hot springs. Banff Hot Springs would be a tourist draw, and generate much-needed dollars for the public purse to help alleviate the debt generated by building the Canadian Pacific Railway. But the wildlife would also be a tourist draw, allowing for visitors interested in seeing the diversity of the natural world, but also bringing in those who wanted to hunt. As Janet Foster stated: "It was a tourist resort, not a wildlife sanctuary, that was being created in 1887."[16]

As the years progressed, Canada, when it came to wildlife preservation, was influenced by more than the United States' park initiatives. Figures such as the writer and naturalist John Muir, himself influenced by Ralph Waldo Emerson and Henry David Thoreau, embodied a preservationist standpoint that became relevant as the frontier was obviously shrinking and opinions of abundant wildlife were replaced by a realization of the natural world's limitations.[17] Gifford Pinchot brought forestry into the forefront of the conservation movement, in 1898, becoming chief of the Department of Agriculture's Division of Forestry (soon after the U.S. Forest Service). Although wildlife was not a priority for him, he prized the wise use of forest resources. His forest management ideas didn't align with the wilderness preservation view, as he believed trees should be harvested, but the ensuing habitat destruction was not a consideration. These men represented polarizing views in the preservationist versus conservationist debate. But it was the U.S. President, Theodore Roosevelt, who would be an enthusiastic supporter of conservation, and work with Pinchot to begin setting aside millions of acres for overseeing by the U.S. Forest Service.[18] In 1909, Roosevelt initiated the North American Conservation Conference, which brought Canadian delegates to Washington to begin talks about natural resource protection, including "game preservation and the protection of bird life."[19]

With Canada lagging behind the United States when it came to "recognition and defence of their national parks as wilderness," in the late 1960s, Roderick Nash reflecting on that era wrote: "the Canadian public's sensitivity to and enthusiasm for wilderness values lags at least two generations behind opinion in the United States."[20] A Declaration of Principles was agreed upon during the North American Conservation Conference, including a statement that "resources were to be developed, used and conserved for the future in the interest of mankind." Another was made on the subject of game, namely that "there should be legislation to ensure game preservation and the protection of bird life."[21] This wasn't a binding treaty, they were merely suggestions that might guide both countries in their management of what the public was seeing increasingly as more than just a commodity or natural resource.

Canada did not have a John Muir or Sierra Club to influence the public, but by 1910, there were growing calls in the United States to make national parks not just places to wisely harvest trees but places to preserve wilderness. In 1916, supporters of this view found success with the National Parks Act, prioritizing preservation and recreation within their boundaries.[22]

Canada did take strides to make its national parks into wildlife refuges, once it was realized that wildlife drew in more tourists. It was thought at one point that Rocky Mountain Park could be stocked with elk, mountain sheep and moose, to name a few.[23] Legislation such as the Unorganized Territories Game Preservation Act in 1894 established precedence in stopping the killing of the over-hunted buffalo and created closed seasons for certain birds and mammals. By the time of the North American Conservation Conference, Canada had six national parks, containing forests that had been set aside and protected, and a refuge for certain kinds of game. But, as Roderick Nash pointed out, "Canadian legislation imposed no preservation function on the parks and did not even distinguish between them and the commercially-oriented forest reserves." This he would apply to legislation such as Canada's Dominion Forest and Parks Act that was passed in 1911.[24] True preservation within the Canadian parks wouldn't take place until after the 1930 National Parks Act. There was a reason behind this delay: "The Canadian wilderness movement lags behind the American for the reason that Canadians (in general, the typical Canadian) still regard themselves as a pioneering people with an overabundance of wild country."[25]

One of Muir's seminal works focused on one of the first parks in the United States. In *The Yosemite*, published in 1912, he wrote about his outings in this wilderness: "Therefore I decided to visit California for a year or two to see its wonderful flora and the famous Yosemite Valley."[26] His words describing the park's landscapes and features included "harmony," "superb" and "beauty." But his descriptions of its birdlife illustrated an apparent scarcity: "Flocks of pigeons are often seen, and about six species of ducks, as the river is never wholly frozen over. Among these are the mallard and the beautiful woodcock, now less common on account of being so often shot at."[27] The discovery that wildlife, including birds, was not unlimited was becoming more apparent to the general public. Although Canada was accomplishing more in its policies, including creating the Parks Branch in 1911 (the first government organization established to focus on managing and developing a national park), the importation of over 700 plains bison to be safeguarded in Buffalo National Park and the protection of a rapidly declining pronghorn antelope herd at Nemiskam National Antelope Park, it was migratory bird conservation that eventually led to international co-operation to save a form of wildlife that had drastically declining populations.

In this time of diminishing wildlife, how could specimen collection be seen to ethically further scientific knowledge? Beyond Percy Taverner's need as an ornithologist to have a specimen collection readily at hand, skins in a museum's collection were often mounted and displayed in exhibition halls and galleries for public viewing. As William Temple Hornaday, perhaps the leading conservationist of the nineteenth century, who was instrumental in re-establishing bison herds in the United States when they were almost extinct, saw it early on in his career: taxidermy allowed for an animal secured in the wild and displayed in a metropolitan museum for the general public to educate many city dwellers on the importance of the natural world and the beauty within it.[28] Prior to photography becoming a conventional means to study wildlife, collecting specimens for museums was a viable trade. His book about a 1905 collecting expedition, *Camp-Fires in the Canadian Rockies*, featured not only Hornaday, director of the New York Zoological Park, but also John M. Phillips, Pennsylvania State Game Commissioner, tramping the hills and mountains of southeastern British Columbia, hunting for grizzly bear and mountain sheep. This they combined with a new quest for high-quality alpine photography of mountain sheep, and prepared prize mountain ram specimens for mounting. Phillips presented one to the Carnegie Museum in Pittsburgh; Hornaday presented the other to the Brooklyn Institute Museum.[29] This was the tradition naturalists working on collecting expeditions were to follow. Hamilton Mack Laing found his niche in this scientific climate.

One of the men to recruit Laing, along with Percy Taverner, was Dr. Rudolph Martin Anderson, who had made his name in zoology partly by accompanying scientist and explorer Vilhjalmur Stefansson, on a 1908–1912 expedition into the arctic. Stefansson immersed himself in Inuit life, and Anderson acted as all-round scientist, writing reports of trees, plants, insects, birds and mammals, travelling "from Point Barrow, Alaska east to the middle portion of Coronation Gulf and Southern Victoria Island."[30] Some parallels can be drawn between Anderson's and Laing's work in northern climes, including Alaska. Anderson collected "a small lot of plants" including the red-purple vetch, observed the golden eagle and Canada jay and found the mosquitos to be "a weariness to the flesh during at least two of the summer months in nearly all parts of the North."[31] He also paid attention to the seasonally fluctuating populations of the Macfarlane varying hare, curious as to why in "certain years the Varying Hares of Rabbits are very numerous, while during other years they are almost lacking."[32] Later on, when heading the biology department at the Victoria Memorial Museum, he may have seen Laing as furthering that work, including that initiated during Anderson's second arctic expedition begun in 1913, when signing him up as naturalist for the Mount Logan Expedition of 1925. In his *Catalogue of Canadian Recent Mammals*, Anderson later credited a long list of "mammalogists, officials in various institutions in Canada and the United States, and numerous naturalists in private life," including "Allan Brooks of Okanagan Landing, B.C. (and) H.M. Laing of Comox."[33] Anderson referred to the report he co-authored with Laing within the pages of the National Museum of Canada's Annual Report for 1927, noting the Canada lynx specimen Laing secured was represented in the National Collection in the National Museum of Canada.[34] He also indicated when it came to red squirrels, "five specimens in the National Museum of Canada from head of Chitina River, Alaska, seem to be referable to *petulans*," the five White Pass red squirrels specimens secured by Laing in May 1925.[35] Further listings indicated Laing's Chitina River specimens made their way into the National Museum, including five Yakutat tundra mice and three collared pikas.[36] But it would be Anderson's and Taverner's assistance several decades earlier in creating an international agreement allowing for migratory bird protection that was a crowning achievement for the growing conservation movement.[37]

The Migratory Birds Convention Act of 1917 had its buildup around the years that Hamilton Mack Laing considered himself a motorcycle-naturalist, riding a Harley-Davidson to access the natural world and write about the birds encountered, building up his own reputation as a writer and naturalist who was self-sufficient in the field. The Act would have its own relevance to Laing's eventual work during the Mount Logan Expedition. But the public outcry about declining birdlife began earlier.

In the nineteenth century, John James Audubon inspired naturalists' clubs and ornithological societies; in 1873, the Nuttall Ornithological Club was created, which would father the American Ornithologists' Union (AOU).[38] The systematic arrangement of classification and nomenclature Taverner used later in his work came from the *American Ornithologists' Union Check-list of North American Birds*, fourth edition from 1931.[39] Worry grew among the general public that birds were on the decline. The Audubon Society, formed in 1886, teamed up with the AOU to fight the growing hunting of birds for their feathers used in the fashionable millinery trade. This kind of hunting eclipsed the usual seasonal market hunting that took place by the turn of the twentieth century.[40]

Since the 1870s, even hunters of conscience in the U.S., encapsulated by the term "sportsman," had been organizing into associations and clubs concerned with the preservation of fish and game. This mirrored the growing focus of federal and state governments, and by 1915, several states had enacted laws, enforced to varying degrees by administrative agencies. National parks were closing to hunting to protect bison and deer. President Theodore Roosevelt was creating game refuges with enthusiasm, and the Lacey Act of 1900 discouraged market hunting by banning interstate transportation of wild game and birds that had been illegally taken.[41] The moral associations with being a "sportsman" were becoming much better defined as a result.

By the late 1910s, the growing political pressure to protect birds and mammals from wanton destruction had begun to create a certain code of ethics among sportsmen. Influenced by conservationists who were hunters, such as William T. Hornaday and Aldo Leopold, this code was borne of a growing sense of responsibility, and the term "sportsman" was a great honour to those who aspired to hunt conscientiously, limit kills and when one did kill, to do so using great "enterprise and skill." As Curt Meine, Aldo Leopold's biographer, put it: "Sportsmanship was a personal matter, referable by the individual to his God, mediated by the human conscience."[42] It was an unwritten contract of sorts between the hunter of conscience, the natural world and what higher power was believed in.

Percy Taverner would further this code of sportsman ethics in his introduction to *Birds of Western Canada*. He stated the discerning hunter was required to determine whether a wild creature was "legitimate game" by its "size, habits, and general food value." He also illustrated the linkage between the hunter and the natural world, the pursuit of fair game being "invigorating sport and tends to the healthful welfare of the sportsman, teaching woodcraft, hardihood, out-of-door adaptability, and marksmanship." This development of skill in the open air would have, as foundation, its own ethical code. "The true sportsman," Taverner wrote, "has a code of ethics of his own founded upon economic as well as humanitarian principles." Reiterating that legitimate game must be used as food, he insisted the ethical sportsman give the game pursued a fair chance: "He is also careful not to deplete the game upon which his future sport depends." However, he took a cautionary tone here, that allowing for liberty among sportsmen did not always have the ideal outcome. "True sportsmanship," he lamented, "has not been universal, and its too common absence has resulted in a gradual but steady depletion of our game." Admitting that regulation had been implemented too late, like the proverbial barn doors being shut long after the horse has left, Taverner hoped that it was not too late for migratory birds, lauding legislation such as the international treaty inherent in the Migratory Birds Convention Act, along with provincial policies that followed suit, but wrote somewhat sheepishly, "the regulations that are enacted today should have been adopted yesterday and the consequence is that, over much of the country, game is a thing of the past."[43]

In the 1939 *Canadian Water Birds: A Pocket Field Guide*, Taverner further took a collaborative tone to begin his extensive and detailed handbook by writing: "it is essential that the sportsman and the shooting fraternity, who exert so powerful a directive influence on public opinion and legislation, should be fully informed upon the species that they seek to perpetuate. It is to them that this volume is especially dedicated."[44] With this somewhat hushed plea, his introduction acknowledged that there "is a common and seemingly justified criticism that our New World sportsmen do not know the birds they shoot as well as do those of the Old Country." He wrote with feeling about the loss of forests, drained swamps, and ploughed prairies being able to revert to their original habitat, but when it came to wildlife, it "is, in fact, a long chain of inter-related factors, many of whose links are so hidden that the continuity between them is often difficult to establish. Tinkering with the unknown or half-known is a dangerous process, no matter how well intentioned it may be."[45] He believed, in order to maintain wildlife at the right level, a problem that required the efforts of Canada as a whole, that crucial was "the recognition and naming of the factors that compose it." Probing even further, Taverner seemed keen to guide the appreciator of winged species to veer away from the rifle, to find pursuits that present altogether an appreciation by identification and aesthetic, stating that "shot-gun collection is not generally desirable with many of the species at any time, or with others in certain close seasons, but the field glass is of invaluable assistance to anyone who wishes to inform himself for sporting, aesthetic or conservational reasons."[46]

Photography, Taverner argued, allowed for many key aspects of the hunt that sportsmen enjoyed, generating the same kind of excitement by "careful stalking and a quick camera shot; erecting a blind in a chosen vicinity from which the operator can photograph subjects unaware of his presence" demanded the same kind of skill and knowledge required while stalking with a gun.[47] Increasingly, banding was becoming a more popular form in capturing birdlife. Banding allowed scientists to learn "more about the movements, matings, age, and migration of birds than we ever hoped before it became an established method of study." This was also a way those who enjoyed outwitting birds in the wild could practice their skills through developing technique and springing traps that could, without causing harm, contribute to the scientific community's knowledge and understanding of birds.[48] Ultimately, Taverner reiterated, it was the Migratory Bird Convention Act that he believed was the clincher, uniting Canada and the United States in coordinated action. Although admonishing how the treaty "has not been easy to administer," he saw the light at the end of the tunnel when it came to depleted birdlife: for the first time "the downward trend in this wild-life population seemed stayed and a little upward movement could be detected." Alas, though he may have continued with this optimism unabated, he realized that it was not enough by itself, but that this upward trend in migratory birds depended on the continued conscientious efforts of "the sporting fraternity." If the ethical sportsman would "restrain himself to harvesting the annual increase without infringing on capital stock, we may have indefinitely a moderate amount of wild-life but in no case can we expect to see again the vast hordes of wild game that our forefathers enjoyed."[49]

In *Birds of Canada*, a revised edition published in 1947 by special permission of the National Museum of Canada, Taverner noted a major change in classifications system, showed appreciation to the creation of national parks and land set aside for wildlife and modified the promising tone of his notes on protection to do with the Migratory Birds Convention Act in his 1926 *Birds of Western Canada*. In his updated version, he wrote in his introduction's "Plan of the Book" section that the "systemic arrangement ... used is that of the American Ornithologists' Union of North American Birds, 4th Edition, 1931." This might seem a trivial alteration to the classification system from his previous works, but he termed it a "radical change," adding that "the old system was antiquated and misleading and the change is already long delayed. The new system will probably be used for the next fifty years, the old one having been accepted for an equal period, so the sooner we learn it the better."[50]

Taverner also tempered his pessimistic forecast for "the future of our waterfowl" with a sincere acknowledgement of "federal and provincial action in the establishment of wild-land reservations in addition to the National and Provincial parks already established." Noting the steady increase in settlement and agricultural practice, he gave thanks for these areas set aside for wildlife, to "give sanctuary, protection, and suitable living conditions in the midst of cultivation and settlement."[51] He hoped that this system might allow for those kinds of native wildlife to flourish. However, his post-war forecast was no longer as optimistic as it was in those heady days of international co-operation that lead to increased migratory bird populations following the activation of the Migratory Birds Convention Act. He wrote of "new factors" having come into play: "With a momentary increase of game more guns have been produced to kill and the killing has been better organized: more marshes have been drained and meadows trodden by cattle." This expanded hunting and destruction of habitat was not the only foe facing bird populations: "Strange diseases have swept in epidemic through the feathered ranks and dry seasons have destroyed thousands." On top of that, Taverner told of the disappearance of eelgrass, the key food source on the Atlantic coast for wintering geese. "The prospects are not promising and, unless means are found to reduce the annual kill or to materially increase production," he warned, "the future of North American migratory game will afford deep concern to sincere conservationist and thoughtful sportsman alike." He clearly did not like to take the alarmist viewpoint, but with so much adversity facing migratory birds, even his earlier faith in the ethical sportsman had waned in recent years. In the introduction for *Birds of Canada*, he wrote: "The only factor that seems possible of direct or immediate control is the legal kill, but this, the generality of sportsmen seem most reluctant to apply to the needs of the case."[52]

As part of Laing's field process, the securing of a bird or mammal specimen included analyzing the stomach contents, which helped determine the specimen's effect on the machinations of the human economy. This, in part, influenced public opinion as to whether a wild creature's existence was detrimental to human prosperity. As Taverner described it: "Stomach examination of what has actually been taken into the alimentary canal is practically the only positive evidence of food habits and in some cases leads to surprising results. No species should be condemned until a thorough study by this method has been made by experienced investigators."[53] Laing's analysis of a specimen's last meal was, by the day's standards, a way of furthering its future, ensuring it was not seen as a pest in agricultural or other economic practice.

In fact, in Taverner's books, each classification included a section on "Economic Status." For example, in 1926's *Birds of Western Canada*, the raven's "Economic Status" indicates it eats "both animal and vegetable food, but has a strong partiality for the former. It seeks the offal from the hunter's dressed game, or the game itself if it be available. It lurks about the outskirts or rookeries and makes dashes for eggs and young. By the sea, it searches the shores at low water for crabs and other sea life and for anything edible that may be washed up. Avoiding cultivation as it does it has little direct economic influence."[54] Perhaps in determining the raven's interest in hunter's offal, Taverner took into account Laing's relationship with a raven family in the Chitina River valley?

Laing, who clearly exhibited the sportsman's ethic, also realized his privilege in collecting specimens, plants, birds and mammals, as the naturalist attached to the Mount Logan Expedition of 1925. He possessed the appropriate permits and collected specimens for the Victoria Memorial Museum. With his days as a motorcycle-naturalist freelancer behind him, he was now a paid museum collector. As Laing biographer Richard Mackie described his adoption of this career, "museum work allowed him to apply and combine the various skills he had learned as a hunter, game warden, teacher, naturalist and writer."[55] His expenses were covered, and he was paid a salary. He also had the chance to record stories, material for his continuing freelance writing for various publications. Prior to 1925, he had been involved in the Smithsonian Institution's 1920 expedition to Lake Athabasca, led by Francis Harper; the "purpose of the expedition was to examine the main breeding grounds of migratory North American waterfowl at or near the Athabasca delta," Mackie wrote. The expedition sponsors hoped naturalists could determine "the number, distribution, and migration patterns of waterfowl, all

The National Museum's British Columbia field party at Vaseux Lake, May 31, 1922.
Back row, left to right: Allan Brooks, P.A. Taverner, Frank Farley. Front row,
left to right: H. M. Laing, George Gartrell, D. Alan Sampson
(PHOTO: H.M. LAING, COURTESY: RICHARD MACKIE)

of which would, theoretically, enable them to administer more effectively the Migratory Birds Convention Treaty of 1917."[56]

In 1921, Taverner recruited Laing to act as his assistant for summer fieldwork in Cypress Lake, Saskatchewan. Laing found success in the expedition, not only with the many specimens he secured for the National Museum but also in the enjoyment of bringing the expedition party to his familiar haunt, Heart's Desire, at Oak Lake, Manitoba, where they received a visit by Hoyes Lloyd.[57] In May 1922, Laing joined the Victoria Memorial Museum's British Columbia field party, beginning in the southern Okanagan Valley, after Taverner introduced him to Allan Brooks. Laing respected Brooks, a prominent bird painter and naturalist, and the two formed a lasting bond.[58] Starting in June, Laing began two months of collecting in and around Comox on Vancouver Island. He really liked the area and decided to settle there, devoting much of the following year to constructing his first home, Baybrook.[59] In 1924, Laing took what became a difficult expedition job, one that Brooks had turned down, as naturalist on board the HMCS *Thiepval*, sailing to Japan via the north Pacific Ocean to bring fuel for the amphibious bi-plane that Archibald Stuart MacLaren was flying in an aerial circumnavigation attempt. The trip was plagued by seasickness and disagreeable shipmates, and Laing learned, by telegram, that his father had died.[60] In March of the next year, Laing, now in his early forties, became naturalist and cinematographer assigned to the Mount Logan Expedition of 1925.[61]

Laing found himself in the Chitina River valley a few months later, having been adopted by a raven family while doing his biological work. Upon discovering he had killed, in the pursuit of his work, the matriarch of a raven family with newly hatched offspring, he became somewhat detached from his role as scientist and began a process of atonement. Perhaps there was a point Laing believed he had made amends for his taking their mother away from them. No matter as, by August, the ravens tired of Hubrick's Camp, and found easy pickings in ripening berries elsewhere. Luckily, he had managed to photograph the raven family at work on the offerings that for a time gave Laing a sense of closeness with his adoptive family.

At Heart's Desire, Oak Lake, Manitoba, in 1921. Left to right:
Hoyes Lloyd, Percy Taverner, D. Alan Sampson and H.M. Laing
(PHOTO H.M. LAING, COURTESY: RICHARD MACKIE)

Laing experienced other exchanges with wildlife he encountered in
his work. The moment when he locked eyes with Napoleon on June 20
and spoke to the little ram, getting within twenty-five feet of him, was
a "pleasing adventure with a wild creature."

Although the creatures he encountered would inspire him to use the
Universal movie camera, by Laing's own admission, the bulkiness of the
equipment was sufficient for him to, over time, leave the motion picture
photography to nearer camp and bring the still camera further afield.

Allen Carpe recorded that the "only cameras available for such use at
the time of the expedition were (a) the [Debrie] 'Sept,' having a magazine capacity of 15 feet of standard gauge film, (b) the Bell & Howell
'Filmo,' chambered for daylight loading 100-foot reels of 16mm, narrow-
gauge film." Using the Filmo in freezing temperatures and poor weather
conditions was more advantageous because its capacity was equivalent
to 250 feet of standard gauge film and the film containers were already
spooled, ready to insert. As Carpe acknowledged, perhaps from previous

experience, "frequent rethreading or manipulation of a change bag is impossible in a storm with frozen fingers; even operation of the camera is difficult." This statement reinforces the fact that his intensive film work taken at higher elevations leading to the summit of Logan was a remarkable achievement.[62] In the *Bulletin of the Geographical Society of Philadelphia*, it was noted that Carpe "accomplished the remarkable feat of taking motion pictures of the entire ascent, at elevations never before attempted by cinema work in this country and exceeded only during the Everest Expeditions."[63]

Laing's greatest accomplishments with the film camera were in wonderful shots of wildlife in their environment. However, sometimes it was in the moments lost to posterity that he had the most appreciation for the natural world. An example is when two rams near Raven Canyon's rim, where, by the time he had put down the camera and readied it for action, the bigger ram appeared before him ready-made for an ideal shot, he noted, "I was standing behind a fallen, leaning spruce and its hundred obstructions blocked my lens." It's hard not to feel his disappointment in what might have been a glorious shot, portraying this hardy animal of the Chitina River valley, that ended up being just a good intention. "And so," Laing lamented, "a wild-life picture of years—the subject, the background, were as perfect as Nature could make them—was not taken; and no such opportunity came again."[64]

Both Carpe and Lambart advocated for the inclusion of motion picture photography in capturing the events leading up to the summiting of Logan. At the Mount Logan Committee meeting in Vancouver on January 11, 1925, Director Wheeler of the Alpine Club of Canada stated that he found such photography to be superfluous, and not a priority for the expedition, wishing for a focus on still photography: "it not being considered that movies would be worth while [sic]." Lambart scribbled on his meeting minutes under this quotation "what rubish [sic] HFL."[65] This was the first sign of friction developing between Lambart and Wheeler on this subject. Despite Wheeler and the committee's apparent lack of interest in motion picture photography during the expedition, Lambart was quietly querying the Eastman Kodak Company and keeping W.W. Foster in the loop about his movie desires. On January

28, on official Mount Logan Expedition stationary, Foster wrote to Lambart that, around February 6, he was "going down to Seattle with Wheeler to see MacCarthy off [for the winter freighting expedition] and will then take up the question of moving-picture man."[66] Apparently, Foster was trying to convince Wheeler at that point. But to take it a step further, Foster wrote supportively "MacCarthy feels that Captain Hulbrick (sic) who is the photographer at MacCarthy (sic) could do all that is required."[67] Is this Captain Hubrick of Hubrick's Camp?

Of course, at this early date, Hamilton Mack Laing had not yet been attached to the Mount Logan Expedition. And by Wheeler's estimation, in a letter to Lambart also dated January 28, there would be no recourse for another hanger-on that would be a "dead weight on the expedition." Wheeler consoles Lambart that the Mount Logan Committee doesn't discount the value of a photographer, but "it does not appear that any suitable Canadian is available for such purpose, and there is no doubt that the moving picture end of it would be very considerable additional expense."[68] Lambart was planning to bring his own Ross camera along on the expedition for still photography.

After this, events started unfolding quite quickly. Requisitions for rolls of Sept moving camera film began to come from Lambart's desk.[69] On March 26, Lambart drafted a letter to ACC Director Wheeler mentioning he was corresponding with Dr. Charles Camsell, Deputy Minister of the Department of Mines, about bringing along a naturalist who could also act as cinematographer.[70] Lambart listed Laing's recent expedition experience, finishing with his 1924 stint as naturalist on board the HMCS *Thiepval*.

On March 26, Chief of the Division of Biology Rudolph M. Anderson waded into the discussion of motion picture photography on the Mount Logan Expedition with a memo, in which he mentions R.S. Peck's recommendation of the Bell & Howell Filmo, but as it was a camera that used 16mm film, he, Percy Taverner and Hoyes Lloyd believed it wouldn't be "practicable for our exhibition purposes as it can not be used in standard size of projecting machine."[71] In other words, they required 35mm film stock to project films for the public. Anderson then went on to mention that enlarging the 16mm film to 35mm would be an additional cost, despite the supposed ease of use suggested by R.S. Peck. Although Anderson suggested that the film captured during the expedition would more likely be of benefit to the mountaineers' lecture tours in future, he acknowledged Lambart's view that "the expedition is helping Mr. Laing out on Museum collecting work, and we can reciprocate by helping the expedition out on motion picture work."[72] Overall, the takeaways from Anderson's memo were that Deputy Minister Camsell request a loan of a Universal camera and outfit from the Department of Trade and Commerce, authorize the purchase of 4,000 feet of film and also authorize that arrangements be made for Laing go to Seattle for instruction on the use of the Universal camera. Anderson suggested Mr. WHE Hudson as instructor, who had been "a press motion picture photographer for Seattle Post-Intelligencer and other papers, and was taking motion pictures in Alaska when we were there in 1913."[73] Also suggested was Asahel Curtis "formerly of Curtis & Miller, has a large firm in Seattle" who had specialized in photographing Indigenous peoples (also by his brother, Edward S. Curtis). Anderson knew him through photographs taken in Victoria for the arctic expedition in 1913 and had worked with him more later.[74] Laing's calendar during his time in Seattle was filling up, and he had not yet officially accepted the offer to accompany the expedition.

Lambart wrote to Foster on March 29 regarding the plan as it pertained to Laing. The young writer and naturalist was to "report at Seattle and be under training with his Universal Motion apparatus until the date of our sailing."[75] He made sure to inform Foster that this camera was on its way from Ottawa to the west coast for Laing's use, with the Department of Mines sorting out the arrangements. But more to the point, Lambart ensured Foster that their cinematographer and naturalist was committed to the expedition. "This morning," Lambart wrote, "the Department phoned me that they had received word from Laing that he is all prepared to accept the offer if so finally decided."[76] Since learning of Laing and his possible inclusion, Lambart had become an advocate for him, continued with ebullient support for their new recruit, no doubt buoyed by the idea that the expedition was all but assured of the cinematographer that he had supported for several months. "I have heard nothing but good things of Laing ever since his name and this offer to join the Expedition came up," Lambart cheered. "He writes very well and has written a great deal in the Globe and other papers on natural history topics. He is a good mixer and is well liked."[77]

The concern with the Logan Committee back in Vancouver didn't seem to be how much he would be liked but under how much control he would be. In a telegram, sent from Vancouver on March 31, W.W. Foster wrote:

Logan Committee met yesterday and appreciate offer Department Mines STOP

Desire to know whether Laing under absolute control leaders and same bases regarding material as others STOP

Committee feel films should belong to club but all information of Departmental nature to Department STOP

Can Laing interview Wheeler

Please advise Wheeler direct

Committee desire cooperate but apprehensive additional weight equipment[78]

Lambart was quite certain that Laing would not want to travel beyond Turn Camp with that heavy motion picture camera apparatus in tow, but what had emerged was where the final film would belong: with the Department of Mines or the Alpine Club of Canada. Lambart wasted no time and replied to Foster's telegram directly to ACC Director A.O. Wheeler that "Laing under control leaders subject to mutual understanding between Mines Department and Expedition Committee that Expedition assists Laing collecting natural history specimens and that Laing act as photographer for expedition STOP."[79] Lambart now assured them he had written the Department of Mines regarding film rights, and assured the committee on the west coast that there were "no difficulties" when it came to the Alpine Club of Canada.

However, it was soon clear to Lambart that Wheeler saw difficulties with the expenses in preparing for the expedition. In a formal letter, written on April 4, 1925, on official "Alpine Club of Canada, Mt. Logan Expedition 1924–1925" stationary, Wheeler outlined his concerns to Lambart. They stemmed from the very expedition MacCarthy had overseen that assured the mountaineers had what they required for the expedition. "MacCarthy's difficulties and increased expenditure render finances and results doubtful," Wheeler wrote with a gloomy tone just prior to a major expedition setting off, especially one on which he was director. He expressed to Lambart, the assistant leader, what was discussed with care at the committee meeting of March 29, specifically that "the carrying capacity of the party now available for the glacier section beyond Trail End would not stand any further strain, and, should MacCarthy not succeed in placing his supplies as he had planned, would be of doubtful sufficiency."[80] Had the compromise to include Laing, on top of MacCarthy's challenges during the freighting expedition pushed the expedition's budget to its limits? "In consequence," Wheeler continued, "it was thought that the addition of Mr. Laing's outfit would be impossible to handle without further carrying power. It would be an easy matter to add an extra pack horse to Trail End, but beyond that is a problem, without adding another porter to the Expedition in addition to Laing, for which we do not see a solution." Had Wheeler, in bending to the will of the expedition members, and certainly foremost Lambart's wishes, to include Laing, found a way to detract his inclusion? He continued by putting more blame on MacCarthy's winter freighting expedition: "MacCarthy's expenses for transport have increased beyond all expectation and financing the Expedition has also become a very serious problem. There is just $4000 available for the party going in on May 2nd, and we have no money to pay for any expense in connection with Laing."[81] It was made clear to Lambart that there was no fat left on the expedition's budget, and Wheeler wrote further of his hope that, even though the Department of Mines was footing the bill for Laing, he would not allow for any more expenses than already agreed upon by the expedition's committee. With that having been expressed, Wheeler wrote that the committee "would be willing to have Laing go with the Expedition, and he would be expected to report to the Chairman of the Committee, Colonel Foster, at the Hotel Seattle, Seattle, on May 1st, or sooner at Vancouver."[82] But in almost a parting shot at Lambart's decision to have an extra man, naturalist and cinematographer, billed as self-sufficient and well-liked, Wheeler could not help but include a final query: "In your letter of March 26th you say that it is not likely that Laing would go farther than Turn. Would it not be beyond that point that motion pictures would be most beneficial?"[83]

On April 11, 1925, a week after Wheeler expressed his concerns in writing to Lambart, Allen Carpe wrote to Lambart letting him know about his departure for Seattle on April 23, and that he would look him up at the Hotel Seattle closer to May 1. After some queries about mountaineering equipment, he asked about the subject at the core of their correspondence: "Were any arrangements finally made for a photographer and motion picture man? I heard nothing more about it, and the showing of the Mt. Everest film here recently made me feel that would be a great loss if good pictures were not obtained on our trip."[84] Films of expeditions were becoming increasingly popular as establishing documents of major achievements in the natural world, and Lambart and Carpe had been corresponding about this subject. "I have been looking into the possibilities of the small 16mm film and Bell & Howell portable camera somewhat, and hope to bring one out unless arrangements have been made for something better." Lambart's answer to Wheeler's question of a week earlier may have been answered. Further, Carpe managed to take matters into his own hands, in regards to institutional concerns of enlarging 16mm film to 35mm for exhibition purposes: "I have arranged with the cinematograph department of the Eastman people at Rochester to try enlarging the 16mm film onto standard size film and should get a test of it in a few days."[85] Lambart must have been rubbing his hands together in anticipation, as Carpe suggested by his enthusiasm that the results should allow for acceptable images when incorporated into a film shot with Laing's 35mm contributions using the Universal motion picture camera. But it was Carpe's final endorsement of the Bell & Howell camera that must have cinched tight the discovery as to which of the mountaineers would continue filming from Trail End to the true summit. "The Bell & Howell camera only weighs 5 lbs. And is a remarkably fine little machine—two speeds, suitable for telephoto lens, daylight loading and runs 4 minutes on one load—but of course I don't want to bring anything out if other arrangements have been made already."[86]

As for how the Debrie Sept would feature in the expedition, and what arrangements with the Department of Mines in acquiring Laing would mean in the eventual film's final use, part of Lambart's letter to Foster would iron that out:

> In any event, whatever happens, Dr. Camsell the Deputy Minister of Mines in conversation with me made it clear that the Department were anxious to cooperate and help the Expedition, which is quite manifest by providing the cost of the 4000 feet of film and arranging for special training at Seattle, all largely to help the Expedition. I brought up the point of our privileges with the use of the film and this was very kindly answered by saying that as far as the Department were concerned it would be only used by them in their own little private series of lectures given in the Museum and that the Expedition would have the first public showing if it wanted it. The Department would have for themselves of course one print (Positive copy): regarding further copies for the Alpine Club or for any other purpose I felt that this would have to work itself out later. If successful, with what Mr. Laing is able to get together, with what we can gather together from the Septs, which I hope there will be two (one Mac [MacCarthy] has now) there ought to be enough to put on quite a good showing. I am bringing 24 reels (18 feet each) for the Sept. The cost of developing and printing one positive is 6 cts. per foot, this exclusive of titles and arrangement of the text, which mounts up to something.[87]

With today's emphasis on photographic excellence, and a plethora of nature documentaries available via a wide variety of media, it might be difficult to appreciate the efforts of these early pioneers in motion picture photography. The viewing of the resulting films, produced by institutions such as the National Museum of Canada, was becoming quite fashionable among naturalists. And its emerging importance might have added emphasis to the pressure felt by Laing in his labours to capture the natural world on film.

Hoyes Lloyd wrote an article in the May 1926 issue of *The Canadian Field-Naturalist*, published by the influential Ottawa Field-Naturalists'

Club, about the growing number of motion pictures, produced by government institutions, on the subject of natural history.[88] An indomitable
figure in the ornithological community, he became president of the
Ottawa Field-Naturalists' Club in 1923, was once president of the
American Ornithologists' Union, and, after having been interviewed by
Rudolph Martin Anderson among others, had been put in charge of
administering the Migratory Bird Regulations under the Convention
Act in 1918.[89] The article listed a number of newly made films, some
produced by the Victoria Memorial Museum (National Museum of
Canada), for hire for the nominal sum of $1.00 from the Canadian
Government Motion Picture Bureau. Lloyd was pointing out to naturalists who may not be fully aware of the growing film industry that
there "are many films that show the scenery of various parts of Canada."
He clarified that some dealt with natural history subjects and featured
the scenery of Canada: "It is suggested that, for most audiences, one
travelogue picture be included with those that deal more strictly with
natural history." The large number of titles listed indicated that this was
a developing industry, and that enterprises like the Mount Logan Expedition would have films made to accompany them. Lloyd himself had
written several, such as *Making Friends with Wild Life*, while Percy
Taverner wrote and photographed others, including *The Birds of a City
Garden*, produced by the National Museum of Canada.

Taverner himself penned an article in the same issue, "Scientific
Advice for Wild Life Conservationists," that tackled the controversial
subject of game production. At that time, some in the growing conservation movement posited that game be raised on farms, rather like the
utilitarian view of forestry put forth by Gifford Pinchot, to make up for
sagging numbers of fair game. He began with a quote, from the previous
fall, by Aldo Leopold, a growing force in conservation in the United
States. Leopold was at pains to point out that this new idea was lacking
in know-how as sportsmen simply didn't know how to execute it: "He
may be a good woodsman but a poor scientist. He is missing a lot, because acquiring a personal skill in raising as well as hunting game dou-
bles the attractiveness of the sport."[90] Taverner, who was just about to
write his introduction for *Birds of Western Canada*, in which he would

argue that "the scientific collector is sympathetic towards the principles of wild-life conservation," saw Leopold's words as a primer for him to discuss wildlife conservation. It would foreshadow his own disappointment in the conduct of certain sportsmen, perhaps not as conscientious as would be desired, when he wrote in his article: "It is not always a fact that the successful hunter or trapper knows much more about his game than is sufficient for its pursuit. In certain directions he may be well informed, but in larger aspects he is usually lacking."[91] With this cautionary tone, Taverner pursued what he would write about in *Birds of Western Canada*, perhaps with naturalists such as Laing recently in mind, having concluded his article with this question:

> Is it not time that those concerned with wild life conservation followed the example set in the less complex subject of forestry and surround their executives with scientifically trained naturalists who can supply ascertained fact instead of guess-work, who can see the subject comprehensively and who have made themselves familiar with the history of the subject, its failures and successes both at home and abroad?[92]

Leopold, whose article "Wilderness as a Form of Land Use" was published in 1925, was moving into a realm of thinking that saw him forwarding wilderness preservation, whereas earlier the value of wilderness was seen as recreational, surrounding its conquest, a view that was firmly rooted in his homelands pioneering mindset. This paradigm shift eventually moved him into the realm of his "land ethic," while Laing in Alaska in 1925 was becoming part of a community rather than conquering it. Over time, he accomplished this through his connection with ravens, a young ram and a red-tailed hawk. He, along with the mountaineers, ceased to be just an objective scientist or conqueror and became part of this land-community.

In *A Sand County Almanac*, Leopold described his vision of a land ethic. He laid out its premise: that an individual is part of a community of interdependent elements; an individual that instinctively competes to gain a foothold in that community also, ethically, must co-operate to ensure that there is still a place to compete for. He extended this premise to cover soil, water, plants and animals: the land. In summary, he wrote:

"a land ethic changes the role of *Homo sapiens* from conqueror of the land-community to plain member and citizen of it. It implies respect for his fellow-members, and also respect for the community as such."[93]

The same year that the Mount Logan Expedition set out and Laing collected his specimens along the Chitina River valley, an organization comprising wildlife scientists, wildlife managers and lovers of the natural world from both sides of the border began secretly assembling. One of their most prominent members was Aldo Leopold; another member was James Harkin, Canada's first Dominion Parks Commissioner. Concerned with increasing resource extraction and land privatization, the Brotherhood of Venery was also worried about wanton wildlife destruction. Many members, such as Leopold, who had been subsistence hunters, knew the importance of striking balance, and opposed predator control tactics as they recognized the risks of overpopulation.

Writer and naturalist Briony Penn, while researching a book, came across a file folder simply marked "B" that sent her down a rabbit hole investigating this secret group, which she credits with the legacy of our current concern of climate change and the modern environmental movement. One of the individuals asked to join the Brotherhood was Hamilton Mack Laing. "Although Laing didn't join in the end," Briony wrote, "he was very much part of the group, was friends with them all and shared all their values of mentoring and education and they all riffed off one another." But it was Leopold, I learned from Briony, who had something to gain from associating with a pool of Canadians embedded in the growing movement. "Far from them being influenced by Leopold," Briony wrote, "Leopold was influenced by the older instigators of Hoyes Lloyd and Percy Taverner and the other Canadians."[94] The concern of development and overuse of national parks would grow.

In 1961, concern grew at the Resources for Tomorrow Conference held in Montreal regarding the increased numbers of visitors at national parks such as Banff as well as road building and similar development within parks. In 1968, a conference held in Calgary was meant to address this, and other issues about proper use of natural resources and protection of wildlife. Jean Chrétien, recently sworn in as Minister for Indian Affairs and Northern Development, was responsible for Canada's national parks. In his opening address in Calgary, he spoke of three concerns. One was that over-development in parks would not strike a balance between visitors' demands for recreation in parks with the need for conservation. The next was that the park system was too concentrated in the west, and he wished for it to extend further east. Lastly, he sought to investigate diversifying the park system to "meet particular needs in particular situations."[95]

Jean-Paul Harroy, then the Chairman of the International Commission on National Parks of the International Union for the Conservation of Nature and Natural Resource, spoke on the national park movement as not particular to Canada, rather one taking place worldwide. But countries each struck their own balance. He had established that "the title 'national park or equivalent reserve' could only be applied to areas which had been accorded a legal status protecting them from all natural resource exploitation by man and from any other threat to the quality of the area."[96] In some cases, this could mean that a national park could prohibit tourists, and was then a nature reserve, which could apply to "private reserves such as those administered by the National Audubon Society or The Nature Conservancy in the United States of America."[97] However, in Canada, and in other nations' parks, tourism was allowed and encouraged; throughout his address, Harroy was firm on the conflict inherent in "social tourism" overwhelming national parks and reserves in industrialized countries. He stated: "social leisure and the increasing mobility of citizens are causing problems which are different, but just as serious and related also to the 'tourism' factor." With a citizenry increasingly in need of a natural playground, it seemed that the very demand for the tourist playground destinations that national parks had become, certainly in Canada via its earliest one at Banff, people ran the risk of destroying the very natural setting with its wildlife they came to see and experience.[98] This takes note of the core conflict throughout conservation: the meeting of recreation, industrialization and preservation. But what was to be made of wildlife's value?

Furthering Taverner's reasoning behind the value of birds, naturalists and ornithologists more recently pointed out how ineffable it is. As W. Earl Godfrey wrote in *The Birds of Canada*, published in 1986, there is "no way of estimating in dollars and cents the total value of our bird life, but we do know it is immense." His introduction clearly stated that birds consume vast numbers of insects each year that would ordinarily devastate crops and forests "and annoy us generally." Certain birds, he noted, specialize in performing tasks for us: "Hawks during the day and owls by night maintain a round-the-clock check on the numbers of rodent pests. Gulls and other birds perform a useful service as scavengers." Remarking on the developing hobby of studying birds, which may be their most measurable societal value, he wrote that it "is an absorbing recreation that is enjoyed regularly by thousands of Canadians in all seasons and in all types of terrain. Their numbers are rapidly increasing." The wide variety of equipment associated with birdwatching or birding ranges from binoculars to cutting-edge camera technology to outdoor apparel. "Many enthusiasts plan their vacation itineraries in the hope of satisfying their particular interest in birds," Godfrey observed, "often joining one of the many elaborate bird tours to various parts of the world." Equally, there was the flip side: hunting of migratory game birds was also an industry that supported the economy, one "involving guns, ammunition, hostelries, special apparel, and transportation."[99] Perhaps the underlying value of birds is that they bring joy to us, however we interpret their presence, and it is by balancing need, conscience and forethought, that determines whether they will continue to be present in such numbers for us to enjoy in future.

A recent visit to the George C. Reifel Migratory Bird Sanctuary in Delta, near Vancouver, reminded me of the underlying value of birds. While walking its trails, I've been fascinated by the diversity of waterfowl and impressed by some visitors' massive and expensive-looking photographic equipment, which dwarf my Nikon D3400 with its 18–55mm lens, aimed at that waterfowl. Sometimes large congregations of these photographers around a particular bird of interest seems to me excessive and invasive, in a competitive bid to get the ideal shot, that perfect nature photograph.

I asked George Reifel, grandson of conservationist George C. Reifel for whom the sanctuary is named, about how it attempts to strike balance between appreciative visitors and conserving the very birdlife they want to protect. Just two years after Laing's expedition in Alaska, in 1927, George C. Reifel purchased land on the northwest corner of Westham Island, where the sanctuary is today. Dykes were established, and so was waterfowl habitat, and soon Reifel had created a desirable property that served as an ideal family retreat. In the 1960s, his son, George H. Reifel, set the machinery in motion to create a bird sanctuary, granting the first lease to the British Columbia Waterfowl Society (founded in the company of Mack Laing's contemporary Ian McTaggart Cowan, in 1961), and Ducks Unlimited Canada collaborated with the Society on water management purposes for the variety of habitat on-site. The Society has managed the sanctuary since 1963, and today George Reifel is its vice-president and takes the time to do community outreach. He said the sanctuary is one of the only places in Canada where visitors, who come in droves every year, pay for the privilege of seeing waterfowl in their natural habitat. Revenue and membership fees go towards fencing, creative facilities and general upkeep, but Reifel admits that the sheer number of waterfowl appreciators threaten the very thing they've come to see: The number of visitors are sometimes a risk to overwhelm the waterfowl:

> Finding balance is a big challenge. What's the right number of people admitted? As a result of Covid, there is now a reservation system. It's based on the number of vehicles that can fit in the parking lot. We put in a gate system with professional gate control. But nowadays visitors will come by with very expensive binoculars and camera equipment and they can crowd in and overwhelm a particular bird while they're trying to get that perfect picture. There is a competition to have their photo on the cover of *Marshnotes*, the newsletter of the British Columbia Waterfowl Society. There are some professional photographers out there and they crowd around the one bird of interest, and so there has to be some field etiquette. We have thousands of images on file from photographers.[100]

Reifel also admits that photography is to thank for ending the practice of collecting specimens for scientific study in the twentieth century. "The quality of photography is light years ahead of where is was then," he told me, referring to Laing's days along the Chitina River in 1925.[101]

"Simply put, we no longer need to collect specimens today." From the long camera lenses that I see at the sanctuary, getting up close and personal with waterfowl no longer requires inanimate specimens for study. Through surveillance, humans are getting to know birdlife.

Reifel explained the role regulations such as the Migratory Birds Convention Act played in wanton destruction of birdlife as it "eliminated market hunting, putting it out of business." With a reduced market, and growing public opinion on the subject, selling one's bagged birds to restaurants and shops came to a swift end, with Reifel noting that "quite a bit of that market hunting was done in the Fraser Delta."[102]

Growing up on the Reifel Farm, a young George Reifel used to, as a young Hamilton Mack Laing did, secure a fair number of birds. "Hunting was something that I would do after school," Reifel told me, "I loved it." Today, the land once occupied by the farm is the Alaksen National Wildlife Area, and his family home is now the Canadian Wildlife Service headquarters, part of Environment Canada. "It was built in 1929 by my grandfather," Reifel said, "and it was 1972 when it was gifted to the federal government." So he admitted, from his boyhood stalks on the family's farm, that much knowledge can be gained from hunting birds: "Sportsmen have an experience of seeing, observing the life cycle of birds." To this, he added that considerable funding of conservation groups such as Ducks Unlimited comes from sportsmen. Today, Reifel believes that, when it comes to hunting, "harvesting has minimal impact," and in fact, he mirrored the sentiment of Percy Taverner in the 1920s when he expressed to me that "birds are very important, they have a different type of value."

When it comes to banding, a practice begun in Taverner's day around the time Laing was hunting in the Chitina River valley, Reifel admitted its importance in understanding migratory birds, as well as its high-tech developments in the twenty-first century: "My grandfather was a conservationist, and he banded 35,000 birds, but today we don't have to band a bird as satellite tracking of birds allows us to see their entire migratory route." This amazing turn of events has, for example, included small plastic neck bands on select lesser snow geese that determine their location in their migratory route from Wrangel Island north of Siberia to the Fraser River estuary. "We get an email a week from birds being tracked," Reifel said, "where they're going and maps." This, paired with extraordinary leaps in photographic technology, have made specimen collecting for scientific bird study a thing of the past. But perhaps even Hamilton Mack Laing and Percy Taverner would be impressed by the sanctuary's Leo Malfet Bird Collection, 509 taxidermy mounted birds housed within the lecture hall. Although Reifel admitted that "some specimens are long in the tooth," they are seen by many urban school programs in a given year, a nod to how things used to be before tracking and photographic technology, as well as wildlife policy, progressed since Laing's days walking the gravel bars at the Chitina. Ironically, Reifel conceded that, with decreased hunting of waterfowl, parts of their habitat, especially for lesser snow geese, "are under siege: they're chewing up the Fraser Delta foreshore." It seems that, with improved science and photography, waterfowl, in some cases, have an overpopulation problem.[103]

In his first book, *Out with the Birds*, Laing recounted several sojourns in the natural world leading from his Heart's Desire, penning adventures intending to highlight Manitoba's birds. In the tenth chapter ("Some Harmless Hunting"), he leads off a search for ducks:

> For the man who has within him that perennial yearning to go afield and kill something who in short, really loves to hunt, yet withal nourishes somewhere in his conscience the counter conviction that no longer should the creatures of the woods and fields be killed for fun, there is no hobby quite so good as the speed kodak [sic]. And of all the numerous kinds of game that he may bring to bag, at all times of the year—for there are no game-laws for the kodak—he will find no more worthy foeman for his lens than the clan of Web-foot.[104]

This passage captured the link between photographer, sportsman and specimen collector: the relationship between the stalker, whether with a gun or a camera, and the subject. As Laing further stated, it was, and still is, this "pitting of himself, his own wit and fiber against that of the birds" that allowed for better study of these creatures that did, and still do, fascinate us so.[105] A visit to the Reifel Migratory Bird Sanctuary shows the current extent of this fascination, sometimes to a point of excess, as in overcrowding a sheltering great horned owl with too many long lenses pointed at it. However, the development of conservation has taken us from needing an inert specimen before us for scientific study to exploring our curiosity with photography. Today this is where we are in our efforts to strike balance.

Acknowledgements

A loving thank you must, as always, go to my wife, Dr. Laura Sauvé, for her patience and understanding as I wrote, spoke ideas aloud and struggled at times, during the writing of this book. Thanks as well to my sons, Michael and Marc, who also heard my ideas spoken aloud, and may have heard me say, from time to time, that I am not a mountaineer.

Thank you to my parents, Michael and Louise Hughes, who heard, on more than one occasion, my synopsis for the book. I may have rambled on a little too much.

A great big thanks to the late Ron Hatch and his widow, Veronica, who heard my pitch for *Capturing the Summit* while we were promoting *Riding the Continent* in Hamilton Mack Laing's parents' town of residence, Portland, Oregon, in 2019. They supported the project from that point on. To Kevin Welsh, assistant publisher, my appreciation and thanks for his patience and perseverance as he has seen many versions of the manuscript I sent him (perhaps more than was necessary) and worked through a pandemic while getting to know Ronsdale Press. Thank you to my own indefatigable guide, editor Judith Brand, for her thorough work on this manuscript. To Julie Cochrane, my thanks for her work in layout and cover design. Thank you to publisher Wendy Atkinson, who I got to know recently during the editing and promotion of this book.

To Elizabeth Kundert-Cameron, Director of Archives and Special Collections; and to Kayla Cazes, Librarian and Reference Archivist at the Whyte Museum of the Canadian Rockies, go my thanks for corresponding with me, answering my questions, and welcoming me into the archives in March 2022 after many failed pandemic attempts to travel to Banff. What a privilege it was to research the expedition in the Rockies. An additional thanks to Michael Coleman-Hughes who was the best research assistant I could have asked for.

My thanks to Katie Sauter, Library Director at the American Alpine Club Library, for helping me locate Allen Carpe's photography under difficult circumstances at the library, as well as Grant Carnie and other volunteers who helped determine locations on the massif where photographs were taken.

Thanks to Patrick Osborne, Senior Rights and Licensing Specialist, Public Services Branch at Library and Archives Canada for answering my queries about *The Conquest of Mount Logan* and several other sources besides.

Thanks to Dion Dhillon, Records and Privacy Manager, Partnerships IT and Digital, at the Royal BC Museum, for his assistance in locating the diaries of Hamilton Mack Laing from the Mount Logan Expedition of 1925. Thanks also to the staff at British Columbia Archives who accommodated me during three days of reading and research there in March 2020.

As with *Riding the Continent*, my thanks for the continued support of Jim Boulter, Gordon Olsen and the members of the Mack Laing Heritage Society. They have faced an unprecedented challenge in preserving the last remaining home of Hamilton Mack Laing in Comox, British Columbia, and my best wishes and hopes for their success in doing so.

Thank you, Lorne Hammond, Curator of History at the Royal BC Museum, for helping me track down an article written by Percy A. Taverner, "Scientific Advice for Wild Life Conservationists," in which he quotes Aldo Leopold on game propagation relating to wildlife protection.

Thanks to the work of Janet Foster, I was able to assemble a snapshot of the growing movement of conservation not only in Canada but also in the United States, before, during and after Laing's time in the Chitina River valley in 1925.

A general appreciation for the collection of the Vancouver Public Library, from which I gathered many sources of information and borrowed many books. May the VPL's collections stay free of charge and accessible to the public. Also, I'm grateful to the Cornell Lab of Ornithology for creating the wonderful online resource allaboutbirds.org which was consulted many times.

Thanks also to Wade Davis, Briony Penn, George C. Reifel, Zac Robinson and, of course, Richard Mackie, for your assistance and support of *Capturing the Summit*.

I'd like to thank H.M. Laing for writing his diaries, on which much of this story was built.

Common and Scientific
Names of Species

Birds

COMMON NAME	SCIENTIFIC NAME
American hawk owl	*Surnia ulula*
American three-toed woodpecker	*Picoides americanus*
American tree sparrow	*Spizzela monticola*
Arctic three-toed woodpecker	*Picoides arcticus*
Barrow's golden-eye duck	*Glaucionetta islandica*
bohemian waxwing	*Bombycilla garrula*
brown-headed chickadee	*Penthestes hudsonicus*
collared pika	*Ochotona collaris*
common redpoll	*Acanthis linaria*
flicker	*Colantes auratus*
golden-crowned kinglet	*Regulus satrapa*
golden-crowned sparrow	*Zonotrichia coronata*
golden eagle	*Aquila chrysaetos*
goshawk	*Astur atricapillus*
green-winged teal	*Nettion carolinense*
hawk owl	*Surnia ulula*
hermit thrush	*Hylocichla guttata*

COMMON NAME	SCIENTIFIC NAME
herring gull	*Larus argentatus*
horned lark	*Otocoris alpestris*
horned owl	*Bubo virginianus*
Hudsonian chickadee	*Penthestes hudsonicus*
lesser yellowlegs	*Totanus flavipes*
magpie	*Pica pica hudsonia*
myrtle warbler	*Dendroica coronata*
northern bald eagle	*Haliaeetus leucocephalus*
northern flicker	*Colaptes auratus*
northern hairy woodpecker	*Dryobates villosus*
northern phalarope	*Lobipes lobatus*
northern raven	*Corvus corax*
olive-backed thrush	*Hylocichia ustulata*
olive-sided flycatcher	*Nuttalornis borealis*
pigeon hawk	*Falco columbarius*
pine siskin	*Spinus pinus*
pipit	*Anthus rubescens*
raven	*Corvus corax*
red-breasted nuthatch	*Sitta canadensis*
red-tailed hawk	*Buteo borealis*
ruby-crowned kinglet	*Regulus calendula*
sandpiper	*Tringa solitaria*
Savannah sparrow	*Passerculus sandwichensis*
slate-coloured junco	*Junco hyemalis*
sparrow hawk	*Cerchneis sparvaria*
spotted sandpiper	*Actitis macularia*
spruce grouse	*Canachites canadensis*
three-toed woodpecker	*Picoides arcticus*
Townsend's solitaire	*Myiadestes townsendi*
varied thrush	*Ixorius naevius*
violet-green swallow	*Tachycineta thalassina*
wheatear	*Saxicola oenanthe*
whisky-jack or Canada jay	*Perisoreus canadensis*
white-crowned sparrow	*Zonotrichia leucophrys*

COMMON NAME	SCIENTIFIC NAME
white-winged crossbill	*Loxia leucoptera*
white-winged scoter	*Oidemia deglandi*
Wilson's warbler	*Wilsonia pusilla*
yellow warbler	*Dendroica aestiva*

Mammals

COMMON NAME	SCIENTIFIC NAME
Alaska porcupine	*Erethizon epixanthum myops*
beaver	*Castor canadensis*
black bear	*Ursus americanus*
Canada lynx	*Lynx canadensis canadensis*
Dall mountain sheep	*Ovis dalli dalli*
Dawson red-backed mouse	*Cleithrionomys dawsoni dawsoni*
Drummond meadow-mouse	*Microtus pennsylvanicus drummondii*
grizzly bear	*Ursus*
Lake Bennett ground squirrel	*Citellus plesius plesius*
Mackenzie varying hare	*Lepus americanus macfarlani*
mountain coyote	*Canis lestes*
mountain goat	*Oreamnos*
mountain long-tailed vole	*Microtus mordax mordax*
red squirrel	*Sciurus hudsonicus petulans*
Yakutat tundra mouse	*Microtus yakutatensis*

Flora

COMMON NAME	SCIENTIFIC NAME
anemone	*Anemone parviflora*
buffalo berry	*Shepherdia*
camas	*Zygadenus elegans*
cranberry	*Vaccinium pauciflorum*
dryas	*Dryas drummondii*
fireweed	*Epilobium angustifolium*
green orchid	*Habenaria*

COMMON NAME	SCIENTIFIC NAME
mountain avens	*Dryas octopetala*
mountain saxifrage	*Saxifraga oppositifolia*
orchid	*Calypso bulbosa*
polygonum	*Polygonum viviparum*
red-purple vetch	*Hedysarum mackenzii*
silverberry	*Elaeagnus comutata*
white lady's slipper orchid	*Cypripedium passerinum*
white spruce	*Picea canadensis*

Notes

INTRODUCTION

1 Laing, "A 'Been-There' Motorcyclist's Touring Outfit."
2 National Museum of Canada, *The Conquest of Mount Logan.*

CHAPTER 1

1 Turner, *Those Beautiful Coastal Liners*, p. 63.
2 Ibid., pp. 67–8.
3 Carpe, "Observations," p. 87.
4 Ibid., p. 88.
5 Ibid.
6 George Eastman to H.F. Lambart, January 10, 1925, WMA & SC.
7 Minutes of Mount Logan Committee meeting, January 11, 1925.
8 Wheeler to JWA Hickson, January 14, 1925, WMA & SC.
9 Lambart to Wheeler, January 20, 1925, WMA & SC.
10 Eastman to Lambart, January 28, 1925, WMA & SC.
11 R.S. Peck to Lambart, February 26, 1925, WMA & SC.
12 Lambart to Wheeler, March 26, 1925, WMA & SC.
13 Memorandum from R.M. Anderson, WMA & SC.
14 Anderson to L.L. Bolton, March 26, 1925, WMA & SC.
15 Telegram, Bolton to Laing, March 27, 1925, WMA & SC.
16 Bolton, Memorandum of Duties of Mr. Hamilton M. Laing.
17 Alpine Club of Canada, *The Gazette*, p. 1.
18 Ibid., pp. 1–2.
19 Ibid., p. 1.

20 *Vancouver Daily Province*, "Farewell Dinner," p. 12.
21 Alpine Club of Canada, *The Gazette*, p. 2.
22 Fraser, *Wheeler*, p. 4.
23 Alpine Club of Canada. *The Gazette*, p. 2.
24 *Vancouver Daily Province*, "Alpine Adventures," p. 16.
25 *Vancouver Daily Province*, "Mount Logan Party Sails," p. 24.
26 Ibid.
27 Ibid.
28 Alpine Club of Canada, *The Gazette*, p. 2.

CHAPTER 2

1 Alpine Club of Canada, *The Gazette*, p. 2.
2 *Vancouver Daily Province*, "Mount Logan Party Sails," p. 24.
3 Ibid.

CHAPTER 3

1 Lambart, Logan Expedition Diary, Friday, May 8, 1925.
2 Lambart to Foster, March 29, 1925, WMA & SC.

CHAPTER 4

1 Laing, Taverner and Anderson, *Birds and Mammals*, pp. 83, 88–91, 100, 104–5.
2 R.S. Peck to Hamilton M. Laing, April 14, 1925, WMA & SC.
3 Foster, W.W., "The Story of the Expedition," pp. 51–52.
4 MacCarthy, "Preliminary Explorations," pp. 26–27.
5 Ibid., pp. 28–29.
6 Ibid., p. 29.
7 Ibid., pp. 27, 29.
8 Ibid., p. 29.
9 Laing, Taverner and Anderson, *Birds and Mammals*, p. 71.
10 Scott, *Pushing the Limits*, p. 99.
11 Laing, Taverner and Anderson, *Birds and Mammals*, p. 87.
12 Ibid., p. 104.
13 Hall, "Notes on Equipment," p. 121.
14 Ibid., p. 122.
15 Scott, *Pushing the Limits*, p. 77.
16 Laing, Taverner and Anderson, *Birds and Mammals*, p. 94.
17 Ibid., p. 81.
18 Lambart, "The Conquest of Mount Logan," p. 6.
19 Laing, Taverner and Anderson, *Birds and Mammals*, p. 81.

20 Wheeler, "A Few More Words of Appreciation," p. 10.

21 Hickson, "An Appreciation," p. 2.

22 Lambart, "Topographic and Geographic Exploration of the Mount Logan Region," p. 15.

23 Ibid., pp. 16–17.

24 Ibid., p. 19.

25 Ibid., pp. 19–20.

26 Lambart, Logan Expedition Diary, Friday, May 8, 1925.

27 Laing, "Wild Life of the Upper Chitina," p. 100.

28 Lambart. "The Conquest of Mount Logan," p. 6.

CHAPTER 5

1 Foster, W.W., "The Story of the Expedition," p. 54.

CHAPTER 6

1 Lambart. "The Conquest of Mount Logan," p. 7.

2 Ibid.

3 Ibid.

4 Ibid.

5 Ibid.

6 Ibid.

7 Ibid.

8 Ibid., p. 8.

9 Hall, "Notes on Equipment," p. 74.

10 Laing, Taverner and Anderson, *Birds and Mammals*, p. 103.

11 Ibid., p. 82.

12 Lambart, Logan Expedition Diary, Monday, May 25, 1925.

13 Lambart, "The Conquest of Mount Logan," p. 8.

14 Lambart, Logan Expedition Diary, Monday, May 25, 1925.

15 Lambart, "The Conquest of Mount Logan," pp. 8–9.

16 Laing, Taverner and Anderson, *Birds and Mammals*, p. 85.

17 Lambart. "The Conquest of Mount Logan," p. 9.

18 Ibid.

19 Ibid.

20 Ibid.

21 Laing, Taverner and Anderson, *Birds and Mammals*, p. 93.

22 Ibid., p. 70.

23 Ibid., p. 106.

24 Ibid.

25 Ibid., p. 102.

26 Ibid., p. 76.

27 Ibid., p. 98.

28 Ibid., p. 79.

29 Ibid., p. 86.

30 Correspondence H.M. Laing to Ethel M. Hart Laing, May 31, 1925. BC Archives, File MS-1309.21.7.

CHAPTER 7

1 Foster, W.W., "The Story of the Expedition," p. 55.

2 Ibid.

3 Ibid.

4 Ibid.

5 Ibid.

6 Lambart, Logan Expedition Diary, Wednesday, May 27, 1925.

7 Ibid., Friday, May 29, 1925.

8 MacCarthy. "The Climb," p. 59.

9 Lambart, Logan Expedition Diary, Friday, May 29, 1925.

10 Lambart, "The Conquest of Mount Logan," p. 10.

11 Lambart, Logan Expedition Diary, May 30, 1925.

12 Ibid.

13 Ibid., Sunday, May 31, 1925.

14 MacCarthy, "The Climb," p. 59.

15 Ibid.

16 Ibid.

17 Lambart, Logan Expedition Diary, Monday, June 1, 1925.

18 Ibid., Tuesday, June 2, 1925.

19 MacCarthy, "The Climb," p. 60.

20 Lambart, "The Conquest of Mount Logan," p. 10.

21 Laing, Taverner and Anderson, *Birds and Mammals*, pp. 101–2.

22 Ibid., p. 104.

23 Ibid.

24 Ibid.

25 Ibid., p. 88.

26 Ibid., p. 92.

27 Ibid., p. 94.

28 Ibid., p. 85.

29 Laing, "Wild Life of the Upper Chitina," p. 112.

30 Laing, Taverner and Anderson, *Birds and Mammals*, p. 105.

31 Laing, "Wild Life of the Upper Chitina," p. 110.

32 Laing, Taverner and Anderson, *Birds and Mammals*, p. 84.

CHAPTER 8

 1 MacCarthy, "The Climb," p. 59.

 2 Ibid.

 3 Ibid., p. 61.

 4 Lambart, Logan Expedition Diary, Thursday, June 4, 1925.

 5 Ibid., p. 61.

 6 Hall, *Mount Logan*, p. 7.

 7 Lambart, "The Conquest of Mount Logan," p. 10.

 8 Bjarnason, Erik, and Cathi Shaw, *Surviving Logan*, p. 23.

 9 Marcus, "Climate: The Supreme Ruler."

10 MacCarthy, "The Climb," p. 62.

11 Lambart, "The Conquest of Mount Logan," p. 10.

12 Laing, Taverner and Anderson, *Birds and Mammals*, p. 87.

13 Laing, "Wild Life of the Upper Chitina," p. 112.

14 Laing, Taverner and Anderson, *Birds and Mammals*, p. 84.

15 Ibid., p. 83.

16 Ibid., p. 97.

17 Ibid., p. 92.

18 Ibid., p. 84.

19 Ibid., p. 87.

20 Ibid., p. 85.

21 Laing, "Wild Life of the Upper Chitina," p. 112.

22 Ibid.

23 Laing, Taverner and Anderson, *Birds and Mammals*, p. 85.

24 Ibid.

25 Ibid., p. 93.

26 Ibid., p. 86.

27 Ibid., p. 95.

28 Laing, "Wild Life of the Upper Chitina," p. 110.

29 Laing, Taverner and Anderson, *Birds and Mammals*, p. 105.

30 Laing, "Wild Life of the Upper Chitina," p. 112.

CHAPTER 9

 1 MacCarthy, "The Climb," p. 62.

 2 Hall, *Mount Logan*, p. 7.

 3 MacCarthy, "The Climb." p. 63.

4 Ibid.

5 Lambart, "The Conquest of Mount Logan," p. 11.

6 Ibid.

7 Ibid.

8 MacCarthy, "The Climb," p. 63.

9 Ibid.

10 Lambart, Logan Expedition Diary, Saturday, June 6, 1925.

11 MacCarthy, "The Climb," p. 63.

12 Ibid.

13 Ibid., p. 64.

14 Mackie, *Hamilton Mack Laing*, pp. 20–23.

15 MacCarthy, "Food," pp. 117–18.

16 Ibid., p. 118.

17 Laing, Taverner and Anderson, *Birds and Mammals*, pp. 103–4.

18 Ibid., p. 101.

19 Ibid., p. 104.

20 Ibid., p. 82.

21 Ibid.

22 Ibid., p. 92.

23 Laing, "Wild Life of the Upper Chitina," p. 112.

CHAPTER 10

1 Lambart, "The Conquest of Mount Logan," p. 11.

2 Lambart, Logan Expedition Diary, Monday, June 8, 1925.

3 Ibid., Tuesday, June 9, 1925.

4 MacCarthy, "The Climb," p. 64.

5 Ibid.

6 Ibid., p. 65.

7 Hall, *Mount Logan*, p. 7.

8 Lambart, Logan Expedition Diary, Tuesday, June 9, 1925.

9 Lambart, "The Conquest of Mount Logan," pp. 11–12.

10 Lambart, Logan Expedition Diary, Wednesday, June 10, 1925.

11 MacCarthy, "The Climb," p. 65.

12 Hall, *Mount Logan*, p. 7.

13 Mackie, *Hamilton Mack Laing*, p. 91.

14 Laing, "Wild Life of the Upper Chitina," pp. 105–6.

15 Laing, Taverner and Anderson, *Birds and Mammals*, p. 70.

16 Ibid., p. 76.

17 Ibid., p. 103.

18 Mackie, *Hamilton Mack Laing*, p. 84.
19 Laing, Taverner and Anderson, *Birds and Mammals*, p. 70.
20 Ibid., p. 87.
21 Ibid.
22 Ibid., pp. 82–83.
23 Ibid., p. 92.
24 Laing, "Wild Life of the Upper Chitina," p. 107.
25 Ibid.
26 Laing, Taverner and Anderson, *Birds and Mammals*, pp. 99–100.
27 Ibid., pp. 103–4.

CHAPTER 11
 1 MacCarthy, "The Climb," p. 65.
 2 Lambart, "The Conquest of Mount Logan," p. 12.
 3 Lambart, Logan Expedition Diary, Thursday, June 11, 1925.
 4 Hall, *Mount Logan*, p. 8.
 5 MacCarthy, "The Climb," p. 65.
 6 Lambart, Logan Expedition Diary, Thursday, June 11, 1925.
 7 Ibid., Friday, June 12, 1925.
 8 Ibid., Saturday, June 13, 1925.
 9 Hall, *Mount Logan*, p. 8.
10 Lambart, "The Conquest of Mount Logan," p. 12.
11 Hall, "Notes on Equipment," p. 123.
12 Ibid., pp. 122–23.
13 Ibid.
14 Ibid., pp. 122–24.
15 MacCarthy, "The Climb," p. 65.
16 Lambart, "The Conquest of Mount Logan," p. 12.
17 MacCarthy, "The Climb," p. 65.
18 Hall, *Mount Logan*, pp. 8–9.
19 Lambart, "The Conquest of Mount Logan," p. 12.
20 MacCarthy, "The Climb," p. 65.
21 Lambart, Logan Expedition Diary, Sunday, June 14, 1925.
22 Lambart, "The Conquest of Mount Logan," p. 12.
23 Laing, Taverner and Anderson, *Birds and Mammals*, p. 93.
24 Ibid., p. 80.
25 Ibid., pp. 85–86.
26 Ibid., p. 77.
27 Ibid., pp. 89, 93.

28 Ibid., p. 98.

29 Ibid.

30 Ibid.

31 Ibid.

32 Laing, "Wild Life of the Upper Chitina," pp. 112–13.

33 Laing, Taverner and Anderson, *Birds and Mammals*, p. 81.

34 Ibid., p. 89.

35 Ibid., p. 94.

36 Ibid., p. 90.

37 Ibid., p. 72.

38 Laing, "Wild Life of the Upper Chitina," p. 106.

CHAPTER 12

1 Lambart, "The Conquest of Mount Logan," p. 12.

2 Ibid.

3 Ibid.

4 MacCarthy, "The Climb," p. 66.

5 Lambart, "The Conquest of Mount Logan," p. 12.

6 MacCarthy, "The Climb," p. 66.

7 Lambart, Logan Expedition Diary, Wednesday, June 17, 1925.

8 MacCarthy, "The Climb," p. 66.

9 Lambart, "The Conquest of Mount Logan," p. 13.

10 Hall, *Mount Logan*, p. 10.

11 Lambart, "The Conquest of Mount Logan," p. 13.

12 MacCarthy, "The Climb," p. 66.

13 Ibid.

14 Ibid.

15 Ibid., p. 67.

16 Lambart, "The Conquest of Mount Logan," p. 13.

17 MacCarthy, "The Climb," p. 67.

18 Lambart, "The Conquest of Mount Logan," p. 13.

19 Lambart, Logan Expedition Diary, Thursday, June 18, 1925.

20 Lambart, "The Conquest of Mount Logan," p. 13.

21 MacCarthy, "The Climb," p. 67.

22 Lambart, "The Conquest of Mount Logan," p. 13.

23 Hall, *Mount Logan*, p. 10.

24 Hall, "Notes on Equipment," p. 125.

25 H.F. Lambart to E.G. Browne, Woods Manufacturing Co., March 18, 1925, WMA & SC.

26 MacCarthy, "The Climb," pp. 67–68.

27 Hall, "Notes on Equipment," pp. 125–26.
28 Hall, *Mount Logan*, p. 10.
29 Lambart, "The Conquest of Mount Logan," p. 14.
30 MacCarthy, "The Climb," p. 68.
31 Lambart, "The Conquest of Mount Logan," p. 14.
32 MacCarthy, "The Climb," p. 68.
33 Ibid.
34 Lambart, "The Conquest of Mount Logan," p. 14.
35 Ibid.
36 Lambart, Logan Expedition Diary, Sunday, June 21, 1925.
37 MacCarthy, "The Climb," p. 68.
38 Hall, *Mount Logan*, p. 11.
39 Lambart, "The Conquest of Mount Logan," p. 14.
40 MacCarthy. "The Climb," pp. 68–69.
41 Lambart, "The Conquest of Mount Logan," p. 14.
42 MacCarthy, "The Climb," p. 69.
43 Lambart, Logan Expedition Diary, Sunday, June 21, 1925.
44 Lambart, "The Conquest of Mount Logan," p. 14.
45 MacCarthy, "The Climb," p. 69.
46 Lambart, Logan Expedition Diary, Monday, June 22, 1925.
47 Lambart, "The Conquest of Mount Logan," p. 14.
48 Lambart, Logan Expedition Diary, Monday, June 22, 1925.
49 MacCarthy, "The Climb," p. 69.
50 Lambart, "The Conquest of Mount Logan," p. 14.
51 MacCarthy. "The Climb," pp. 69–70.
52 Lambart, "The Conquest of Mount Logan," p. 15.
53 MacCarthy, "The Climb," p. 70.
54 Lambart, "The Conquest of Mount Logan," p. 15.
55 MacCarthy, "The Climb," p. 70.
56 Lambart. "The Conquest of Mount Logan," p. 15.
57 MacCarthy, "The Climb," p. 70.
58 Ibid., p. 71.
59 Ibid.
60 Lambart, Logan Expedition Diary, Tuesday, June 23, 1925.
61 MacCarthy. "The Climb," p. 71.
62 Lambart, "The Conquest of Mount Logan," p. 15.
63 MacCarthy, "The Climb," p. 71.
64 Lambart, Logan Expedition Diary, Tuesday, June 23, 1925.
65 Lambart, "The Conquest of Mount Logan," p. 15.
66 Lambart, Logan Expedition Diary, Tuesday, June 23, 1925.

67 MacCarthy, "The Climb," p. 72.
68 Lambart, "The Conquest of Mount Logan," p. 16.
69 Laing, "Wild Life of the Upper Chitina," p. 106.
70 Laing, Taverner and Anderson, *Birds and Mammals*, p. 73.
71 Ibid., pp. 86–87.
72 Ibid., p. 105.
73 Ibid., p. 101.
74 Ibid., p. 82.
75 Ibid., p. 81.
76 Ibid., p. 97.
77 Ibid., p. 94.
78 Hall, *Mount Logan*, p. 11.
79 Laing, Taverner and Anderson, *Birds and Mammals*, pp. 75, 91, 104.

CHAPTER 13
1 MacCarthy, "The Climb," p. 72.
2 Ibid.
3 Ibid.
4 Lambart, Logan Expedition Diary, Tuesday, June 23, 1925.
5 MacCarthy, "The Climb," p. 72.
6 Ibid.
7 Ibid., p. 73.
8 Lambart, Logan Expedition Diary, Tuesday, June 23, 1925.
9 Lambart, "The Conquest of Mount Logan," p. 16.
10 MacCarthy, "The Climb," p. 73.
11 Carpe, "Observations," p. 82.
12 Lambart, "The Conquest of Mount Logan," p. 16
13 Ibid.
14 MacCarthy, "The Climb," pp. 73–74.
15 Lambart, "The Conquest of Mount Logan," pp. 16–17.
16 Lambart, Logan Expedition Diary, Tuesday, June 23, 1925.
17 MacCarthy, "The Climb," p. 74.
18 Lambart, Logan Expedition Diary, Tuesday, June 23, 1925.
19 Lambart, "The Conquest of Mount Logan," p. 17.
20 Lambart, Logan Expedition Diary, Tuesday, June 23, 1925.
21 MacCarthy, "The Climb," p. 74.
22 Lambart, "The Conquest of Mount Logan," p. 17.
23 MacCarthy, "The Climb," p. 74.
24 Ibid., p. 75.
25 Lambart, Logan Expedition Diary, Wednesday, June 24, 1925.

26 Lambart, "The Conquest of Mount Logan," p. 17.
27 MacCarthy, "The Climb," p. 76.
28 Lambart, "The Conquest of Mount Logan," p. 17.
29 MacCarthy, "The Climb," p. 76.
30 Lambart, "The Conquest of Mount Logan," p. 17.
31 MacCarthy, "The Climb," p. 77.
32 Lambart, Logan Expedition Diary, Wednesday, June 24, 1925.
33 Lambart, "The Conquest of Mount Logan," p. 18.
34 MacCarthy, "The Climb," p. 77.
35 Lambart, "The Conquest of Mount Logan," p. 18.
36 MacCarthy, "The Climb," p. 77.
37 Lambart. "The Conquest of Mount Logan," p. 18.
38 MacCarthy, "The Climb," p. 77.
39 Lambart, "The Conquest of Mount Logan," p. 18.
40 MacCarthy, "The Climb," p. 77.
41 Lambart. "The Conquest of Mount Logan," p. 18.
42 MacCarthy, "The Climb," p. 78.
43 Lambart, Logan Expedition Diary, Friday, June 26, 1925.
44 MacCarthy, "The Climb," p. 78.
45 Ibid., p. 78.
46 Lambart, "The Conquest of Mount Logan," pp. 18–19.
47 Ibid., p. 19.
48 Lambart, Logan Expedition Diary, Friday, June 26, 1925.
49 MacCarthy, "The Climb," p. 78.
50 Ibid.
51 Lambart, "The Conquest of Mount Logan," p. 19.
52 MacCarthy. "The Climb," pp. 78–79.
53 Lambart, "The Conquest of Mount Logan," p. 19.
54 Ibid.
55 Ibid.
56 Ibid.
57 Wheeler, "A Few More Words of Appreciation," p. 10.
58 MacCarthy, "The Climb," p. 79.
59 Wheeler, "A Few More Words of Appreciation," p. 10.
60 MacCarthy, "The Climb," p. 79.
61 Ibid.
62 Lambart, "The Conquest of Mount Logan," p. 20.
63 Ibid.
64 Lambart, Logan Expedition Diary, Friday, June 26, 1925.
65 Ibid., Sunday, June 28, 1925.

66 Lambart, "The Conquest of Mount Logan," p. 20.

67 Laing, Taverner and Anderson, *Birds and Mammals*, pp. 81–82.

68 Ibid., p. 93.

69 Ibid., p. 89.

70 Ibid., p. 71.

71 Ibid., p. 73.

72 Ibid., p. 73.

73 Ibid., p. 78.

CHAPTER 14

1 Lambart, "The Conquest of Mount Logan," p. 20.

2 Foster, W.W. "The Mount Logan Expedition," p. 56.

3 Lambart, Logan Expedition Diary, Wednesday, July 1, 1925.

4 Foster, W.W. "The Story of the Expedition," p. 56.

5 Ibid.

6 Lambart, Logan Expedition Diary, Thursday, July 2, 1925.

7 Lambart, "The Conquest of Mount Logan," p. 21.

8 Lambart, Logan Expedition Diary, Friday, July 3, 1925.

9 Lambart, "The Conquest of Mount Logan," p. 21.

10 Ibid.

11 Foster, W.W., "The Story of the Expedition," p. 56.

12 Lambart, "The Conquest of Mount Logan," p. 21.

13 Lambart, Logan Expedition Diary, Sunday, July 5, 1925.

14 Foster, W.W., "The Story of the Expedition," p. 56.

15 Lambart, "The Conquest of Mount Logan," p. 21.

16 Ibid., pp. 21–22.

17 Laing, Taverner and Anderson, *Birds and Mammals*, p. 96.

18 Ibid., p. 91.

19 Ibid., p. 72.

20 Lambart, "The Conquest of Mount Logan," p. 22.

21 Lambart, Logan Expedition Diary, Friday, July 10, 1925.

22 Foster, W.W., "The Story of the Expedition," p. 56.

23 Ibid.

CHAPTER 15

1 Lambart, "The Conquest of Mount Logan," p. 22.

2 Lambart, Logan Expedition Diary, Saturday, July 11, 1925.

3 Lambart, "The Conquest of Mount Logan," p. 22.

4 Lambart, Logan Expedition Diary, Saturday, July 11, 1925.

5 Foster, W.W., "The Story of the Expedition," p. 57.

6 Lambart, "The Conquest of Mount Logan," p. 23.

7 Foster, W.W., "The Story of the Expedition," p. 57.

8 Lambart, "The Conquest of Mount Logan," p. 22.

9 Ibid.

10 Lambart, Logan Expedition Diary, Sunday, July 12, 1925.

11 Lambart, "The Conquest of Mount Logan," p. 22.

12 Lambart, Logan Expedition Diary, Sunday, July 12, 1925.

13 Lambart, "The Conquest of Mount Logan," pp. 22–23.

14 Lambart, Logan Expedition Diary, Sunday, July 12, 1925.

15 Lambart, "The Conquest of Mount Logan," p. 23.

16 Foster, W.W., "The Story of the Expedition," p. 57.

17 Lambart, Logan Expedition Diary, Monday, July 13, 1925.

18 Hall, *Mount Logan*, pp. 14–15.

19 Lambart, "The Conquest of Mount Logan," p. 23.

20 Lambart, Logan Expedition Diary, Monday, July 13, 1925.

21 Lambart, "The Conquest of Mount Logan," p. 23.

22 Lambart, Logan Expedition Diary, Monday, July 13, 1925.

23 Lambart, Logan Expedition Diary, Friday, July 13, 1925.

24 Ibid.

25 Ibid.

26 Ibid.

27 Ibid.

28 Lambart, "The Conquest of Mount Logan," p. 23.

29 Ibid.

30 Foster, W.W., "The Story of the Expedition," p. 57.

31 Lambart, "The Conquest of Mount Logan," p. 23.

32 Lambart, Logan Expedition Diary, Saturday, July 18, 1925.

33 Foster, W.W., "The Story of the Expedition," p. 58.

34 Ibid., pp. 57–58.

35 Laing, Taverner and Anderson, *Birds and Mammals*, p. 93.

36 Laing, "Wild Life of the Upper Chitina," p. 106.

37 Laing, Taverner and Anderson, *Birds and Mammals*, p. 94.

38 Ibid., p. 73.

39 Ibid., p. 72.

40 Ibid., p. 82.

AFTERWORD

1 Taverner, *Birds of Western Canada*, p. 4.

2 Ibid.

3 Mackie, *Hamilton Mack Laing*, p. 94.

4 Taverner, *Birds of Western Canada*, pp. 12, 15–16.

5 Ibid., p. 16.

6 Ibid.

7 Ibid.

8 Mackie, *Hamilton Mack Laing*, p. 18.

9 Ibid., pp. 20–3.

10 Haig-Brown, "The Land's Wealth," pp. 410–11.

11 Udall, *The Quiet Crisis*, pp. 21–22.

12 Craig Brown, "The Doctrine of Usefulness," p. 95.

13 Foster, Janet, *Working for Wildlife*, p. 12.

14 Ibid., pp. 65–66.

15 Ibid., pp. 17–18.

16 Foster, Janet, *Working for Wildlife*, pp. 25, 28.

17 Meine, *Aldo Leopold*, p. 75.

18 Ibid., pp. 76–77.

19 Foster, Janet, *Working for Wildlife*, pp. 36–37.

20 Nash, "Wilderness and Man in North America," p. 75.

21 Foster, Janet, *Working for Wildlife*, pp. 36–37.

22 Nash, "Wilderness and Man in North America," pp. 76–77.

23 Foster, Janet, *Working for Wildlife*, pp. 56–57.

24 Nash, "Wilderness and Man in North America," p. 77.

25 Ibid., p. 79.

26 Muir, *The Yosemite*, p. 33.

27 Ibid., p. 145.

28 Bechtel, *Mr. Hornaday's War*, p. 81.

29 Hornaday, *Camp-Fires in the Canadian Rockies*, p. 250.

30 Stefansson, *My Life With the Eskimo*, pp. 436–37.

31 Ibid., pp. 447–48, 478, 481.

32 Ibid., p. 514.

33 Anderson, *Catalogue of Canadian Recent Mammals*, p. 7.

34 Ibid., p. 75.

35 Ibid., p. 119.

36 Ibid., pp. 94, 200.

37 Foster, Janet, *Working for Wildlife*, pp. 129–30.

38 Ibid., pp. 120–21.

39 Taverner, *Birds of Western Canada*, p. 1.

40 Foster, Janet, *Working for Wildlife*, p. 122.

41 Meine, *Aldo Leopold*, pp. 147–48.

42 Ibid., p. 163.

43 Taverner, *Birds of Western Canada*, p. 13.

44 Taverner, *Canadian Water Birds*, p. 7.

45 Ibid., pp. 9–10.

46 Ibid., p. 11.

47 Ibid., p. 12.

48 Ibid., pp. 12–13.

49 Ibid., p. 14.

50 Taverner, *Birds of Canada*, pp. 1–2.

51 Ibid., p. 13.

52 Ibid.

53 Taverner, *Birds of Western Canada*, p. 15.

54 Ibid., pp. 258–59.

55 Mackie, *Hamilton Mack Laing*, p. 77.

56 Ibid., p. 78.

57 Ibid., pp. 80–81.

58 Ibid., p. 83.

59 Ibid., pp. 86–87.

60 Ibid., pp. 88–89.

61 Ibid., p. 91.

62 Carpe, "Observations," pp. 87–88.

63 Carpe, "The Ascent of Mount Logan," p. 135.

64 Laing, "Wild Life of the Upper Chitina," p. 111.

65 Minutes of Mount Logan Committee, Vancouver, B.C., January 11, 1925, WMA & SC.

66 Foster to Lambart, January 28, 1925, WMA & SC.

67 Ibid.

68 Wheeler to Lambart, January 28, 1925, WMA & SC.

69 Requisition copy, Lambart to Director, Geodetic Surveys, Ottawa, March 23, 1925, WMA & SC.

70 Lambart to Wheeler, March 26, 1925, WMA & SC.

71 R.M. Anderson Memorandum re motion picture camera for Mount Logan Expedition, March 26, 1925, WMA & SC.

72 Ibid.

73 R.M. Anderson to L.L. Bolton, March 26, 1925, WMA & SC.

74 Ibid.

75 Lambart to Foster, March 29, 1925, WMA & SC.

76 Ibid.

77 Ibid.

78 Telegraph, Foster to Lambart, March 31, 1925, WMA & SC.

79 Telegraph, Lambart to Wheeler, April 1, 1925, WMA & SC.

80 Wheeler to Lambart, April 4, 1925, WMA & SC.

81 Ibid.

82 Ibid.

83 Ibid.

84 Carpe to Lambart, April 11, 1925, WMA & SC.

85 Ibid.

86 Ibid.

87 Lambart to Foster, March 29, 1925, WMA & SC.

88 Lloyd, "Canadian Government Motion Picture Films," pp. 100–102.

89 Foster, Janet, *Working for Wildlife*, pp. 159–60.

90 Taverner, "Scientific Advice," p. 105.

91 Ibid.

92 Ibid., p. 106.

93 Leopold, *A Sand County Almanac*, pp. 239–40.

94 Email interview with Briony Penn, December 15, 2020.

95 Nelson and Scace, *Canadian National Parks*, p. 13.

96 Ibid., p. 19.

97 Ibid., p. 24.

98 Ibid., p. 33.

99 Godfrey, *The Birds of Canada*, p. 9.

100 Phone interview, George C. Reifel, March 31, 2021.

101 Ibid.

102 Ibid.

103 Ibid.

104 Laing, *Out With the Birds*, p. 139.

105 Ibid., p. 140.

Bibliography

Alford, Monty. *The Raven and the Mountaineer: Explorations of the St. Elias Mountains*. Surrey, B.C.: Hancock House, 2005.

Alpine Club of Canada. *The Gazette*, No. 9, June 1925.

Anderson, Rudolph Martin. *Catalogue of Canadian Recent Mammals*. National Museum of Canada, Museum Bulletin No. 102. Ottawa: King's Printer, 1946.

Bechtel, Stefan. *Mr. Hornaday's War: How a Peculiar Victorian Zookeeper Waged a Lonely Crusade for Wildlife that Changed the World*. Boston: Beacon Press, 2012.

Bjarnason, Erik and Cathi Shaw. *Surviving Logan*. Victoria, B.C.: Rocky Mountain Books, 2016.

Bolton, L.L. Memorandum of Duties of Mr. Hamilton M. Laing on Mount Logan Expedition. Victoria Memorial Museum, Department of Mines, April 1925. WMA & SC.

Careless, J.M.S., and Robert Craig Brown, eds. *The Canadians, 1867–1967*. Toronto: Macmillan, 1967.

Carpe, Allen. "The Ascent of Mount Logan." Reprinted from *Bulletin of the Geographical Society of Philadelphia*, Vol. XXIII, No. 4, October 1925.

Carpe, Allen. "The Mount Logan Expedition: Observations." *Canadian Alpine Journal*, Vol. XV, 1925.

Clasen, Colin, ed. *The Birder's Guide to Vancouver and the Lower Mainland*. Madeira Park, B.C.: Harbour, 2016.

Craig Brown, Robert. "The Doctrine of Usefulness: Natural Resource and National Park Policy in Canada, 1887–1914." In *The Canadian National Parks: Today and Tomorrow*, Vol. 1., J.G. Nelson and R.C. Scace, eds. Calgary: University of Calgary, 1968.

Department of the Interior, Ottawa. "Canadian Alpinists' Brilliant Conquest of Mount Logan." *Natural Resources Canada*, Vol. 4, No. 9, September 1925.

Devine, Bob. *National Geographic Traveler: Alaska.* Washington, DC: National Geographic, 2013.

Fisher, Marnie, ed. *Expedition Yukon.* Don Mills, ON: Thomas Nelson & Sons, 1972.

Foster, Janet. *Working for Wildlife: The Beginning of Preservation in Canada.* 2nd ed. Toronto: University of Toronto Press, 1998.

Foster, W.W. "Mount Logan." *Canadian Defence Quarterly*, Vol. IV, No. 1, October 1926.

Foster, W.W. "Mount Logan Conquered: An Epic of Canadian Heroism, Victory Over Fearful Odds." *Vancouver Sunday Province*, August 23, 1925.

Foster, W.W. "The Mount Logan Expedition: The Story of the Expedition." *Canadian Alpine Journal*, Vol. XV, 1925.

Fraser, Esther. *Wheeler.* Banff, AB: Summerthought, 1978.

Godfrey, W. Earl. *The Birds of Canada.* Revised Edition. Ottawa, ON: National Museums of Canada, 1986.

Grinev, Andrei Val'terovich. *The Tlingit Indians in Russian America, 1741–1867.* Lincoln: University of Nebraska Press, 2005.

Haig-Brown, Roderick. "The Land's Wealth." In *The Canadians 1867–1967*, J.M.S. Careless and Robert Craig Brown, eds. Toronto: Macmillan, 1967,

Hall, H.S. "The Mount Logan Expedition: Notes on Equipment." *Canadian Alpine Journal*, Vol. XV, 1925.

Hall Jr., Henry S. *Mount Logan.* Reprinted from *Appalachia*, Vol. XIX, Bulletin No. 7. Boston: Appalachian Mountain Club, February, 1926.

Hickson, J.W.A. "The Mount Logan Expedition: An Appreciation." *Canadian Alpine Journal*, Vol. XV, 1925.

Hornaday, William T. *Camp-Fires in the Canadian Rockies.* New York: Charles Scribner's Sons, 1907.

Ise, John. *Our National Park Policy: A Critical History.* Baltimore: Johns Hopkins Press, 1961.

Laing, Hamilton M. "A 'Been-There' Motorcyclists' Touring Outfit." *Recreation*, July 1916.

Laing, Hamilton M. *Allan Brooks: Artist Naturalist.* Victoria, BC: Royal British Columbia Museum, 1979.

Laing, Hamilton M. Logan Expedition Diary. BC Archives, Item P2-DIA; 22 Diary 1925 (1) Mount Logan Expedition, A P2: Box 2 (April 15-June 22).

Laing, Hamilton M. Logan Expedition Diary. BC Archives, Item P2-DIA; 23 Diary 1925 (2) Mount Logan Expedition, J P2: Box 2 (June 28-August 9).

Laing, Hamilton M. Logan Expedition Diary. BC Archives, Item P2-DIA; 24 Diary 1925 (3) Mount Logan Expedition, A P2: Box 2 (August 10-September 4).

Laing, Hamilton M. *Out With The Birds*. New York: Outing Publishing, 1913.

Laing, Hamilton M. "The Mount Logan Expedition: Wild Life of the Upper Chitina." *Canadian Alpine Journal*, Vol. XV, 1925.

Laing, Hamilton M., P.A. Taverner and R.M. Anderson. *Birds and Mammals of the Mount Logan Expedition*. Department of Mines, National Museum of Canada. Bulletin No. 56, Annual Report for 1927, Ottawa: King's Printer, 1929.

Lambart, H.F. "The Conquest of Mount Logan." *The Geographical Journal*, Vol. 68, July–December 1926.

Lambart, H.F. Logan Expedition Diary, 1925. Archives / Collections and Fonds, R1570–2–7–E, MG30–B74, Vol. 2, accession number: 1973–385 NPC, Library and Archives Canada.

Lambart, H.F. "The Mount Logan Expedition: Topographic and Geographic Exploration of the Mount Logan Region." *Canadian Alpine Journal*, Vol. XV, 1925.

Leopold, Aldo. *A Sand County Almanac: With Essays on Conservation from Round River*. New York: Random House, 1966.

Lloyd, Hoyes. "Canadian Government Motion Picture Films Showing Natural History Subjects." *The Canadian Field-Naturalist*, Vol. XL, No. 5, May 1926.

MacCarthy, A.H. "The Mount Logan Expedition: Food." *Canadian Alpine Journal*, Vol. XV, 1925.

MacCarthy, A.H. "The Mount Logan Expedition: Preliminary Explorations." *Canadian Alpine Journal*, Vol. XV, 1925.

MacCarthy, A.H. "The Mount Logan Expedition: The Climb." *Canadian Alpine Journal*, Vol. XV, 1925.

Mackie, Richard. *Hamilton Mack Laing: Hunter-Naturalist*. Victoria, B.C.: Sono Nis, 1985.

Marcus, Melvin G. "Climate: The Supreme Ruler." In *Kluane: Pinnacle of the Yukon*, John Theberge, ed. Toronto: Doubleday Canada, 1980.

Meine, Curt. *Aldo Leopold: His Life and Work*. Madison: University of Wisconsin Press, 1988.

Moon, Barbara. "How Mount Logan Was Conquered." *Maclean's Magazine*, July 1, 1952.

Muir, John. *The Yosemite*. San Francisco: Sierra Club Books, 1989. Photographs by Galen Rowell.

Munro, J.A. *Birds of Canada's Mountain Parks*. Ottawa: Queen's Printer, 1963.

Nash, Roderick. "Wilderness and Man in North America." *The Canadian National Parks: Today and Tomorrow*, Vol. 1. Calgary: University of Calgary, 1968.

National Museum of Canada. *The Conquest of Mount Logan*, 1925. Film, 44 minutes. Library and Archives Canada/National Museums of Canada fonds/ISN 105485. www.youtube.com/watch?v=DeSuFqQ733Q

Nelson, J.G. and R.C. Scace, eds. *The Canadian National Parks: Today and Tomorrow*, Vol. 1. Calgary: University of Calgary, 1968.

Robinson, Zac. "Last Icy Stand." *Canadian Geographic*, March/April 2022.

Scott, Chic. *Pushing the Limits: The Story of Canadian Mountaineering*. Calgary, AB: Rocky Mountain Books, 2000.

Sherman, Paddy. *Cloud Walkers: Six Climbs on Major Canadian Peaks*. Toronto: Macmillan, 1965.

Stefansson, Vilhjalmur. *My Life With the Eskimo*. Natural history appendix by Dr. Rudolph M. Anderson. New York: Macmillan, 1951.

Taverner, P.A. *Birds of Canada*. Toronto: Musson Book Company (by special permission of The National Museum of Canada), 1947.

Taverner, P.A. *Birds of Western Canada*. Victoria Memorial Museum, Museum Bulletin No. 41. Ottawa: King's Printer, 1926.

Taverner, P.A. *Canadian Water Birds: A Pocket Field Guide*. Toronto: Musson Book Company, 1939.

Taverner, P.A. "Scientific Advice for Wild Life Conservationists." *The Canadian Field-Naturalist*, Vol. XL, No. 5, May 1926.

Theberge, John, ed. *Kluane: Pinnacle of the Yukon*. Toronto: Doubleday, 1980.

Turner, Robert D. *The Pacific Princesses: An Illustrated History of Canadian Pacific Railway's Princess Fleet on the Northwest Coast*. Winlaw, B.C.: Sono Nis, 2004.

Turner, Robert D. *Those Beautiful Coastal Liners: The Canadian Pacific Princesses*. Victoria, B.C.: Sono Nis, 2001.

Udall, Stewart L. *The Quiet Crisis: A History of Environmental Conservation in the USA, from the Native Americans to the Modern Day*. Adansonia Press, 1963.

Vancouver Daily Province. "Alpine Adventures." May 4, 1925.

Vancouver Daily Province. "Farewell Dinner to Mt. Logan Climbers." May 1, 1925.

Vancouver Daily Province. "Mount Logan Party Sails: Canadian Alpine Expedition Bound North on Hazardous Task." May 4, 1925.

Wheeler, Arthur O. "The Mount Logan Expedition: A Few More Words of Appreciation." *Canadian Alpine Journal*, Vol. XV, 1925.

WMA & SC (Whyte Museum Archives & Special Collections): https://archives.whyte.org

ADDITIONAL RESOURCES

All About Birds. Cornell Lab of Ornithology: Allaboutbirds.org

Digital Museums Canada: www.virtualmuseum.ca/sgc-cms/expositions-exhibitions/logan/

George C. Reifel Migratory Bird Sanctuary: reifelbirdsanctuary.com

Green Fire: Aldo Leopold and a Land Ethic for Our Time. Film, 73 minutes. Aldo Leopold Foundation, 2011.

Kluane National Park & Reserve. Government of Canada: www.pc.gc.ca/en/pn-np/yt/kluane

"The Bison and the 'B.'" *Ideas.* CBC Radio. Originally aired September 21, 2018.

About the Author

Trevor Marc Hughes expanded his research into the archived diaries and papers of writer and naturalist Hamilton Mack Laing after editing *Riding the Continent* (Ronsdale Press, 2019). *Capturing the Summit* is the result, following Laing's inclusion in the high-profile Mount Logan Expedition of 1925, as naturalist and cinematographer. Trevor explored British Columbia by motorcycle for over a decade and wrote many magazine articles as well as the books *Nearly 40 on the 37: Triumph and Trepidation on the Stewart-Cassiar Highway* and *Zero Avenue to Peace Park: Confidence and Collapse on the 49th Parallel* in which he combined historical non-fiction and adventure travel-writing. He plans a third installment in the series. He is also a documentary filmmaker, and has produced *Classic & Vintage*, *The Young Hustler* and is working on the upcoming *The North Arm*. Trevor lives in Vancouver with his wife, Laura, and his two sons, Michael and Marc.

Index